From the Ground Up

CRITICAL AMERICA

General Editors: RICHARD DELGADO and JEAN STEFANCIC

Luke W. Cole and
Sheila R. Foster

FROM THE
GROUND UP

ENVIRONMENTAL RACISM
AND THE RISE OF THE
ENVIRONMENTAL
JUSTICE MOVEMENT

New York University Press

New York and London

NEW YORK UNIVERSITY PRESS
New York and London

Library of Congress Cataloging-in-Publication Data
Cole, Luke W., 1962–
From the ground up : environmental racism and the rise of the
environmental justice movement / Luke W. Cole and Sheila R. Foster.
p.   cm. — (Critical America)
Includes bibliographical references and index.
ISBN 0-8147-1537-0 (pbk.) — ISBN 0-8147-1536-2 (cloth)
1. Environmental justice—United States. 2. Environmental
policy—United States. 3. Minorities—United States—Political
activity.   I. Foster, Sheila R., 1963– II. Title. III. Series.
GE180 .C65 2001
363.7'0089'00973—dc21   00-010595

New York University Press books are printed on acid-free paper,
and their binding materials are chosen for strength and durability.

Manufactured in the United States of America

10 9 8 7 6 5 4

For Ralph Santiago Abascal
LUKE W. COLE

For My Family
SHEILA R. FOSTER

CONTENTS

ACKNOWLEDGMENTS

This book is the product of the work and input of many people over the past six years. We particularly thank Maricela Alatorre, Bineshi Albert, Bradley Angel, Jerome Balter, Francisco Beltran, Lydia Beltran, Arnold Cohen, Joseph Della Fave, Juanita Fernandez, Lorenzo Garcia, Tom Goldtooth, June Kruszewski, Mary Lou Mares, Lupe Martinez, Esperanza Maya, Joe Maya, Zulene Mayfield, Dora Montoya, Eduardo Montoya, Saul Moreno, Sylvia Moreno, Dennis Palla, Juan Reyes, Rosa Solorio-Garcia, Tiwana M. Steward-Griffin, and Jackie Warledo for their help in the case studies found in the Preface and chapters 2, 4, 6, and 7, and for teaching us about environmental justice. Judith Lurie and Miriam Montesinos conducted field interviews for chapter 4; Henry Komansky provided invaluable research for chapter 2 and parts of chapter 7; Jen Gadbow and Sergio Garza helped transcribe interviews. Ralph Abascal, Skip Cole, Giovanna Di Chiro, Michel Gelobter, Nancy Shelby, and Katie Silberman provided insightful feedback and editorial advice. Charles Lee, himself a one-person history of the Environmental Justice Movement, has been an invaluable colleague and source of information. Dana Alston, Carl Anthony, Robert Bullard, Deeohn Ferris, Tom Goldtooth, Vernice Miller, and Richard Moore have all provided important direction both to the Movement and to us at various stages of our thinking about environmental justice. Our editors, Richard Delgado and Jean Stefancic, have been unwavering in their support of this project during its long gestation period. Rutgers University School of Law-Camden also provided crucial support, both tangible and intangible, toward the completion of this book.

Parts of this book were adapted from the following previously published articles: Luke W. Cole, *The Theory and Reality of Community-Based Environmental Decision-Making: The Failure of California's Tanner Act and its Implications for Environmental Justice*, 25 ECOLOGY LAW QUARTERLY 733 (1999); Luke W. Cole, *Environmental Justice and the*

Three Great Myths of White Americana, 3 HASTINGS WEST-NORTHWEST JOURNAL 449 (1996); Luke W. Cole, *Macho Law Brains, Public Citizens, and Grassroots Activists: Three Models of Environmental Advocacy*, 14 VIRGINIA ENVIRONMENTAL LAW JOURNAL 687 (1995); Luke W. Cole, *Civil Rights, Environmental Justice and the EPA: The Brief History of Administrative Complaints under Title VI*, 9 JOURNAL OF ENVIRONMENTAL LAW AND LITIGATION 309 (1994); Luke W. Cole, *Environmental Justice Litigation: Another Stone in David's Sling*, 21 FORDHAM URBAN LAW JOURNAL 523 (1994); Luke W. Cole, *The Struggle of Kettleman City for Environmental Justice: Lessons for the Movement*, 5 MARYLAND JOURNAL OF CONTEMPORARY LEGAL ISSUES 67 (1994); Luke W. Cole, *Empowerment as the Key to Environmental Protection: The Need for Environmental Poverty Law*, 19 ECOLOGY LAW QUARTERLY 619 (1992); Luke W. Cole, *Remedies for Environmental Racism: A View from the Field*, 90 MICHIGAN LAW REVIEW 1991 (1992); Sheila Foster, *Justice from the Ground Up: Distributive Inequities, Grassroots Resistance, and the Transformative Politics of the Environmental Justice Movement*, 86 CALIFORNIA LAW REVIEW 775 (1998); and Sheila Foster, *Impact Assesment* and *Public Participation* in THE LAW OF ENVIRONMENTAL JUSTICE: THEORIES AND PROCEDURES TO ADDRESS DISPROPORTIONATE RISKS (Michael B. Gerrard, ed., 1999).

We Speak for Ourselves

The Struggle of Kettleman City

El pueblo unido jamas sera vencido ("The people united shall
never be defeated")
—Chant and slogan from the farm-worker justice movement

Stories are one way we transmit our history, share our successes, and
learn from our losses. Stories are also an important part of the movement
for environmental justice, which has as one of its central tenets the idea
"We speak for ourselves." This book tells the stories of ordinary men and
women thrust into extraordinary roles as community leaders, grassroots
experts, and national policymakers. We invoke these stories to illustrate
the human reality behind the numerous studies that chart the disproportionate distribution of environmental hazards, and the burgeoning
grassroots movement for environmental justice that has sprung up
around the country.

The first story is about Kettleman City, one of the defining struggles
of the early days of the Environmental Justice Movement. The story is a
classic David-and-Goliath tale, in which a small farm-worker town took
on the largest toxic waste dumping company in the world—and won.

Kettleman City is a tiny farm-worker community of 1,100 residents in
Kings County, in California's San Joaquin Valley.[1] Ninety-five percent of
Kettleman residents are Latino, 70 percent of the residents speak Spanish at home, and roughly 40 percent are monolingual Spanish speakers.
They are primarily farm-workers who work in the fields that spread out
in three directions from Kettleman City. Kettleman City is much like
many other rural communities in the Southwest, and few people would
know about it were it not for the fact that Kettleman City is also host to

the largest toxic waste dump west of Alabama, a landfill that is owned and run by Chemical Waste Management, Inc, about three and a half miles from town, hidden behind some low hills. The dump was created in the late 1970s without the community's knowledge or consent.

People marvel that a gigantic toxic waste site can be placed just miles from a community without the community's knowledge. In California, under state environmental laws, government agencies are required to provide public notice in three ways: (1) through notices printed in a newspaper of general circulation, which in Kettleman City means a small box in the classified ads in the Hanford *Sentinel*, published forty miles away; (2) by posting signs on and off the site, which means on a fence post three and a half miles from Kettleman City; and (3) by sending notices through the mail to adjacent landowners.[2] The adjacent landowners to the Chem Waste facility are large agribusiness and oil companies such as Chevron.

Residents of Kettleman City found out about the dump in the early 1980s, after reading in the local paper about multimillion-dollar fines levied against the Chem Waste facility for violations of environmental laws. While residents were unhappy to find out their town was host to a huge toxic waste facility, they saw few ways in which they could challenge the dump.

Things changed in 1988, when Chem Waste proposed to build a toxic waste incinerator at the dump site. Residents in Kettleman City heard about this proposal not from Chem Waste, not from Kings County or state officials, but from a phone call from a Greenpeace organizer in San Francisco. Bradley Angel, Southwest campaigner for Greenpeace's toxics campaign, had received a phone call from the Kings County sheriff one afternoon in January 1988, asking him whether Greenpeace planned to demonstrate at the hearing in Kettleman City that night. After finding out about the hearing, Angel called one of the few people he knew in Kettleman City at the time, Esperanza Maya, and said, "Espy, did you know that there's a hearing tonight in your community about a toxic waste incinerator?" She said, "I haven't heard a thing about it."

Maya grabbed a few of her neighbors and went to the hearing. They were shocked to find out that Chem Waste was proposing to build an incinerator that would burn up to 108,000 tons—216,000,000 pounds—of toxic waste every year. That translates to about 5,000 truckloads of toxic waste that would pass through the Kettleman area each year, in addition to the hundreds of daily truckloads bound for the existing toxic dump.

After the hearing, many Kettleman City residents began to do their homework about the dump, the incinerator, and the company, Chemical Waste Management. They formed a community group, El Pueblo para el Aire y Agua Limpio (People for Clean Air and Water). The group found out that the air in the San Joaquin Valley was already contaminated, that the Valley is considered the second-worst polluted air basin in the United States, ranking behind only Los Angeles. And, whereas Los Angeles has ocean breezes to cleanse it, the San Joaquin Valley, because of its unique bathtub shape, is a closed system, so pollutants stay put and fill the Valley.

Members of El Pueblo also found out about a 1984 report done for the California Waste Management Board. That report, known popularly as the Cerrell Report, and paid for California taxpayers' dollars, suggested to companies and localities that were seeking to site garbage incinerators that the communities that would offer the least resistance to such incinerators were rural communities, poor communities, communities whose residents had low educational levels, communities that were highly Catholic, communities with fewer than 25,000 residents, and communities whose residents were employed in resource-extractive jobs like mining, timber, or agriculture.[3] When members of El Pueblo looked around Kettleman City, they were startled. "The Cerell report fit us to a T," says Mary Lou Mares, one of the leaders of El Pueblo. The incinerator proposal suddenly also made sense to Kettleman residents: "If there's a report that specifically tells them what to look for, of course they're going to target us," observes Mares.

El Pueblo also looked at California's other toxic waste dumps. California has three Class I toxic waste dumps—the dumps that can take just about every toxic substance known to science. The group found out that in addition to Kettleman (95 percent Latino), the two other dumps were in Buttonwillow, where 63 percent of the residents are people of color, primarily Latino, and in Westmorland, which is 72 percent Latino.[4] "It seemed like a conspiracy," says Mary Lou Mares, "although it's logical if they are using the Cerell report." Both Buttonwillow and Westmorland look just like Kettleman: they are small, predominantly Latino, rural farm-worker communities marked by high levels of poverty. People in Kettleman City began to put two and two together.

The Pattern

Then El Pueblo looked at the company, Chemical Waste Management, the largest toxic waste dumping company in the U.S. Chem Waste runs the largest toxic waste dump in the country (and, probably, the world) in Emelle, Alabama, which is in the heart of Alabama's black belt, in a community that is about 95 percent African American.[5] Emelle actually looks a great deal like Kettleman City—small, rural, poverty-stricken— but the residents are black instead of brown.

Even more interesting were the locations of Chem Waste's other incinerators. At the time, Chem Waste owned three other toxic waste incinerators: one on the south side of Chicago in a neighborhood that is 55 percent African American and 24 percent Latino;[6] one in Port Arthur, Texas, in a community that is about 80 percent black and Latino;[7] and one in Sauget, Illinois, which is surrounded by neighborhoods that are 95 percent or more African American,[8] including East St. Louis, an overwhelmingly African American community that has been called "America's Soweto."

The residents of Kettleman City started to see a pattern. "Our initial reaction was outrage," says Maricela Alatorre, a student leader during El Pueblo's struggle who has lived in Kettleman City her entire life. "We felt we were being targeted, that Chem Waste as a corporation was targeting these communities on purpose because their ethnic make-up would make people least likely to protest." Every single community where Chem Waste operated its toxic waste incinerators is a community of color, and substantially so: 79 percent in Chicago and Port Arthur, in the 90s in Sauget, and 95 percent in Kettleman City. They found out later that Chem Waste had planned to build an incinerator in Tijuana, Mexico, thereby hitting the 100 percent mark.[9]

The residents of Kettleman City then turned to Chem Waste's compliance record. At the Kettleman City facility, Chem Waste had been fined $3.2 million for more than 1,500 incidents of dumping too much waste into its evaporation ponds.[10] Chem Waste's incinerator in Chicago had blown up and been shut down by the Illinois EPA.[11] Illinois State Representative Clem Balanoff came to Kettleman City and told residents about Chem Waste's overfilling of the Chicago incinerator, which then spewed black smoke plumes, and about the fine Chem Waste faced for having turning off the incinerator's air monitoring equipment so that nobody would know what was coming out. And it did so once, not twice, but many times over a period of months.[12] In Vickery, Ohio, Chem Waste took in PCB-contaminated oil for disposal and then turned around and resold it to a company that used it to repave streets and as fuel oil in nearby communities.[13] The residents took note of Chem Waste's actions in Louisiana, where the company was caught storing toxic waste in one of those store-yourself rental lockers.[14]

El Pueblo also discovered that Chem Waste and its parent company, Waste Management, had paid more than $50,000,000 in fines, settlements, and penalties for price fixing, bribery, and related environmental crimes. "They could get away with all this because they were a multimillion dollar corporation," notes Alatorre. "These fines meant nothing to them." The company, they found out, was such an environmental bad actor that the San Diego District Attorney's Office had told the San Diego Board of Supervisors that "the company's history requires extreme caution by the San Diego County Board of Supervisors or any other governmental entity contemplating any contractual or business relationship with Waste Management" because of a pattern of continuing criminal behavior.[15]

Nor was Chem Waste's behavior ancient history. In the fall of 1992, as the incinerator project was under consideration, Chem Waste was fined a record $11.5 million for a botched Superfund cleanup in Pennsylvania.[16] In Kettleman City, Chem Waste was caught "sample packing." Ten trucks of waste would show up at the gate of the dump; by law Chem Waste was required to sample each truck to determine its contents to ensure that incompatible wastes were not disposed of together. What Chem Waste was doing, however, was taking ten samples from the first truck and then waving all the other trucks through.

Kettleman City residents felt justified in being a little alarmed by the prospect of having this company run yet another facility near their town. The residents figured that if the company can't run a hole in the ground correctly, it shouldn't be given the ability to do something worse.

The Process

As part of the permitting process for the incinerator, Kings County issued an Environmental Impact Report (EIR). The Environmental Impact Report was about 300 pages long, with another 700 pages of appendices, for a total of about 1,000 pages. Kettleman City residents, 40 percent monolingual Spanish speakers, 95 percent Latino, said to Kings County, "Look, to include us in this decision, you need to translate these documents into Spanish." Kings County was unresponsive. The County decision makers likely did not want to set a precedent; if they translated the EIR, they would have to translate documents in other situations, which is something the people of Kettleman City thought would probably be a good idea. Chem Waste, in a generous offer, translated a five-page executive summary and distributed that to every household in Kettleman City. English speakers in Kings County thus had about 1,000 pages of data to pore over, while Spanish speakers had five pages.

Despite being shut out by the lack of environmental review in their own language, Kettleman City residents nevertheless attempted to take part in the process. "We thought if we could get enough people to write and express their opinion, it would be important," says El Pueblo leader Mary Lou Mares. Mares and her allies generated almost 120 letters from the tiny community, and more than two-thirds of all the comments by individuals on the EIR were from the people of Kettleman City—in Spanish. Residents wrote in saying, in effect, "Hey, translate this document. Include us in the process. Let us know what you are proposing to do up on the hill. If you say it's safe, why won't you let us know what you are doing? Why won't you translate this document?"

The public hearing on the incinerator was scheduled not in Kettleman City but forty miles away, in the county seat of Hanford. It was held in the largest venue in Kings County, the County Fairground building, which is about the size of a football field. The hearing room was set up with a raised dais in the front, with a table at which sat the Planning Commission, looking down on the room. Then there was an open space; beyond that, two microphones set up for the public. Behind the microphones were about fifty rows of seats, and there were some bleacher seats at the back of the room. Behind the bleachers was empty concrete floor back to the very rear of the auditorium, about 300 feet from the Planning Commission.

Kettleman City residents showed up at the meeting in force. About 200 people came by bus and carpool from Kettleman City, and, as one of the their leaders made clear, "We're here, we want to testify on this project, and we brought our own translator." The chair of the Kings County Planning Commission looked down on the crowd and said, "That request has been denied. The translation is taking place in the back of the room and it won't happen up here."[17] Residents looked at where the Planning Commissioner was pointing: they looked from the Planning Commission up on their dais, they looked at the open space and the microphones, they looked at all the rows of chairs, and they looked at the bleachers. And then they looked way back behind the bleachers, nearly at the rear of the room, where there was one forlorn man sitting surrounded by a little circle of about twenty-five empty chairs. The Planning Commission chair said again, "Why don't you go back there? There are monitors back there. We are all in the same room." The 200 people from Kettleman City looked around, and they looked at the back of the room at those twenty-five chairs, and they looked at the empty chairs up front, and they said, "Adelante, adelante" ("forward, forward"), and they moved up to the front of the room. Residents testified in Spanish, from the front of the room, that the last time they had heard about people being sent to the back of the room was when African Americans were sent to the back of the bus—a policy dumped in the dustbin of history a generation ago. They said they weren't going to stand for that.[18] "The incident summed up what the County felt for the people out here in Kettleman City," notes Maricela Alatorre. "Our rights were second to this huge corporation."

The public hearing on the project brought to a close the public's ability to comment on the incinerator. Subsequently, the Planning Commission voted to approve the incinerator, and El Pueblo appealed that decision to the Kings County Board of Supervisors.

The Benefits and Burdens of Waste

California has a compensated siting law.[19] Under the law, local governments can tax hazardous waste facilities up to 10 percent of their gross revenues. What does this have to do with the story? As Kettleman activist Mary Lou Mares sums it up, "When it comes to politics, the ones that have the money win out."

Kings County, which is about 65 percent white, has five members on the Board of Supervisors. At the time of El Pueblo's appeal, all the board members were white. Most white residents in Kings County live in one area, while most of the Latinos live in another part of the County. If this page were a map of Kings County, almost all the white people would live up in the upper right corner of the page, in and around the county seat of Hanford. And most of the Latino people would live at the bottom of the page—Kettleman City would be in the lower left of the page, and the Chem Waste dump would be next to it. Every single town in Kings County is majority white except for Kettleman City, which is 95 percent Latino, way down in the lower left of the page. Under the California law that provides for compensated siting, Kings County was receiving about $7 million per year in revenue from Chem Waste's preexisting dump. That $7 million was about 8 percent of the County's annual budget.[20] Most of the money is spent up near Hanford (in the upper right of the page), in the white community, and very little of it trickles down to the people of Kettleman City (down in the lower left of the page). The incinerator promised to almost double that tax revenue, so the County would be receiving about one-sixth of its annual revenue from this single company. "The County knew people in Hanford didn't give a damn one way or the other," points out Joe Maya, a leader of El Pueblo. Not surprisingly, the white Supervisors voted for the incinerator on a three-to-one vote.

The Lawsuit

Faced with this situation, the residents felt they had no choice but to file a lawsuit. The lawsuit was successful when the judge ruled that the Environmental Impact Report had not sufficiently analyzed the toxic waste incinerator's impacts on air quality and on agriculture in the San Joaquin Valley and, most importantly, that the residents of Kettleman City had not been meaningfully included in the permitting process.[21] As the Court eloquently stated: "The residents of Kettleman City, almost 40 percent of whom were monolingual in Spanish, expressed continuous and strong interest in participating in the CEQA [California Environmental Quality Act] review process for the incinerator project at [Chem Waste's] Kettleman Hills Facility, just four miles from their homes. Their meaningful involvement in the CEQA review process was effectively precluded by the absence of Spanish translation."

Kings County decided not to appeal the lawsuit, largely because of the political pressure the Kings County Board of Supervisors was receiving from Kings County residents and from their supporters across California. A postcard campaign targeting the Board of Supervisors and the local Farm Bureau, orchestrated by El Pueblo and Greenpeace, generated more than 5,000 postcards to the Board and the Farm Bureau, while a petition campaign in the San Joaquin Valley by Citizen Action generated more than 17,000 signatures in opposition to the incinerator. Chemical Waste Management did not fold as easily, however, and appealed the judgment.[22] Rather than go back and do the environmental study right in order to respond to the judge's (and the residents') concerns, the company was more comfortable staying in court. But Kettleman City's struggle had become a national struggle. The residents of Kettleman City and their representatives were telling Kettleman City's story at meetings, conferences, symposia, and rallies across the country. "I think they thought we would go away," observes Mary Lou Mares, the Kettleman City housewife who appeared on national television to tell the Kettleman story. "But it was too dangerous to let an incinerator come in here—we had to do something about it." The press loved the story, and soon people all around the country knew about the struggles of Kettleman City.[23]

The Community Is Heard

On September 7, 1993, Chem Waste announced that it was withdrawing its application to construct the toxic waste incinerator near Kettleman City.[24] Although Chem Waste cited changing economic conditions and a new public policy turn away from incineration,[25] the General Manager of the Kettleman Hills Facility personally hand-delivered the news to one of the leaders of the community group El Pueblo, acknowledging the group's role in the decision.[26] As the El Pueblo leader Espy Maya said, "I don't care how they word it; we won."[27]

INTRODUCTION

Environmental hazards are inequitably distributed in the United States, with poor people and people of color bearing a greater share of pollution than richer people and white people. This intuitive idea—think for a moment about the most polluted parts of your region—has been borne out by dozens of studies completed over the past two decades.[1] The disparate impact documented in studies has given birth to the term "environmental racism." When President Clinton signed an Executive Order on Environmental Justice in 1994, the phenomenon of environmental racism gained unprecedented recognition.[2] Fueling this recognition is a remarkable rise in grassroots activism communities across the country. Thousands of activists in hundreds of communities are fighting for their children, their communities, their quality of life, their health—and for "environmental justice."

This book is about both the phenomenon of environmental racism and the movement that propelled environmental racism into national consciousness and forced action at the highest levels of government. The events and strategies chronicled here ultimately developed out of an alliance of grassroots activists, lawyers, other professionals, and concerned citizens whose efforts constitute the broad movement for social and economic justice known as the Environmental Justice Movement. The movement continues to shape environmental policy while creating increased opportunities for marginalized communities to speak out about their own disenfranchisement and the social and economic policies that subject them to daily environmental hazards.

We approach the subject from both an external and internal perspective. The internal perspective looks at the movement from the "ground up"—from the experience of communities that struggle daily with environmental degradation and with their disenfranchisement from the institutions and structures that control their living environments. The external perspective casts a critical eye on the political economy of environmental degradation, including the structure of environmental decision making in disaffected communities. We believe both perspectives are crucial to understanding the scope of the problem and the shape of solutions.

These perspectives—internal and external—also mirror our respective positions vis-à-vis the Environmental Justice Movement. One of us has spent more than ten years primarily working with, and providing legal representation to, grassroots groups in their struggles for environmental justice in their communities. The other author is a legal academic who has spent more than five years primarily studying and observing the phenomenon of environmental racism. Our goal in writing this book is to bring together, in one place, an analysis that reflects the disparate elements of the movement for environmental justice and that combines our individual and collective insights.

Our Perspective

In bringing our insights to bear on the subject of environmental racism, we are mindful of the lens(es) through which we view this problem. Both of us are lawyers by training, though our combined experience with communities struggling with environmental degradation has broadened our perspective. Our legal background thus undoubtedly colors, but does not unduly constrain, our analysis. We recognize, and call to our readers' attention, the rich body of existing literature on this subject, written from a variety of disciplines and viewpoints. However, since so much of environmental decision making is structured by legal institutions, it is important to understand the way in which environmental laws can both contribute to and mitigate the injustice experienced by many communities.

The law, however, is part of a larger social structure. Understanding environmental racism and injustice requires a broader, structural perspective. This broader perspective, what we call the "political economy" of environmental racism, is crucial both to framing the issue and to addressing the injustice so many communities experience. This perspective examines the relationship among economic, political/legal, and social forces as they influence environmental decision-making processes and environmental outcomes. Part and parcel of a political economic perspective on the issue of environmental racism is an understanding of the

experience of people in those communities that bear the disproportionate impact of environmental hazards.

The Importance of Grassroots Experiences

The stories of communities like Kettleman City (profiled in the Preface)
are spread throughout the book. These stories, or case studies, are not
intended to be representative of all aspects of the grassroots movement
for environmental justice (though we chose case studies with regional,
racial, organizational, and strategic diversity in mind). Rather, our case
studies are illustrative of some of the facets of this diverse, complex, and
evolving movement, which has its roots in previous social justice grassroots movements. In chapter 1, we trace the origins of environmental
justice activism to various social reform movements, such as the Civil
Rights and the anti-toxics movements. These movements have sought
self-determination and power for different groups and communities
much like those profiled in this book.

Grassroots experiences are critical to our understanding of environmental racism and justice for both our internal and our external perspectives. For our internal perspective, grassroots accounts tell a crucial
narrative that "reveals the particular experiences of those in social locations, experiences that cannot be shared by those situated differently but
that they must understand in order to do justice to the others."[3] Grassroots struggles can help us understand, and "unmask,"[4] the way in which
individuals in disenfranchised communities experience the very social
and structural constraints upon which, as we argue in chapter 3, the environmental decision-making process relies. For our external perspective,
grassroots struggles are a window into the social relations and processes
that underlie distributive outcomes. A view from the ground (or the
field) allows us to see the many dimensions of power struggles, the relationships of actors within these struggles, and the role of the legal and
regulatory framework in structuring those relationships.

Focusing on the structural dynamics of grassroots struggles, particularly as these struggles interact with the state/public apparatus, also shifts
the attention away from individual actors and the fruitless search for
clearly identified perpetrators. As we explain in chapter 3, the insistence
on establishing a linear, causal connection between disproportionate

outcomes and a "single bad actor" permeates our society's legal and social understandings of racism and injustice.[5] This prevailing understanding obscures the forces at work in producing environmental racism, however, by disaggregating communities and institutions and by isolating them from their social settings. By looking at the political economy of distributional outcomes, we hope to articulate a broader causal analysis and understanding of environmental racism. This broader analysis, in turn, forces us to go beyond framing the problem as merely a distributive one—certain communities get an unfair environmental burden—and to reconceptualize grassroots activism as more than an attempt to disrupt the decisions of private corporations and state agencies. Instead, grassroots struggles are a crucial arena in which to restructure social relations through systems of localized environmental decision making.

We map out some of the processes of struggle, in chapter 5, as way of giving context to the grassroots accounts. In mapping these processes, we do so with both our own experiences working with and observing grassroots efforts in mind and with the benefit of countless struggles memorialized in the impressive, and growing, body of environmental justice literature. The processes of grassroots struggle involve the formal and informal mechanisms of environmental decision making and the various obstacles experienced by community residents after they discover that a private company or government official has made the decision to locate an environmentally hazardous facility in their neighborhood. These processes also involve a community's decision to organize and become involved in the decisions that shape its lives and health. In their efforts to take control of their environment, grassroots groups inevitably run up against a system of environmental decision making that was not designed with their full participation in mind, as our case studies in the following chapters illustrate. Understanding the structure of environmental decision making, particularly on the state and local levels, where these struggles occur, is crucial to understanding the motivation, stages, and strategies of grassroots activism.

Transformative Politics

In portraying and analyzing environmental justice grassroots activism, we do not intend to reduce grassroots struggles to a new consciousness on the part of the poor and people of color about environmental concerns, even as that term is broadly construed. What is important about the communities that we portray, and the grassroots movement as a whole, is the self-representation and agency inherent in "speaking for ourselves." As Giovanna Di Chiro writes, what is "new" about the Environmental Justice Movement is not the "elevated environmental consciousness" of its members but the ways that it transforms the possibilities for fundamental social and environmental change through redefinition, reinvention, and construction of innovative political and cultural discourses and practices. This includes, among other things, the articulation of concepts of environmental justice and environmental racism and the forging of new forms of grassroots political organization.[6] These exciting developments are what we call the transformative politics of the Environmental Justice Movement. This transformation takes place on a number of levels—the individual, the group, the community—and ultimately influences institutions, government, and social structure.

Individuals are transformed through the process of struggle by learning about, and participating in, a decision that will fundamentally affect their quality of life. Using lawyers and other technicians, residents in embattled communities both build upon their knowledge of their community's environmental problems and acquire knowledge about the substantive and procedural aspects of environmental decision making. Their home-grown, and acquired, expertise empowers local residents and helps them to develop a grassroots base to influence environmental decision making.

The community is transformed by the grassroots environmental justice groups established in the midst of environmental struggles. These groups help to transform marginal communities from passive victims to significant actors in environmental decision-making processes. Grassroots groups are often fighting against a decision already made to place a toxic site in their neighborhood without any negotiation or consultation with those most affected by that decision—community residents. The groups rightly challenge, first and foremost, the legitimacy of the decision-making process and the social structures that allow such decisions to be made without the involvement of those most intimately concerned.

Part of what also empowers individuals and communities to demand participation in decisions that fundamentally affect their lives is the realization that power relationships within a decision-making structure are fluid and open to contestation. Once this realization takes hold, community residents can move from a reactive mode to one in which they take the initiative and decision makers begin to respond to their concerns. In this way, decision-making bodies—government institutions and corporations—are also transformed. This mutually transformative power dynamic in disaffected communities reveals an important facet of environmental justice politics. That disaffected communities are both vulnerable to disproportionate siting practices and, simultaneously, often successful at halting those practices suggests a paradoxical combination of socially oppressive sociopolitical constraints and self-determining capacities at work in these communities.

The transformation of environmental justice participants, and their local communities, ultimately lies in the forging of coalitions and the networking of grassroots organizations across substantive areas. Environmental justice groups are networking with other groups to provide information and technical expertise to grassroots constituencies on various issues of interest to disenfranchised communities, beyond environmental justice. Because of these networks, residents in marginal communities will continue to shape environmental policy, both locally and nationally, as well as create more opportunities for community input into the spectrum of policy making that affects their material conditions.

Words Have Power: A Note on Our Terminology

We use the terms "environmental racism" and "environmental injustice" interchangeably in the book. While "environmental racism" is the better-known term, "environmental injustice" is broader and encompasses both the racial and the class aspects of the political economy at work in communities that face toxic assault.[7]

We use the term "environmental justice" deliberately. Some government agencies and industry groups prefer the term "environmental equity," because they feel it "most readily lends itself to scientific risk analysis"[8] and avoids those sometimes controversial terms "racism" and "justice." We use the term "environmental justice" because it both expresses our aspiration and encompasses the political economy of environmental decision making. That is, environmental justice requires democratic decision making, community empowerment, and the incorporation of social structure—for example, existing community health problems, cumulative impacts of preexisting environmental hazards, the effect of segregative housing patterns—in environmental decision-making processes.

Most important in our concept of environmental justice is the element of democratic decision making, or community self-determination. Current environmental decision-making processes have not been effective in providing meaningful participation opportunities for those most burdened by environmental decisions.[9] "Meaningful," in this context, means substantive dialogue among administrators, experts, and affected communities along with the opportunity for affected communities to influence the decision-making process.[10] This means early, direct, and collaborative public participation. More important, it presupposes a power-sharing process in which government is but one party to the ultimate decision or agreement.[11]

We refer to the "environment" in a broader context than many environmental groups traditionally have defined it, using the Movement definition: the environment is where we live, where we work, where we play, and where we learn.[12] Historically, poor communities of color have been marginalized within the environmental movement. These communities view traditional environmentalism as associated with the preservation of wildlife and wilderness—concerns that are just not central to the everyday survival of poor communities and communities of color.[13] The Civil Rights Movement, the movement most closely aligned with these communities, also has not viewed environmental concerns as a priority. Consequently, until recently there has been a noticeable dearth of knowledge regarding environmental policy and processes of decision making in disaffected communities. Grassroots environmental justice activists recognize this neglect and are constructing a new meaning of "environmentalism" that links environmental preservation to their material environment and community.

The notion of "environment" for environmental justice groups and networks has come to mean home and community.[14] These are the places that need to be preserved and protected from pollutants and other harms. This community preservation principle[15] recognizes that the harms that result from the disenfranchisement of the most vulnerable communities from environmental decision making are not only health related but include other, broader consequences, such as the reduction of community cohesion, the feeling of powerlessness, and socioeconomic damage that result from the loss of businesses, homes, and schools.

A Final Note: The Focus on Waste

The movement for environmental justice seeks much more than merely to *stop* the siting of waste facilities, and other locally undesirable land uses in low-income communities and communities of color. Waste facility siting battles are but one aspect of the movement for environmental justice, which also concerns itself with the cleanup of contaminated industrial sites, the elimination of occupational hazards, lead abatement, enforcement of existing environmental regulations, and the guarantee of representation in the environmental decision-making process. The movement for environmental justice is also about creating clean jobs, building a sustainable economy, guaranteeing safe and affordable housing, and achieving racial and social justice.[16]

Given the diversity of various community struggles, and the complexity of issues represented in environmental decision making, it is difficult to capture, in one place, the multifacetedness of the Environmental Justice Movement. We do not pretend to attempt such a feat. Our structural analysis and profiles of grassroots struggles in this book focus, in large part, on decisions regarding commercial waste facilities. The distribution of hazardous, or potentially hazardous, facilities is important enough to environmental justice issues, and central enough to grassroots struggles, that it deserves the focus of our stories and analysis.

Waste facility siting is also the arena in which a great deal of grassroots action takes place. It is no coincidence that some of the first major environmental justice studies to chart disproportionate impact focused on commercial waste facilities. These facilities can pose great risk to human health and the environment and are the subject of ongoing public scrutiny and concern. Moreover, the siting of hazardous waste facilities is at the heart of the anti-toxics movement, a movement that, as we explain in chapter 1, is an important predecessor to the Environmental Justice Movement.

The stories, analysis, and lessons contained here are equally applicable to other types of environmental justice struggles, and indeed to social justice struggles in general. On one level, the issues are the same—community empowerment, the structure of institutional decision making, policy reforms that address our most vulnerable communities. It is our hope that the lessons learned in the communities we profile, and the analysis offered here, can be translated into, and replicated within, other struggles for justice.

| ONE |

A History of the Environmental Justice Movement

The determination and persistence of residents in communities like Kettleman City is firmly rooted in past social justice movements in the United States. Many of the techniques employed by groups like El Pueblo in Kettleman City did not, of course, originate in those struggles. Coalition building, mastery of technical language, development of technical expertise, direct action, litigation, and direct participatory democracy have all been used in various social reform movements for decades. Nevertheless, as applied to environmental struggles in poor communities and communities of color, these techniques are helping to redefine both ecological awareness and the meaning of the "environment" itself.

Pointing to a particular date or event that launched the Environmental Justice Movement is impossible, as the movement grew organically out of dozens, even hundreds, of local struggles and events and out of a variety of other social movements. Nevertheless, certain incidents loom large in the history of the movement as galvanizing events.

Many observers point to protests by African Americans against a toxic dump in Warren County, North Carolina, in 1982 as the beginning of the movement. The sociologist Robert Bullard points to African American student protests over the drowning death of an eight-year-old girl in a garbage dump in a residential area of Houston in 1967.[1] Others note that the Rev. Dr. Martin Luther King Jr. was traveling to Memphis to support striking garbage workers in what is now considered an environmental justice struggle when he was assassinated in 1968.[2] The United

Farm Workers' struggle against pesticide poisoning in the workplace, beginning in the 1960s (and continuing to this day), is the starting point for some. Some Native American activists and others consider the first environmental justice struggles on the North American continent to have taken place 500 years ago with the initial invasion by Europeans.

Rather than an incident-focused history of the movement, however, we think it more useful to think metaphorically of the movement as a river, fed over time by many tributaries.[3] No one tributary made the river the force that it is today; indeed, it is difficult to point to the headwaters, since so many tributaries have nourished the movement. Particular events can be seen as high-water marks (or perhaps, to push the metaphor, exciting rapids) in each stream, or the main river. With this idea in mind, we discuss here some of the most important tributaries of the river of the Environmental Justice Movement.

Foundations of the Environmental Justice Movement

The Civil Rights Movement

Perhaps the most significant source feeding into today's Environmental Justice Movement is the Civil Rights Movement of the 1950s, 1960s, and 1970s. Through that movement, hundreds of thousands of African Americans and their allies, primarily but not solely in the southern United States, pressed for social change and experienced empowerment through grassroots activism.[4]

The spirit and experience of resistance through the Civil Rights Movement was widespread in the southern United States and in many northern urban areas. The movement was strongly church-based; many of its leaders, like the Rev. Dr. Martin Luther King Jr. and the Rev. Ralph Abernathy, were ministers. When the Environmental Justice Movement began building momentum in the early 1980s, it was church-based civil rights leaders, seasoned in the Civil Rights Movement, who were at its fore. The 1982 protests in Warren County, North Carolina, against a PCB dump were led by local church officials and by the Rev. Benjamin Chavis, a longtime civil rights activist and at that time the head of the United Church of Christ's Commission for Racial Justice.[5] The Environmental Justice Movement's roots in civil rights and church-based advocacy is evidenced in the United Church of Christ Commission for Racial Justice's landmark 1987 study, *Toxic Wastes and Race in the United States.* Perhaps the single best-known work documenting the disproportionate impact of environmental hazards on people of color, *Toxic Wastes and Race* galvanized the movement. (Its author, Charles Lee, while working for a church-based civil rights group, also helped organize early meetings of academics to talk about environmental justice issues.)

Environmental Justice Movement leaders coming out of civil rights organizing include not only those who advocated for the rights of African Americans but also Latino activists. Movement leaders like Jean Gauna and Richard Moore of Albuquerque came out of Chicano political organizing in the Southwest, which involved mass protests against the Vietnam War, police brutality, and racism in housing and education.[6]

Civil rights activists brought three things to the Environmental Justice Movement: a history of, and experience with, direct action, which led to similar exercises of grassroots power by the Environmental Justice Movement; a perspective that recognized that the disproportionate impact of environmental hazards was not random or the result of "neutral" decisions but a product of the same social and economic structure which had produced de jure and de facto segregation and other racial oppression; and the experience of empowerment through political action. The seasoned civil rights leaders recognized environmental racism and set about using the tools and techniques they knew in their effort to combat it. The Warren County protests, for example, in which more than 500 people were arrested in acts of civil disobedience,[7] directly echoed the sit-ins and civil disobedience of the 1960s. Similarly, marches, a signature of the Civil Rights Movement, have become a fixture in local environmental justice struggles.

Civil Rights Movement leaders now in positions of power have also lent assistance to the Environmental Justice Movement. For instance, in 1992, Representative John Lewis of Georgia, a prominent participant in the protests of the 1960s, introduced the Environmental Justice Act.[8] Though the Act did not pass Congress, it raised environmental justice issues to a new stature in Washington. Lewis, in speaking about the bill, recognized that "the quest for environmental justice has helped to renew the civil rights movement" through its call for environmental protection as a "right of all, not a privilege for a few."[9]

The Anti-Toxics Movement

The second major tributary to the river is the grassroots anti-toxics movement. Communities have long resisted and organized against hazardous waste facilities, landfills, and incinerators.[10] The grassroots anti-toxics movement burst into national prominence in the late 1970s, when President Jimmy Carter declared Love Canal, New York, a disaster area and evacuated residents of a housing development built on a former toxic waste dump.[11] While Love Canal and the subsequent evacuation and relocation of another contaminated community at Times Beach, Missouri, are perhaps the best-known early examples of "grassroots environmentalism," similar stories have taken place across the United States. The proliferation of local actions marked an important shift in environmental activism when it began in the late 1970s: as Andrew Szasz notes, these local environmental conflicts "tended not to be about nature, per se, but about land use, social impact, [and] human health."[12] These local actions and activists also transformed toxic waste from a "nonentity to a full-fledged issue."[13]

The grassroots anti-toxics movement grew to prominence after the Civil Rights Movement; in contrast to that movement, its leadership is generally characterized by a lack of political organizing experience before a particular toxic struggle. "I have never been an activist before this fight" is a common story in the anti-toxics movement, in which residents, primarily women, are galvanized to action by threats to their health, their families, and their communities. As these grassroots leaders heard about other, similar anti-toxics fights in nearby communities, they slowly linked their local struggles together into a larger "movement."[14]

The anti-toxics movement became loosely organized under several national umbrella organizations in the 1980s, which helped make its actions more technically sophisticated and strategically coherent. For example, Citizens Clearinghouse for Hazardous Wastes (CCHW), an organization founded by former residents of Love Canal, has assisted grassroots activists nationwide for the past fifteen years, working with more than 7,000 local groups.[15] Thousands of these groups used (and continue to use) direct action protests to effectuate their demands. National groups like CCHW and regional groups that sprang up, such as the Environmental Health Coalition in San Diego, California, also used science and technical information, placing a high premium on demystifying arcane documents such as environmental impact statements and processes such as risk assessment. The anti-toxics movement sought to understand, and then restructure, the system of toxic waste production in the United States. Growing out of their concrete experiences in their own communities, anti-toxics activists came up with the idea of "pollution prevention"—that is, eliminating the use of toxic chemicals in industrial practices so that the production of toxic waste is stopped as well. Under the force of years of organizing, pollution prevention has moved from being a movement demand to being national policy.[16]

Like the Civil Rights Movement, the grassroots anti-toxics movement also brought the experiential base of direct action into the Environmental Justice Movement. It further contributed both the experience of using (and, when need be, discrediting) scientific and technical information and the conceptual framework that pushed pollution prevention and toxics use reduction as policy goals. Anti-toxics groups also had built national networks by linking local activists, an experience that they brought to the movement.

The grassroots anti-toxics movement also contributed a structural understanding of power, albeit different from civil rights leaders'. Civil rights advocates came, through the process of the civil rights struggles, to understand discrete racial assaults (from epithets to lynchings to segregation laws) as part of a social structure of racial oppression that ultimately had to be dismantled if racial justice was to be achieved. Anti-toxics activists, through the process of local fights against polluting facilities, came to understand discrete toxic assaults as part of an economic structure in which, as part of the "natural" functioning of the economy, certain communities would be polluted. Anti-toxics leaders thus focused on corporate power and the structure of the U.S. and the global economies and on strategies for changing that structure. It was when, in the 1980s, civil rights leaders began to embrace the anti-toxics movement's economic analysis and the anti-toxics leaders embraced the civil rights activists' racial critique that the conceptual fusion took place that helped create the Environmental Justice Movement.[17]

Academics

A third important contributory stream to the Environmental Justice Movement comes from a seemingly unlikely spot: academia. Academics, however, have played a crucial role in both sparking and shaping the Environmental Justice Movement, perhaps a larger one than they have played in any other broad-based social movement in the United States. Beginning in the 1960s, isolated researchers discovered that environmental hazards had a disproportionate impact on people of color and low-income people.[18] Dr. Robert Bullard, studying Houston land use patterns, found in the late 1970s that garbage dumps had a disproportionate impact on African Americans; this research led to Bullard's pioneering work in the field. In the late 1980s, Bullard did a literature search using the terms "minority" and "environment" and found twelve articles—six of which he had written. At that time, several academics, led by Bunyan Bryant at the University of Michigan, Bullard (then at the University of California-Riverside), and Charles Lee of the United Church of Christ, began to discuss the findings of disparate impact among themselves and held conferences on the subject.

In 1990, a group of academics convened at the University of Michigan to discuss their most recent findings. At that meeting, they decided that the energy and the momentum generated in their weekend together were too exciting to let dissipate in the usual academic papers. Instead, the group wrote letters to Louis Sullivan, the Secretary of the U.S. Department of Health and Human Services, and to William Reilly, head of the U.S. Environmental Protection Agency. In the letters, the professors, who came to be known as the Michigan Group, set out some of their findings of disproportionate impact and asked for a meeting with the officials to discuss a government response. As Bullard reports, the group never heard from Secretary Sullivan. William Reilly, however, agreed to meet with the Michigan Group, and, later in 1990, seven professors met with Reilly and EPA staffers in Washington, D.C.[19] The result of the Michigan Group's advocacy with Administrator Reilly was EPA's creation of a Work Group on Environmental Equity.[20] Reilly later created an Office of Environmental Equity, which newly appointed EPA Administrator Carol Browner renamed the Office of Environmental Justice in 1993.

Beyond lobbying the federal government, the academics researched and wrote (and continue to produce) studies that demonstrate the disproportionate impact of environmental hazards on people of color and on low-income people. These studies, dialectically fueled by and fueling the movement, played a series of roles. For one, the studies sparked and moved forward local struggles. In Los Angeles, for example, a community struggle led by Concerned Citizens of South Central Los Angeles against a giant garbage incinerator received what its leaders call crucial support when, before a key vote of the City Council, the UCLA School of Urban Planning released a 700-page critique of the incinerator project and its disproportionate impact on people of color in Los Angeles.

The academics' work also shaped or reaffirmed movement leaders' consciousness about the structural or systemic nature of environmental oppression. "I thought it was just us until I began to hear about the United Church of Christ study and the other studies," says Mary Lou Mares, an activist who has fought for more than ten years against Chemical Waste Management's toxic dump near her Latino community of Kettleman City. "Then I realized we were part of a national pattern."[21]

At other times, the academics have provided expertise to community groups during litigation or administrative advocacy in a local environmental justice struggle. In fact, the career of the most prolific and influential academic, Dr. Robert Bullard, was launched by a court case in Houston in the late 1970s in which his wife needed an expert witness.[22] Bullard and others have since prepared studies and testified for dozens of community groups nationwide. In perhaps the best known example, Professor Bullard's documentation of racially biased decision-making criteria in the siting of a nuclear waste processing facility in rural Louisiana was directly responsible for the federal government's decision to deny a permit to the facility.[23]

The concrete victories achieved in Los Angeles, Louisiana, and elsewhere were marked by the synergy between community activism and the academic support that played a critical role in each fight. On a local level, the education went both ways: the academics learned from community residents the situation on the ground, while local residents came to understand their community's struggle in the context of a larger regional or national pattern and movement.

Finally, the academics' work provides a basis for policy changes at the local, state, and national levels. In signing the Executive Order on Environmental Justice, for example, President Clinton acknowledged the need to "focus Federal attention on the environmental and human health conditions in minority communities and low-income communities with the goal of achieving environmental justice."[24] Without the previous decade of studies that had established the scope of the environmental injustice in these communities, the problem never would have reached the attention of the White House.

Today, academics continue to play a crucial supporting role through such institutions as the Environmental Justice Resource Center at Clark-Atlanta University, founded and run by Robert Bullard, and the Deep South Center for Environmental Justice at Xavier University in New Orleans, run by Beverly Hendrix Wright. These centers, and others like them, provide crucial research that aids local struggles, as well as train a new generation of professionals of color.

Native American Struggles

A fourth significant stream feeding the Environmental Justice Movement has been organizing by Native Americans. Native Americans have struggled for self-determination in land use decisions since their first encounters with Europeans more than 500 years ago.[25] Activism by Native Americans in the late 1960s and early 1970s was the precursor to today's organizing around environmental issues by Indians on and off the reservations, organizing that contributes one of the most vibrant and ever expanding tributaries to the movement. The struggles that led to the creation of the American Indian Movement were often focused around land and environmental exploitation, including such well-known and iconic incidents of Indian resistance as the shootout at Pine Ridge in 1975, which took place on the very day that the corrupt Pine Ridge Tribal Chair Dickie Wilson was in Washington, D.C., signing away rights to mineral exploration in the sacred Black Hills to major oil companies.[26]

Native American activists brought to the Environmental Justice Movement the experiences of centuries of struggle for self-determination and resistance to resource-extractive land use. The struggles of the 1870s to protect tribal land honed skills that would be useful later. As the first victims of environmental racism, Native Americans brought a deep understanding of the concept to the Environmental Justice Movement. The Native American tributary to the movement also helped define one of its central philosophies, the concept of self-determination. The centuries-old Native American idea of sovereignty echoed with, and helped create, the Environmental Justice Movement's credo, "We speak for ourselves." While for some other communities the slogan was an attempt to take back environmental policy decisions from traditional environmental groups, for Native Americans the slogan defined their relationship to state and federal governments.

The significant contributions of Native Americans to the Environmental Justice Movement were institutionalized in the formation of the Indigenous Environmental Network in 1990, the history and function of which is the subject of chapter 6.

The Labor Movement

Various strands of the labor movement have also contributed to the Environmental Justice Movement. The largest labor tributary has been the historical struggle of farm-workers to gain control over their working conditions. The farm-worker movement of the 1960s, led by Cesar Chavez, was perhaps the first nationally known effort by people of color to address an environmental issue. Much of the activity took the form of union organizing drives. For instance, the United Farm Workers (UFW) included in its initial organizing and contractual demands the ban of certain dangerous pesticides, including DDT. Union contracts in the late 1960s prohibited the use of such pesticides, and the lawsuits that ultimately led the U.S. government to ban the chemical outright were brought by migrant farm-workers.[27] Farm-workers' struggle for self-determination in the workplace—for the power to control decisions that affected their lives, such as the use of pesticides—mirrored the struggles by Native Americans and African Americans for political self-determination and by the grassroots anti-toxics movement for a role in local decisions. Unionization and protection of farm-workers' health and safety were integrally linked from the earliest days of the farm-worker organizing drives, and they continue to be linked today; it was thus natural for farm-workers to become active participants in the movement for environmental justice.

A second, and much less significant, labor tributary, one fed by the public health activism of the 1970s, is the occupational safety and health movement. The rise of Committees on Occupational Safety and Health (COSHs) across the country in the 1970s and 1980s brought increased attention to the environmental hazards faced by workers in the workplace. The COSHs were active in regions of the country—the South, for example—and in industry sectors—such as textiles and high-technology—that traditionally had little or no union representation. COSH activists, such as Mandy Hawes in San Jose, California, became early organizers of and advocates in the Environmental Justice Movement.

A third labor tributary is the increased attention paid to occupational safety and health by industrial unions. Led by sometimes renegade union activists such as Tony Mazzochi, unions such as the Oil, Chemical, and Atomic Workers Union have paid increased attention to environmental justice issues. While industrial unions have often believed that their interests lay with further development or expansion of industrial plants, some visionary union leaders have understood that the push for safer jobs and a cleaner workplace can help build political support for labor from fence line communities and environmentalists. This awareness has led to an important collaboration between the Environmental Justice Movement and organized labor in the Campaign for a Just Transition; through this campaign, movement and union leaders have been exploring common ground in phasing out the use of dangerous chemicals. This tributary is still a trickle, but it is an exciting addition to the movement.

Traditional Environmentalists

A very small, and late, tributary to the Environmental Justice Movement is the traditional environmental movement. Perhaps it is the history of the traditional environmental movement that has made it such a small contributor to the Environmental Justice Movement.

Two major waves of traditional environmentalism have swept the United States. The first wave began around the turn of the century, when John Muir, Theodore Roosevelt, and other lovers of wilderness advocated the preservation of natural spaces in the United States. Like the second wave, the first wave encompassed two divergent views that even today remain in tension: the preservationists, who advocate preserving wilderness from humans, and the conservationists, who want to preserve nature for human use through wise stewardship.[28]

Modern environmentalism, or the second wave, began after World War II with the rapid expansion in the use of petrochemical products. When the consequences of the shift to petrochemical production began to be felt, a new wave of activism sprang up, fueled by searing critiques of industrial practices such as Rachel Carson's *Silent Spring*. This wave of environmentalism coalesced around Earth Day in 1970 and was institutionalized in the proliferation of legal-scientific groups such as the Natural Resources Defense Council (NRDC), the Sierra Club Legal Defense Fund (SCLDF), and the Environmental Defense Fund (EDF), organizations that currently dominate the national scene.[29] The second wave— what we call the traditional environmental movement[30]—and the body of statutes and case law known today as environmental law grew out of the social ferment of the 1960s. The Civil Rights Movement and the anti–Vietnam War movement, the two movements in which the second wave has its roots, were explicitly oriented toward social justice.

The second-wave environmentalists have moved away from this social justice orientation, however. In particular, they have moved from a participatory strategy based on broad mobilization of the interested public, such as that used in the civil rights and the anti-war movements, to an insider strategy based on litigation, lobbying, and technical evaluation.[31] The movement away from a participatory strategy paralleled the movement away from the social justice issues that dominated the speeches given on Earth Day in 1970.[32] It also coincided with the traditional groups' desire to control the environmental establishment or at least to have power within it; as one commentator observes, "Shedding the radical skin of their amateur past seemed necessary to achieve that goal."[33]

The second wave, made up overwhelmingly of lawyers, focused primarily on legal and scientific approaches to environmental problems.[34] Second-wave lawyers helped write most of the environmental legislation on the books today, from the National Environmental Policy Act (NEPA), to the Clean Air Act (CAA), the Clean Water Act (CWA), the Resource Conservation and Recovery Act (RCRA), the Comprehensive Environmental Response, Compensation, and Liability Act (CERCLA), the Federal Insecticide, Fungicide, Rodenticide Act (FIFRA), the Toxic Substances Control Act (TSCA), and the Superfund Amendment and Reauthorization Act (SARA). These laws created complex administrative processes that exclude most people who do not have training in the field and necessitate specific technical expertise. The laws, while in some cases successful in cleaning up the environment, have also had an unintended consequence—the exclusion of those without expertise from much of environmental decision making.

Having designed and helped implement most of the nation's environmental laws, the second wave has spent the past twenty-five years in court litigating. Lawsuits are now the primary, and sometimes the only, strategy employed by traditional groups.[35] As the executive director of the Sierra Club Legal Defense Fund stated in 1988, "Litigation is the most important thing the environmental movement has done over the past fifteen years."[36]

Until relatively recently, the traditional environmental law community has largely ignored environmental justice issues.[37] In some cases, the lack of attention has been intentional: in a 1971 national membership survey, the Sierra Club asked its members, "Should the Club concern itself with the conservation problems of such special groups as the urban poor and ethnic minorities?" According to the Club's Bulletin, "[t]he balance of sentiment was against the Club so involving itself," with "58 percent of all members either strongly or somewhat opposed" to the idea.[38]

Racism and other prejudices have historically excluded activists of color and grassroots activists from the traditional environmental movement.[39] In fact, some of these activists regard the traditional environmental groups as obstacles to progress, if not outright enemies.[40] Some in traditional environmental groups have pushed for a greater focus on environmental justice—one hired an environmental justice coordinator, another hired several environmental justice fellows and announced a new focus on such cases—but, for the most part, the Environmental Justice Movement has operated without the input or assistance of the traditional environmental groups, perhaps to its benefit.[41] Given the second wave of environmental activism's roots in the grassroots activism of the 1960s, this disconnect is ironic, and poignant.

Some have described the grassroots movement for environmental justice as the third wave of environmental activism,[42] but we see the Environmental Justice Movement as separate from and as transcending the environmental movement—as a movement based on environmental issues but situated within the history of movements for social justice.

The Summit

The disparate strands of the Environmental Justice Movement—civil rights, grassroots anti-toxics, academic, labor, indigenous—were consciously brought together for the first time in 1991 at the First National People of Color Environmental Leadership Summit. The Summit served notice that the Environmental Justice Movement had arrived as a force to be reckoned with on the national level. It was also, in some ways, a declaration of independence from the traditional environmental movement; a telling statement from attendees was, "I don't care to join the environmental movement, I belong to a movement already."

Ironically, the Summit grew out of the Environmental Justice Movement's challenge to traditional environmental groups. In early 1990, Richard Moore, of the SouthWest Organizing Project, and Pat Bryant, of the Gulf Coast Tenants Organization, drafted a letter, ultimately signed by more than 100 community leaders, to the ten largest traditional environmental groups in which they accused the groups of racism in their hiring and policy development processes.[43] An article in the *New York Times* on the letter[44] initiated a media firestorm around the issue, and in an interview on CNN, the Rev. Ben Chavis, one of the signatories of the letter and at the time the head of the United Church of Christ's Commission for Racial Justice, called for an emergency summit of environmental, civil rights, and community groups. "In his mind, he was thinking about a small group of people getting together to negotiate it out," says Charles Lee, who directed the environmental justice program at the Commission for Racial Justice. Lee had other ideas, however, and, as he put together a planning committee, the summit quickly evolved from a small negotiating session into an event at which people of color could actively put forward their own environmental agenda.

The Summit was the product of eighteen months of intensive organizing by movement leaders, including Lee, Bryant, Moore, Dana Alston of the Panos Institute, the Indian activist Donna Chavis of North Carolina, and the academic Robert Bullard. Chavis's initial idea of a small gathering ended up a national event that brought together more than 300 delegates and 400 observers and supporters for three heady days in Washington, D.C. There were speeches by leaders in the national social justice movement, such as Jesse Jackson and Dolores Huerta, strategy sessions on issues such as toxic dumps and legal challenges, and caucuses for delegates organized by region and by race.

Unprecedented alliances were formed at the Summit, and participants made conceptual linkages between seemingly different struggles, identifying common themes of racism and economic exploitation of people and land. Many there came to understand their issues in the context of a larger movement, and on a deeper level than before. Latinos saw the racism African Americans had experienced and likened it to their own experiences; foes of toxic waste dumps understood the fights of those who opposed uranium mining. The raised consciousness took place at a variety of levels: "Native Americans stressing a spiritual connection with the environment were able to find a common ground with Christian African Americans and Mexican Americans," recalls Tom Goldtooth, a delegate to the Summit who now coordinates the Indigenous Environmental Network.

Some say that from October 21–24, 1991, the environmental movement in the United States changed forever. Certainly, those in attendance went back to their communities across the country with a renewed understanding of the need for environmental justice and with new ideas on how to fight for it; nascent environmental justice networks (such as the Indigenous Environmental Network profiled in chapter 6) gained momentum. Environmental justice as a concept had reached the national stage, and it was not long afterward that two key planners of the Summit, Ben Chavis and Robert Bullard, were appointed to President-elect Clinton's transition team. On a more tangible level, perhaps the most important result of the Summit were the Principles of Environmental Justice, seventeen principles agreed to by the delegates.

Environmental Justice Activists

Despite the many tributaries from which they come to the Environmental Justice Movement, at least three characteristics unite the movement's activists: motives, background, and perspective. With respect to motives, grassroots activists are often fighting for their health and homes. Environmental justice activists usually have an immediate and material stake in solving the environmental problems they confront; they realize the hazards they face affect the communities where they *live* and may be sickening or even killing them or their children. Because grassroots activists have such a personal stake in the outcome of particular environmental battles, they are often willing to explore a wider range of strategies than other advocates, including traditional environmental advocates.

Second, with respect to background, grassroots environmentalists are largely, though not entirely, poor or working-class people. Many are people of color who come from communities that are disenfranchised from most major societal institutions. Because of their backgrounds, these activists often have a distrust for the law and are often experienced in the use of nonlegal strategies, such as protest and other direct action.

The third trait, perspective, is an outgrowth of the first two. Most environmental justice activists have a social justice orientation, seeing environmental degradation as just one of many ways their communities are under attack. Because of their experiences, grassroots activists often lose faith in government agencies and elected officials,[45] leading those activists to view environmental problems in their communities as connected to larger structural failings—inner-city disinvestment, residential segregation, lack of decent health care, joblessness, and poor education. Similarly, many activists also seek remedies that are more fundamental than simply stopping a local polluter or toxic dumper. Instead, many view the need for broader, structural reforms as a way to alleviate many of the problems, including environmental degradation, that their communities endure.

These shared traits influence the tactics and strategies used by local activists, as we explore throughout the stories in this book. The motives, backgrounds, and perspectives of most environmental justice activists are shaped by their experiences in a deeply racially and economically stratified society, a stratification that we explore in more detail in chapter 3.

The Political Economy of Environmental Racism

Chester Residents Concerned for Quality of Life

The story of Chester, Pennsylvania, is in many ways a classic case of environmental racism: it is emblematic of the social, political, and economic forces that shape the disproportionate distribution of environmental hazards in poor communities of color. Chester also illustrates the extraordinary grassroots activism that has arisen in response to environmental racism. It is the tale of an otherwise disenfranchised community's political will and energy, its persistent organizing, and the long odds faced by low-income people and people of color who are fighting for environmental justice.

Located along the Delaware River, approximately fifteen miles southwest of Philadelphia, Chester is a small enclave of people of color within predominantly white Delaware County. While Delaware County, excluding Chester, is only 6.2 percent African American, 65 percent of Chester's 39,000 residents are African American. The median family income in Chester is 45 percent lower than the rest of Delaware County, and its 25 percent poverty rate is more than three times the rate in Delaware County. Unemployment and crime rates are high in Chester, as is the rate of health problems: Chester has a mortality rate 40 percent higher than the rest of Delaware County, as well as the state's highest child mortality rate.[1]

Waste facilities that once promised needed jobs have instead brought many forms of pollution. From 1986 to 1996, the Pennsylvania Department of Environmental Protection (DEP) issued seven permits for commercial waste facilities in Delaware County, five of which were to be located in Chester. All of the municipal waste and sewage in Delaware County is processed in Chester, even though only 7.5 percent of the county population lives in Chester. Moreover, more than 60 percent of the waste-processing industries in Delaware County are located in Chester.[2]

Living in Chester today can best be described as an assault on the senses—a toxic assault. During the summer, the stench and the noise force residents to retreat into their houses. Recent visitors to Chester have said that the "air is thick with acrid smells and, often, smoke. Dump trucks rumble through throughout the day,"[3] and "the first thing you notice is the smell."[4]

These conditions have prompted a citizen uprising against the facilities. Concerned residents began meeting privately in 1992, spurred by the noise and dust generated by trucks that brought trash to one of the largest garbage incinerators in the country, located only eighty feet from some peoples' homes in Chester's West End neighborhood. The residents were most irritated by the huge trucks that roared through their neighborhoods at all times of the day and night, disturbing their sleep and their children's recreational time and damaging the overall character and peace of their community. Noise and vibration from the constant stream of waste trucks had caused the foundations of houses near the main roads to crack and property values to plummet. Residents felt imprisoned in their own community. Only later would they fully appreciate the damaging effects these facilities might have on the health of their community. "We are not against profit or gain, but we want to gain in our own areas," said one resident. "We want to live."[5]

Toxic Assault

The recent incursion of waste treatment facilities into Chester began in the late 1980s. In 1987, the LCA Leasing Corporation, now defunct, began operating a waste transfer station in Chester that brought hundreds of truckloads of trash into Chester each day. Shortly thereafter, Abbonizio Recycling Corporation, a demolition debris recycling company, arrived, creating an enormous amount of dust in the residential neighborhood around it. In 1988, despite objections from many Chester residents, and without their input, the DEP granted a permit for the operation of the Westinghouse Resource Recovery Facility (a garbage incinerator). The Westinghouse incinerator is one of the largest in the country[6] and is permitted to burn more than 2,000 tons of trash per day. As well as burning 100 percent of Delaware County's own waste, the incinerator draws trash from three surrounding states—Delaware, New Jersey and New York—and from as far away as Ohio to feed its massive burners. "Since 1991, when the incinerator opened, trucks . . . barreled down Thurlow Street, once a quiet residential road, six days each week, often fifteen or more hours a day."[7] The Westinghouse incinerator brought not only trucks and dust, but also odor and, according to residents, more illness. Adults in the neighborhood began to experience respiratory problems, and their children missed more school than usual due to unexplained illness that the residents believe resulted from the incinerator.

The Westinghouse incinerator and Abbonizio Recycling operate in a community already surrounded by older industries such as Witco Chemicals, Scott Paper, British Petroleum, Sunoco Oil, and a twenty-year-old sewage treatment facility owned by Delaware County Regional Water Control (DELCORA). Recently, the state has issued permits to two other facilities to operate in Chester: Thermal Pure Systems, an infectious medical waste treatment facility, and Soil Remediation Systems, a contaminated-soil burning plant. Chester's environmental problems today are largely a result of this continuing stream of toxic facilities.

When President Clinton issued his Executive Order on Environmental Justice in February 1994, the United States Environmental Protection Agency (EPA) chose Chester as the subject of a six-month cumulative risk assessment. This study, released in the summer of 1995, found unacceptable cancer and noncancer risks, such as kidney and liver disease and respiratory problems, from the pollution sources in Chester.[8] The EPA also concluded that (1) blood lead levels in Chester's children are unacceptably high, with the level in more than 60 percent of the children's blood samples above the maximum level recommended by the Centers for Disease Control (CDC) and (2) air emissions from facilities in and around Chester account for a large component of the cancer and noncancer risk to the citizens of Chester. Peter Kostmayer, then head of the EPA Mid-Atlantic Region, pointed out that, although there was a correlation between the facilities in Chester and poor health in the community, causation was difficult to prove scientifically, because of other compounding factors.[9] Nevertheless, the clustering of facilities in Chester heightens the perception that the community's poor health status is linked to the surrounding waste processing facilities.

Tracing the Development of the Toxic Waste Industry in Chester

At first, the facilities in Chester seemed to appear "out of nowhere."[10] However, Chester's vulnerability to becoming a wasteland for toxic disposal can be traced to its economic, social, and political history. As with many urban areas in which toxic waste facilities are located, Chester's history as a former industrial haven helped to shape its destiny.

Chester's modern history begins in 1682, when William Penn rowed his boat ashore at a sandy stretch along the Delaware River, his first landfall in the Americas.[11] Chester's location along the Delaware River "made it ideal for small-scale manufacturing."[12] By the 1770s, Chester was a successful mill town, and it prospered as a manufacturing center until the 1940s. During this time, many southern blacks and immigrants from Poland and the Ukraine moved to Chester.[13] Shortly thereafter, however, the city began a decline in prosperity that ultimately led to the Chester of today. Like many other urban cities, Chester suffered from the postwar flight of its manufacturing industry overseas and the flight of middle-class whites to surrounding suburban neighborhoods. Between 1950 and 1980, 32 percent of the jobs in Chester disappeared. During the same time period, the African American proportion of the population increased from 20 percent to 65 percent.[14]

Chester is now one of the most economically depressed communities in Pennsylvania.[15] Predictably, social decline soon followed on the heels of the economic decline. Chester's school district is one of the worst in the state.[16] Chester also has the highest crime rate in the state.[17] Desperation accompanied this economic and social decline, with the city government "[e]ncourag[ing] everything and anything to come to town to provide jobs."[18]

Chester did not become a toxic wasteland on its own, however. Although its history foretold its social and economic vulnerability, the situation in Chester seems partly the result of its unique *political* history: a corrupt Republican political machine that has long controlled many aspects of local decision making, and some behind-the-scenes political machinations.[19] Peter Kostmayer, former head of the EPA Mid-Atlantic Region, recalled hearing from a DEP official that "there were political figures and their allies that had financial investments in Chester" and thus supported Chester as a home to the waste industry.[20] A close examination of the present scenario in Chester, including the issuance of waste treatment facility permits, seems to corroborate this assessment.

The most recent waste treatment facility permits issued in Chester can be traced to 1985, when Russell, Rea, and Zappala (RR&Z), an investment banking firm from Pittsburgh, together with Westinghouse, formed Chester Solid Waste Associates and purchased land in Chester.[21] Chester Solid Waste Associates has, as its name implies, brought waste to Chester—tons of it. RR&Z spoke with Delaware County officials about the possibility of incineration as a solution to the county's rising waste disposal costs and the region's dwindling landfill space; it also established the initial facilities that "brought the first glimpse of waste, trucks, and trash odors to the neighborhood."[22] From there, RR&Z's deal with Delaware County officials, who are predominantly white, laid the groundwork for the issuance of a permit for construction of the massive Westinghouse incinerator. According to Chester residents, RR&Z has retained control over every facility that has been permitted to locate in Chester, exerting direct influence over its waste-processing tenants. RR&Z owns the land where the Westinghouse and the Thermal Pure waste treatment facilities now sit. Moreover, most of the recently permitted facilities in Chester—LCA Leasing, Westinghouse, Thermal Pure, and the proposed Soil Remediation Systems—appear to share a corporate relationship under the purview of RR&Z officers.[23]

Not surprisingly, RR&Z has been the focus of two direct protests by outraged Chester residents. The documentary video *Laid to Waste*[24] documented the first protest, which took place in the summer of 1995. Community activists drove to RR&Z's Pittsburgh office and demanded a meeting. RR&Z refused to comply. RR&Z's indifferent attitude infuses a recent press quote: "If a site is economically feasible and passes all regulatory and zoning inquiries, then it's a viable project."[25] Responding to environmental racism charges, an RR&Z consultant quipped,

"It's not the firm's business to feel anything about commercial transactions, all of which were legally aboveboard and ethical."[26]

This attitude is not unique to RR&Z's spokesman. It also underlies the inadequacies of current siting laws, which allow this type of toxic proliferation in communities such as Chester. In Pennsylvania, the siting process does not consider the cumulative impact of preexisting facilities and the proposed facility, the disproportionate location of facilities in the host community, or the demographics of the targeted community. Each permit is considered in a vacuum, requiring only that the individual facility at issue comply with applicable emission regulations and other environmental assessments and technical requirements.[27] Moreover, once a facility is located in a host community, it is easy to expand that facility, allowing even more waste to be processed in the community.[28] As we explain later, this has happened in Chester, where the Westinghouse incinerator continues to expand its operations and import more waste.

The established pattern of waste treatment facilities essentially seals the community's reputation as a toxic wasteland. As EPA's Peter Kostmayer explains, "The presence of facilities molds the aesthetics and the economy. Other businesses are reluctant to locate where there are so many waste treatment plants."[29] Unfortunately, this has proven true in Chester. The new businesses that were supposed to locate near the Westinghouse incinerator have not arrived. Instead, according to a resident-activist, Zulene Mayfield, the only new businesses have been prostitution and drugs.

Taking Direct Action

In the early 1990s, Chester's residents banded together to fight back against what they viewed as an all-out attack on their community's quality of life and health. At that time, Chester was home to the Westinghouse incinerator, which is one of the country's largest waste incinerators, the DELCORA sewage waste treatment facility, the Abbonizio Concrete Recycling facility, and various older industrial operations. The DEP was on the verge of permitting an infectious medical-waste sterilization plant next to the Westinghouse incinerator. In October 1992, concerned residents attended a public meeting convened by the city's first Democratic mayor. Billed as a town meeting, it drew representatives from the EPA and the DEP, local government officials, and private industry. The residents aired their complaints about the facilities, odors, dust, noise, and trucks that carried trash to the facilities. Industry and government representatives offered responses such as, "Do you think your government would do something wrong to you? Do you think [we would allow this facility if it did not] meet all of the federal and state regulations?"[30] At least one resident found the attitude of the representatives condescending. Zulene Mayfield stood up, introduced herself, and told the representatives, "I can't understand why you bright, college-educated people can't come down here and tell a better lie than what you're telling. [W]e are people from probably the worst school district in the state and we can see [and] understand these lies." Mayfield got up and left. From that point on, Mayfield and other concerned residents of Chester began having weekly meetings. Eventually, a group of citizens formed Chester Residents Concerned about Quality of Life (CRCQL), with Mayfield at its helm.

CRCQL first set out to have one-on-one meetings with individual facility owners, city officials, and state officials. All these meetings, however, ended in a similarly disappointing fashion. The residents came to the meetings to complain about existing problems, yet the same problems re-surfaced week after week. Meetings ended with no resolution in sight and residents' questions left unanswered. No one seemed willing to take any responsibility for the problems the residents of Chester faced. A facility representative would tell CRCQL members, "Well, your problem is not exactly our problem," and then direct them somewhere else. Zulene Mayfield recounts that she felt like she was "a gerbil on a habitrail," running and running, and never getting anywhere. These initial meetings with industry and government officials foreshadowed a pattern of stonewalling that emerged every time the community sought information and solutions from industry and government.

Eventually, the residents got fed up with the stonewalling. They decided to gather the facility and government representatives together and "watch them point fingers at each other" instead of telling the residents to go talk to someone else. CRCQL arranged another meeting of local and state agency officials, as well as representatives from the Chester facilities. The confrontational dynamic expected at the meeting never materialized. Government and industry representatives seemingly agreed to divulge as little information as possible. For example, prior to the meeting, there was a fire at the Westinghouse incinerator. Many people from the community came out in force to photograph and tape the commotion surrounding the numerous pieces of emergency equipment employed to fight the fire. At the meeting, when the Westinghouse representative was asked about the fire, he denied that any fire had occurred. The residents were dumbfounded; they had photographed and videotaped a fire at the facility. Now, the company's representative was denying its occurrence. During subsequent meetings, CRCQL continued to challenge Westinghouse's denial. However, even when the fire chief presented CRCQL and the Westinghouse representatives with documentation of the fire, the company still denied there had been a fire. This and other incidents made the residents feel belittled, as if Westinghouse had deliberately decided: "Well, we had a fire, but let's tell them, 'We didn't have a fire,' and that's it. We'll offer no explanation to them." As Mayfield recalled, it was "very demeaning."

The government and industry officials' conduct at the meetings exemplified the ways in which the decision makers had treated the residents all along—as if they did not matter. Moreover, it seemed as if government and industry officials employed various tactics to keep the residents in the dark about issues that fundamentally affected their health and quality of life. For instance, one of the barriers the residents initially faced stemmed from their inability to understand the highly technical language the facility representatives used. When a resident attempted to speak in an open meeting to a Westinghouse representative about the incinerator, the representative immediately corrected the resident, telling her that it was a "resource recovery facility," a technical term for an incinerator.[31] This tactic played on the lack of sophistication of the Chester residents and effectively silenced them. As one resident remarked, "Every meeting we left feeling like our tail was between our legs, because they always tried to make us think that what was happening was not happening."[32] Believing that "intelligence" is an "equalizer," CRCQL members sought to familiarize themselves and other Chester residents with the terminology and technology of the facilities. Nevertheless, even as the residents educated themselves, government and industry representatives continued to ignore them. Meetings with facility representatives were completely unsatisfactory; the residents felt unacknowledged and unheard.

Refusing to surrender to government and industry stonewalling, and seeing no other alternative, CRCQL took more direct action after arriving at two important realizations. First, although concerned residents had tried to work through the system, acquiring technical knowledge about the facilities, reading all of the public documents, and requesting information from decision makers, they had come to realize that their concerns would not be addressed, much less resolved, if they continued to rely on that tactic alone. Second, CRCQL members had come to feel that decision makers had consistently demonstrated a lack of respect toward residents who were trying to obtain further information about the facilities.

On a cold day in December 1992, the residents held their first protest, focusing on one of the most visible and audible invasions into their city— the trucks carrying waste to the Westinghouse incinerator. On the morning of December 22, ten to fifteen residents, mostly senior citizens, lined Thurlow Street in Chester to stop the trucks from reaching their destination. Other residents joined in the protest on their lunch breaks. Westinghouse finally responded after residents physically refused to let the trucks take their load to the Westinghouse facility for up to two hours. Westinghouse's chief financial officer flew to Chester during the protest to meet with the residents. After hearing their story, Westinghouse officers agreed to build a new road for the trucks that hauled trash to the incinerator. Although the new route was built only one block away from the old one, the residents felt this protest was a success. For the first time since they had begun to stand up and voice their opinions, they felt empowered. As Mayfield, the head of CRCQL, explained, "It was really important [for Westinghouse] to understand that . . . this is important enough to stop Christmas shopping, to stop the season, . . . to let [them] know that we have a problem and we don't care how cold it is." The residents also realized that they needed to hit Westinghouse where it hurt— in its bank account. Thwarting normal business operations furthered this objective.

Despite the message of resistance sent by the protests, in July 1993 the DEP issued a permit for the construction and operation of yet another waste treatment facility in Chester. The community learned that Midlantic BioWaste Systems, Inc., a subsidiary of Thermal Pure Systems

(Thermal Pure), planned to build an infectious medical waste sterilization plant next to the Westinghouse incinerator. The proposed facility's
operators planned to sterilize medical chemotherapeutic waste through
a process called autoclaving.[33] They would then package and ship the
waste to a landfill. For Chester residents, this was the last straw—the
Thermal Pure facility compounded an already intolerable situation.
CRCQL mobilized the Chester residents and gathered more than 500
signatures in opposition to the project. It gave these signatures to the
DEP and the City Council as evidence of citizens' opposition to the facility. In response, the company withdrew its permit application, originally filed under the corporate name of Midlantic BioWaste Systems, and
reapplied under the name Thermal Pure. Again, this was nothing new.
Mayfield and CRCQL easily realized that the company was "hiding behind names."

Unfortunately, the residents then uncovered an even more en-
trenched barrier—local politics. All of the City Council members except
for the Mayor sent a letter to the Governor and to the DEP asking them
to expedite the permitting of Thermal Pure. Not surprisingly, the DEP
granted Thermal Pure's permit without holding a public hearing, virtually ignoring the residents' concerns. To the residents' dismay, the legal
requirement designed to include them in the decision-making process
ultimately denied the residents any opportunity to participate in the
process. In Pennsylvania, as in other states, permit applicants must publish formal notice of their proposed facility in local newspapers to give
the public an opportunity to comment on and learn about the facility.[34]
However, this form of notice often proves inadequate for low-income
communities, where literacy levels are low and it is unlikely that many citizens will become aware of or read the official notice. For instance, as
happened in Chester, it is not uncommon for notice of a permit application to be placed in a minuscule space at the back of the local newspaper.
On the other hand, "local [officials] are given a separate, formal opportunity to comment on municipal waste facility permit applications."[35]
Once again, the residents felt the decision makers had excluded them.
The residents believed that "[b]y not holding a public hearing, the DEP
was saying that there was no known public opposition to Thermal Pure,
in spite of the 500 plus signatures they had in opposition."[36]

A Hard Lesson: Environmental Justice as a Political, Not a Legal, Issue

A Philadelphia public interest lawyer, Jerome Balter, read an article about the Chester protest and decided to call CRCQL. This call began a long-term relationship between Balter and CRCQL. Through Balter's efforts, the residents discovered yet another weapon in their fight against the facilities—legal action. In August 1993, one month after the Thermal Pure permit was issued, Balter appealed the Thermal Pure permit on CRCQL's behalf. In its appeal, CRCQL claimed that the permit issued to Thermal Pure and the accompanying regulations promulgated by the DEP violated the Pennsylvania Infectious and Chemotherapeutic Waste Disposal Act (Disposal Act), which the legislature enacted to control waste flow in Pennsylvania.

Pursuant to the Disposal Act, the DEP promulgated the Infectious and Chemotherapeutic Waste Plan (Waste Plan). The effect of the Waste Plan was to divide Pennsylvania into three zones—eastern, central, and western—in order to regulate "incineration or other disposal" of infectious wastes.[37] The DEP found that the eastern zone, which includes Chester and Philadelphia, generated 13,335 tons of infectious waste per year.[38] Under the Waste Plan, covered facilities must obtain 70 percent of their waste from the zone in which the facility is located. The maximum capacity of a covered facility located within the eastern zone could be no greater than 10,765 tons per year.[39] Thermal Pure's permit nevertheless allowed the facility to handle 105,000 tons per year, nearly ten times the maximum allowed by the Waste Plan for a facility in the eastern region and nearly four times the waste produced by the entire state of Pennsylvania.[40] In its appeal, CRCQL questioned how a facility with the capacity to treat four times the waste produced in the entire state could be legal under a statute that was intended to minimize waste transportation in Pennsylvania.

In February 1994, the state Environmental Hearing Board summarily dismissed CRCQL's claims. The Board ruled that the DEP Waste Plan did not govern the Thermal Pure infectious waste sterilization process and that its permit was valid. CRCQL refused to give up. It appealed the decision to the Pennsylvania Commonwealth Court. In February 1995, the Commonwealth Court adopted CRCQL's reasoning, overturned the Environmental Hearing Board ruling, and declared that the Thermal Pure permit was invalid. The Court rejected the DEP's and Thermal Pure's argument that the Disposal Act did not cover the type of activity—autoclaving, a type of medical sterilization—conducted by the Thermal Pure facility. Thermal Pure then appealed to both the Commonwealth Court and the Pennsylvania Supreme Court for a stay of the ruling against them. Both requests were denied. Accordingly, the DEP issued a cease-and-desist order to Thermal Pure, forcing the company to suspend all further operations in Chester.

To CRCQL's amazement, its victory and the closure of Thermal Pure was short lived. Under Pennsylvania law, Thermal Pure had the right to appeal the DEP closure order to the Environmental Hearing Board. Instead, the company directly appealed the DEP order to the Commonwealth Court. Thermal Pure filed a petition asking the Court to review its previous decision not to stay the cease-and-desist order. At the same time, Thermal Pure asked the Pennsylvania Supreme Court to exercise special jurisdiction and to hear arguments on the stay. To everyone's surprise, the Supreme Court granted Thermal Pure's request, issuing a stay of the cease-and-desist order pending its review of the case.

In taking the case from the Commonwealth Court, the Supreme Court employed an extraordinary, and controversial, legal maneuver. The Supreme Court invoked its "King's Bench" power to take the case from the Commonwealth Court. The King's Bench power originates from the Act that created the Supreme Court of the Commonwealth of Pennsylvania in 1722 and gave the court power coterminous with the highest courts in England. An 1836 revision of the Act established the King's Bench power that gave the court the power to stop all existing proceedings in a lower court while it conducts its own review of a case.[41] A later constitutional provision, entitled "extraordinary jurisdiction," seemed to limit the Supreme Court's King's Bench jurisdiction to cases of "immediate public importance," consistent with the power's early beginnings.[42] In spite of its normal conservative practice, there have been "a number of remarkable occasions" in which the Supreme Court has invoked its jurisdiction in a manner that has expanded the Kings Bench power "beyond its original parameters."[43] This arguable overreaching has prompted the state legislature to revisit the question of the King's Bench power.[44] Nevertheless, the Supreme Court took the case before the Commonwealth Court was able to hear Thermal Pure's appeal. The effect of this exercise of the King's Bench power was to deny CRCQL any chance at an appeal.

Prior to making its final decision, the Pennsylvania Supreme Court held a hearing on the DEP regulations and the Thermal Pure permit. CRCQL was invited to attend the hearing and chartered a bus to Harrisburg. The group arrived with high hopes because, as Zulene Mayfield puts it, they believed that "the law is the law and whatever the law says is right. Everybody has to adhere to the law." Sadly, for Mayfield and CRCQL, the community activists were about to confront yet another tangible experience of institutional racism. Mayfield recalls the look of "contempt" in the eyes of the justices as the group entered the courtroom. "I can't say it was a look of hate," she explains, but she "knew before we sat down in that court what the outcome was going to be."

Jerome Balter represented CRCQL at the hearing and has his own view of the proceedings. Noting that there was no transcript or recording of the hearing, Balter relates the atmosphere that prevailed in the room. A justice said to Balter, "Mr. Balter, if it were up to you a lot of companies would lose their permits." To which Balter replied, "I don't take any permits away. That's the DEP's job." The justice did not relent: "Yes, but you start those cases, don't you?" Balter responded, "Well, that's right. I would think, your Honor, that you'd be interested in having the law defended and applied properly." The justice had the final word: "Mr. Balter, around here I am the law."[45]

In November 1995, the Pennsylvania Supreme Court overturned the commonwealth court ruling by a vote of 5-0, allowing Thermal Pure to reopen.[46] In its decision, the Supreme Court ruled that the Commonwealth Court lacked jurisdiction over the matter and that the Waste Disposal Act addressed merely incineration and other disposal and did not cover sterilization—Thermal Pure's process. Accordingly, the permit was deemed valid.

The decision stands under a cloud of illegitimacy for many Chester residents. According to CRCQL, the Supreme Court's initial use of the King Bench's power, and its ultimate disposition of the case, may have been influenced by the firm responsible for the recent proliferation of waste sites in Chester. Pennsylvania Supreme Court Justice Stephen Zappala is the brother of a partner in Russell, Rea, and Zappala, owner of most of the facilities located in Chester.[47] Justice Zappala rescued himself from the Chester case, but CRCQL believes he "exercised his influence" by "convincing the court to use the outdated King's Bench statute."[48] While this accusation has yet to be proven (though it has been repeated in the press),[49] the appearance of impropriety sounded the death knell for CRCQL members' belief that the law would provide justice for people like themselves. In their eyes, this was yet another example of the structural power of racism. As Mayfield summarized it, "racism is real," and it is "the determining factor [in] whether or not you're going to get justice."

Jerome Balter, in contrast, believes the community relied too heavily on the legal system. "There is a reliance on legal action, and no matter how much the lawyer says 'don't count on it,' they count on it." CRCQL learned a powerful lesson: while legal action brings much-needed attention to environmental justice struggles, legal strategies rarely address what is, in essence, a larger political and structural problem.[50] As the struggle surrounding the Thermal Pure case illustrates, lawsuits take place in a forum in which the resources of private corporations and government entities far outweigh community resources. Given its experience with the Pennsylvania Supreme Court, the Chester community is unlikely to rely solely on legal strategies in the future. In fact, the group realizes that legal strategies are merely "another stone in David's sling," a way to bolster their political struggle for empowerment and inclusion.[51]

Avoiding the Slippery Slope: Becoming Political Actors

In late 1994, CRCQL members became aware of yet another potential hazard targeted at their community. Remarkably, even with knowledge of the community residents' overall poor health and despite the stringent opposition of local officials, the DEP granted a permit to Soil Remediation Systems (SRS) to treat 960 tons of petroleum-contaminated soil each day at very high temperatures in order to burn off contaminants so that the soil can be land filled. Once again, the community mobilized. Petitions, protests, and a well-attended public hearing sent the message to SRS and the DEP that the community did not want another facility.

Yet again, residents ran into questionable tactics employed by the facility proponents. For example, early in the public hearing, a young man from the community stood up and said, "I don't care what they do, I need a job." After the resident spoke, one of Zulene Mayfield's friends—a man she considered to be like a nephew—approached her and explained what was happening. Pointing to the man who had just spoken, he hugged her and said, "I'll tell you what's up; he's paid. And they paid me, too, but I'm not going to talk." This tactic, of course, was not new. In a sense, it was the classic jobs-for-environment tradeoff that faces opponents of hazardous facilities.[52] The facilities were following the time-honored practice employed by businesses that hope to move into financially ailing communities: offering financial incentives and increased employment opportunities. CRCQL was well aware that the community needed more jobs and more economic development. Yet the group members were unwilling to sacrifice the quality of their homes, neighborhood, and health for the illusory gains the facility promised. Most of the residents had seen enough waste facilities move into Chester to realize the hollowness of such incentives and job offers. Fortunately, CRCQL had gained powerful allies by this time. In 1992, after decades of Republican party reign that kept "tight control over the city's votes by controlling public funds in such a way that every government function was delivered as a personal favor," the Democratic party overthrew the Republicans in what CRCQL calls "one of the most impressive political campaigns in the city's history."[53] CRCQL benefited from this change of leadership: the group convinced all five members of the City Council to oppose the SRS permit. Seemingly, the political tide had turned in CRCQL's favor. However, once again, its optimism and victory was short-lived. CRCQL, in a meeting with the Secretary of the DEP about the SRS permit, had convinced the agency to delay the permit decision until the EPA completed its health study of Chester. However, despite the public outcry, the opposition by the City Council, and the EPA's troubling conclusions in its health assessment of Chester, in the end the DEP granted the SRS permit.

Group members eventually shifted the focus of their political actions from the state level to the local. Instead of "reacting to the actions of the industries and the government" and "trying to convince the power brokers to act on their behalf," the residents moved proactively to "cut these industries off at the pass."[54] CRCQL again rallied the residents to the cause. CRCQL's first successful step in this direction was to convince the City Council to amend the zoning code so that waste management industries would encounter greater difficulty when attempting to site facilities in Chester. The group then canvassed the city for signatures on a petition to amend the zoning ordinance. It collected 3,000 signatures and presented them to the City Council. The Council dragged its feet until CRCQL confronted it and said, "If every meeting we have to call all 3,000 people and tell them the ordinance is not signed, we will do that."

In June 1994, the City Council passed an ordinance requiring any waste company hoping to locate in Chester to prove that the operation of its proposed facility would not increase overall pollution levels in the city. SRS failed to meet the burden of proof under the ordinance. As a result, SRS lost its DEP permit because it could not get a building license from the city and therefore failed to break ground by the permit's specified deadline. As one CRCQL member remarked, "Finally, the government was forced to react to the residents, instead of the other way around."[55]

The Importance of Building Coalitions

Even before CRCQL's brief victory and its stinging legal defeat in the Thermal Pure case, its leaders had realized that, to be effective, CRCQL needed to broaden its appeal beyond the African American community that accounted for most of its membership and that determined how it was presented in the local media. It had not always been that way, however.

When it was formed in 1992, CRCQL had two co-chairs: the Reverend Strand, from the African American community, and Monsignor Probaski, head of the local Ukrainian and Polish Catholic congregation. Monsignor Probaski was one of the primary organizers of the Westinghouse demonstration. However, during the demonstration, Probaski's secretary came to Thurlow Street and told him that the Archdiocese in Philadelphia wanted to speak to him right away. Shortly thereafter, Probaski returned to the protesters and insisted they disband. The protesters initially refused but eventually agreed to march down to the facility and then disband. At CRCQL's meeting after the protest, Probaski disclosed that he had received a $500 check from Westinghouse to renovate his church. He then told the group that he had ripped up the check and sent it back to Westinghouse. Curiously, the week following the meeting, Probaski resigned as co-chair of CRCQL and withdrew from the group. When he left, so did many of his Ukrainian and Polish parishioners. With the loss of Monsignor Probaski, CRCQL became primarily an African American organization. Currently, approximately 70 percent of the group membership is African American; the rest of the group consists of Latinos, elderly Polish women, and other whites.

In addition to its changing identity, other events forced CRCQL to reevaluate itself. For instance, during the legal battle against Thermal Pure, CRCQL experienced numerous forms of intimidation. The CRCQL office was vandalized twice. In one of the incidents, featured prominently in the video *Laid to Waste,* CRCQL's office was vandalized, and "KKK" was scrawled prominently above Mayfield's desk. As the group's leader, Mayfield received the brunt of many threats against CRCQL. She recalls a neighbor "telling all the little old ladies I better be careful or else somebody is going to firebomb my house." Her home and car were vandalized repeatedly, and she occasionally received expletive-laden threats, including death threats, on her answering machine. To top it off, Westinghouse threatened to bring a $250,000 lawsuit against her personally for blocking its trucks during CRCQL's protest.[56]

The loss of many of its non-African American members, its legal loss to Thermal Pure, and the intimidation tactics used against CRCQL members slowly took their toll. Many group members asked themselves, "How effective are we going to be if this machinery still views us in a negative way?" CRCQL sought to find a way to recast itself and to sidestep the racism that was destroying its effectiveness as a citizens' group. To expand its base, CRCQL sent out invitations over the Internet to an environmental justice retreat that it sponsored at Swarthmore College in February 1995. The conference not only informed and educated students about the concept of environmental justice but also created the Campus Coalition Concerning Chester, known as C4. Eventually, this student group grew to consist of students from more than fifteen campuses in four states, including Swarthmore College, located not far from Chester. The purpose of the group is to assist CRCQL in its battle to educate and fight against environmental injustice in the Chester community. The group wanted to get people the decision makers could "relate to." If it could not get the parents, then "let's get the children," the group reasoned. The goal was to "educate the kids and let the kids go home" and ask their parents the kinds of questions that were confronting the Chester community.

By broadening CRCQL's base, its members believed they could build a more politically sustainable partnership, as well as "take the focus off" CRCQL as an African American organization. According to Mayfield, the partnership with C4 has been "wonderful"—educating people on campus, in Chester, and in surrounding communities. C4 has also been involved in protests with CRCQL. Soon after C4 was formed, its members joined a protest against RR&Z at the firm's Pittsburgh offices. In the summer of 1995, CRCQL and C4 conducted a door-to-door health survey of Chester, which helped to document the poor public health of the community and to bolster the residents' claims of environmental damage. Their partnership has also spawned the Chester-Swarthmore College Community Coalition. Established by grant money, the coalition encourages college students and faculty to work in the Chester community to establish a broad range of social service programs.[57]

The Ongoing Struggle

The ebb and flow of toxic assault and political protest has become part of the reality of living in Chester. Residents once again mobilized to fight the Cherokee Environmental Group's application for a permit to burn contaminated soil in Chester. More than 200 concerned residents, suburban neighbors, and other interested citizens attended a public hearing on the application held in February 1997. CRCQL's efforts paid off when the DEP denied the Cherokee permit on various technical grounds.[58] The denial of the Cherokee permit, perhaps not coincidentally, came at a time when CRCQL had achieved other significant victories.

In December 1997, CRCQL successfully settled an environmental lawsuit, brought under the Clean Air Act, against the county's twenty-year-old DELCORA sewage treatment facility, which receives and treats waste for all of Delaware County. After a year-and-a-half-long negotiation among CRCQL, EPA, DEP, and DELCORA finally came to an end, DELCORA agreed to pay a $320,000 penalty, divided into two parts: $120,000 to go to the EPA and DEP and $200,000 to be used to fund a children's lead poisoning prevention program that Chester residents will manage.[59] Settlement discussions with Westinghouse over Clean Air Act violations ended in a similar settlement.

Shortly thereafter, in January 1998, CRCQL received more good news. A federal court ruled that residents have a "private right of action," under Title VI of the Civil Rights Act, to challenge the proliferation of waste treatment facilities on grounds of racial discrimination. Chester residents had sued the Pennsylvania DEP, claiming that its pattern of granting permits in Delaware County is racially discriminatory. As evidence, they pointed to the clustering of waste facility permits in Chester's predominantly African American community. The residents claimed that the DEP violated Title VI regulations, implemented to enforce Title VI, that mandate that any jurisdiction receiving federal EPA money "shall not use criteria or methods of administering its program which have the effect of subjecting individuals to discrimination because of their race, color, national origin, or sex."[60] The State, however, appealed the case to the United States Supreme Court. In August 1998, the Supreme Court declared the case moot and vacated the favorable federal court ruling.[61]

In the wake of the Court's decision, it appeared that the political tide might also be turning against CRCQL. In 1996, Republicans regained control of Chester after the city's residents had a mixed reaction to the city's short-lived Democratic administration. The turnover at City Hall may be attributable in part to low voter turnout, not surprising in low-income communities of color, and in part to the tumultuous Democratic administration.[62] Residents were understandably concerned that the Republican-controlled City Council would overturn the recently enacted zoning ordinance. The extent to which the tide is turning against CRCQL is unclear, however. The zoning ordinance remains intact, and despite the fact that the Republican mayor of Chester announced his full support of the Cherokee permit application, that application was denied by the DEP. The DEP subsequently denied an application submitted by Ogborne Waste Removal for a proposed construction and demolition transfer station in Chester.

CRCQL also faced a complex, continuing fight over the importation of waste from three states to feed Chester's massive Westinghouse incinerator. CRCQL scored a major, but short-lived, victory through the demonstration it staged at the State of Delaware's Solid Waste Authority's (SWA) offices.[63] When the SWA met in January 1997 to reconsider its export of 225,000 tons of trash per year to the Westinghouse incinerator, it voted to discontinue its shipments to the Westinghouse incinerator. Those responsible for feeding the Westinghouse incinerator did not remain idle, however. Shortly after the incinerator was sold to new owners, the SWA reversed its decision and signed a new contract in May 1997 with the incinerator's new owners, American Ref-Fuel. Under this agreement, 300,000 tons of waste per year is burned at the Chester incinerator.

Despite some setbacks and an uncertain future, CRCQL has created a venerable legacy; it is now a political force to be reckoned with in Chester. What began as a small group of residents concerned with their quality of life and their health has grown into an organization with the power to engage decision makers on issues that affect the residents' fundamental well-being. Indeed, CRCQL's biggest victories may be that it is a cohesive, healthy group and it is in coalition with C4. A self-taught community organizer, Zulene Mayfield recognizes that the importance of CRCQL's struggle goes beyond the individual victories and defeats in its campaign against the toxic facilities in Chester. "Historically, black people haven't realized the power they have. The people who have realized it, who have the knowledge, have to teach the others. We have to start using our own power."[64]

THREE

Environmental Racism

Beyond the Distributive Paradigm

The pattern of siting a disproportionate number of waste facilities in places like Chester, established empirically by national and regional studies, has provided substance to claims of environmental racism. But, as the Chester case study illustrates, the empirical studies and their important conclusions are part of a much larger picture. Chester is not unique as magnet for toxic waste facilities; it shares a social, political, and economic history with other communities that are experiencing a proliferation of unwanted toxic waste sites. Like them, it is a former industrial town now populated by low-income people of color after the flight of businesses and its white, middle-class population. Distributional outcomes are thus produced by, and within, an institutional context and a particular social structure. To understand fully the phenomenon of environmental racism, one must understand the structural processes that underlie the well-documented distributive outcomes. In this sense, unequal distribution is not the sine qua non of environmental racism. Instead, it is a crucial entry point for exploring the social and institutional processes underlying distributional patterns.

The Unequal Distribution of Environmental Hazards

Since the 1960s, researchers have analyzed the distribution of numerous environmental hazards: garbage dumps, air pollution, lead poisoning, toxic waste production and disposal, pesticide poisoning, noise pollution, occupational hazards, and rat bites. Their overwhelming conclusion is that these environmental hazards are inequitably distributed by income or race. In studies that looked at distribution of these hazards by income *and* race, race was most often found to be the better predictor of exposure to environmental dangers. Later studies have in large part confirmed these conclusions.

Appendix A contains an annotated bibliography of studies and articles that document the disproportionate impact of environmental hazards by race and, to a lesser extent, by income. These studies are best taken as a starting point, however: the inequitable distribution of environmental hazards should mandate closer, site-specific analyses of the underlying social processes that continue to produce such outcomes in the most disenfranchised communities.

Because waste facility siting is the focus of this book, our starting point is the seminal study that documents disproportionate distribution of toxic waste sites on a national level. The 1987 study *Toxic Waste and Race in the United States*, performed by the United Church of Christ's Commission for Racial Justice (CRJ), measured the demographic patterns associated with commercial hazardous waste facilities and uncontrolled toxic sites.[1] The CRJ study found that race was the most significant variable in determining the location of commercial hazardous waste facilities; communities with the greatest number of commercial hazardous waste facilities had the highest percentage of nonwhite residents. The CRJ's study of uncontrolled waste sites produced similar findings: three out of every five African American and Latino residents lived in communities with uncontrolled toxic waste sites. Furthermore, African Americans were heavily overrepresented in the populations of metropolitan areas with the largest number of such sites.[2]

More recent national studies, with a handful of exceptions, continue to document the persistence of racial disparities in the location of waste facilities; some studies report that results vary by ethnic group.[3] Most notably, in 1994, the CRJ updated its 1987 study. Based on its assessment of 530 commercial hazardous waste sites, the CRJ found even greater racial disparities in the demographics of people who live around such facilities. In particular, it found that from 1980 to 1993 the concentration of people of color (defined as the total population less non-Hispanic whites) in all zip codes with toxic waste sites increased from 25 percent to 31 percent. Similarly, in 1993, as in 1980, the percentage of people of color in a community increased as commercial hazardous waste management activity increased. The 1994 CRJ study found the increases statistically significant and concluded that there was little probability that the increase could be attributed to merely random fluctuation.[4] The CRJ was careful to note that the study had measured only the outcomes of environmental hazard distribution and did not determine "the root causes of this pattern."[5] Regardless of the causes, the report advocates toxic use reduction as a solution to disproportionate environmental impacts.

Researchers at the Social and Demographic Research Institute (SADRI) of the University of Massachusetts challenged the findings of the 1987 CRJ study. The SADRI study found that there was *not* a statistically significant pattern of racial or ethnic disparity in the distribution of commercial hazardous waste sites.[6] Though the SADRI study analyzed data similar to those used in the recent CRJ study, its methodology was significantly different. For example, the SADRI study used census tracts from 1980 and 1990, instead of zip codes, as the geographic unit of analysis. The SADRI researchers also used data from only metropolitan or rural counties, not from the entire United States, as their comparison group (nonhost tracts), possibly understating the relationship among race, ethnicity, and siting choices.[7] Moreover, the study looked only at African American and Latino populations and did not measure the proximity of other racial groups, such as Asians and Native Americans, to existing toxic waste sites. Hence, the researchers' conclusions leave out a not-insignificant percentage of the people of color population in the United States and possibly understate racial and ethnic disparities.

The most recent study, by Professor Vicki Been, supports the conclusions of both the 1987 and the 1994 CRJ studies, though it uses census tract data as in the SADRI study.[8] Like the previous studies, Been measured the location of commercial hazardous waste facilities and the demographics of people who live near those facilities. In particular, Been set out to analyze how the demographics of neighborhoods that host toxic waste facilities have changed over time. To do this, she used census data from the past three decades (1970, 1980, and 1990). Unlike the researchers in the SADRI study, who used a limited pool of nonhost tracts, Been compared the demographics of host tracts to those of *all* nonhost tracts. However, similar to that in the SADRI study, her analysis seems to have included only disparities that involved African Americans and

Latinos, not those that involved members of other racial groups as defined by the census, such as Native Americans and Asians.

Been's study found that toxic waste sites were disproportionately located near African American and Latino populations. In particular, Been's analysis demonstrated that the percentage of African Americans or Latinos in a census tract in 1990 is a significant predictor of whether or not that tract hosted a toxic waste facility. Been attributed the current inequitable distribution of toxic waste sites in African American neighborhoods to the existence of facilities sited before 1970. On the other hand, she attributed the current inequitable distribution of toxic waste sites in Latino neighborhoods to facilities that were sited after 1970. As to class disparities, Been's study indicated that high poverty rates were "negatively correlated" with the location of toxic waste facilities. Instead, the study concluded, it was working-class and lower-middle-income neighborhoods that contained a disproportionate share of facilities. The study did not measure the effect of the intersection of race and class (e.g., poor African American neighborhoods) on the probability that the tract hosts a facility.

Studies also document the government's unequal enforcement of environmental laws in the waste siting context. A 1992 study by the *National Law Journal* confirmed what environmental justice activists have known for years, that people of color are not protected as vigorously by enforcement of environmental laws as whites. The *National Law Journal* study found that "[t]here is a racial divide in the way the U.S. government cleans up toxic waste sites and punishes polluters. White communities see faster action, better results and stiffer penalties than communities where blacks, Hispanics and other minorities live. This unequal protection often occurs whether the community is wealthy or poor."[9] The Journal's study found that penalties applied under hazardous waste laws at sites in white communities were about 500 percent higher than were penalties applied at similar sites in communities of color; that for all violations of pollution laws, penalties in white communities were about 46 percent higher than in communities of color; and that under Superfund, the law designed to clean up toxic sites, it took communities of color 20 percent longer to be listed as priority clean-up sites than white communities. The disproportionately greater exposure in communities of color to environmental hazards is undoubtedly exacerbated by unequal enforcement of environmental laws in such communities.

Taken together, the national studies conducted to date provide evidence that people of color bear a disproportionate burden of environmental hazards, particularly toxic waste sites. Numerous local studies, with some exceptions, have, on the basis of their assessment of particular cities, counties or regions, similarly concluded that racial disparities exist in the location of toxic waste facilities. Though researchers will continue to study the distribution of environmental hazards, including toxic waste sites, there is already ample evidence to warrant a closer look at the factors that might lead to the outcomes thus far documented.

The Problem of Causation: Naming the Outcomes as Racism

As with most statistical research, studies that chart the disproportionate distribution of waste facilities simply establish *correlations*, not *causation*. Some commentators therefore question whether the maldistribution of environmental hazards is appropriately attributed to racism or other injustice or to a more benign explanation. Among the alternative explanations offered to explain the racial disparities are (1) that the social status or lifestyle choices of certain racial and ethnic groups result in maldistribution and (2) that maldistribution is a result of the operation of the "free market." What both explanations have in common is their description of existing social practices and social structure as a cause of current distributions. By accepting the existing social structure and practices as the "baseline" for causal analysis, these explanations tend to obscure the injustice of current distributions and dangerously suggest that the inequitable outcomes are a natural and inevitable feature of social and economic life.[10]

"Lifestyle" as Causation

The first explanation, what we call the "lifestyle" explanation, invokes a description of a social situation or status as the causal element explaining the distribution of hazardous wastes and other toxics. The United States Environmental Protection Agency's Environmental

Equity Workgroup, for example, after reviewing much of the evidence then available on the disproportionate impact of environmental hazards on people of color, concluded in 1992 that a "person's activity" is the main determinant of how much environmental exposure she bears.[11] The Workgroup further concluded that racially disparate environmental hazard exposure results from the fact that "a large proportion of racial minorities reside in metropolitan areas" and "are more likely to live near a commercial or uncontrolled waste site," that higher levels of certain pesticides in Latinos results from the fact that "racial and ethnic minorities comprise the majority of the documented and undocumented farm work force," and that racial disparities in exposure to contaminated fish result from the fact that some racial groups "consume more fish than the average population."

There is no doubt that certain groups of people, such as recent immigrants with poor English language skills, are concentrated in the most dangerous sectors of our workforce, agriculture and heavy industry. These same people are, not surprisingly, more likely than others to have multiple exposures to environmental dangers; they face more severe hazards on the job, in the home, in the air they breathe, in the water they drink, in the food they eat. Nor is there any dispute that many poor people and people of color are relegated to urban areas; as we explain later, their residential choices are limited by their poverty and by various forms of discrimination. Moreover, while they live with the greatest dangers, poor people and people of color have the least access to health care and often can not get it at all.[12]

That the current social location of certain people overexposes them to contaminated environments raises, rather than answers, important questions about the injustice that underlies environmental distributions. *Why* are African Americans disproportionately segregated in cities and thus overexposed to a variety of pollutants? *Why* are farm-workers disproportionately poor and Latino? *Why* do current environmental laws leave farm-workers unprotected? Why are certain racial groups forced to rely on subsistence fishing or on poisoned fish stocks? Without a further causal analysis of the social processes that constitute the current situatedness of various groups, the tautological "lifestyle" explanation amounts to little more than "blaming the victim."[13] The "lifestyle" approach plays an important social role in naturalizing the unequal distribution of environmental hazards, however, by describing dispro-portionate exposure as a choice those exposed have made, a decision that could, presumably, be changed. It allows the observer to acknowledge the unequal environmental protection of certain groups and, at the same time, to keep a safe distance from the social context and structural dy-namics that produce those outcomes. It also relieves the observer of any culpability for, or responsibility for changing, the unjust situation.

"Market Dynamics" as Causation

The second explanation—"market dynamics"—is by far the most com-mon, and important, causation objection to the empirical evidence of disproportionate impact. Market dynamics adherents ask the question "Which came first, the environmental hazard or the racial/class makeup of the neighborhood?" The suspicion underlying this question is that re-searchers have failed to compare the demographics of the neighborhoods at the time the facilities were sited and at the time measured by the study. This failure "leaves open the possibility that [the facilities] were not dis-parately sited in poor and minority neighborhoods" but that the "dy-namics of the housing and job markets" led people of color and the poor to "come to the nuisance"—for example, to move to areas that surround waste facilities because those neighborhoods offered the cheapest avail-able housing.[14] A waste facility, for instance, may "cause those who can afford to move to become dissatisfied and leave the neighborhood," or it may "decrease the value of the neighborhood's property, making the housing more available to lower income households and less attractive to higher income households."[15]

Again, the explanation is volitional: people, as rational economic ac-tors, are *choosing* to live in neighborhoods that host dangerous facili-ties.[16] There is inconclusive empirical support to date for the "market dy-namics" explanation for racial or economic disparities in the distribution of hazardous waste facilities.[17] Nevertheless, the market dynamics expla-nation is continually invoked to account for the racial disparities in envi-ronmental hazard distribution, as an alternative to the assumption that racially biased practices account for the disparities. As one commentator sums up, "by failing to address how [facilities] have affected the demo-graphics of their host communities, the current research has ignored the possibility that the correlation between the location of [facilities] and the socio-economic characteristics of neighborhoods may be a function of aspects of our *free market* system."[18] The implications of this alternative causal account is that where market dynamics produce current distributions, this fact renders the outcomes somehow more benign. This implication stands on its own terms, however, only if the market is unaffected by racial discrimination and other unjust processes.

"Free market" explanations, however, are notoriously incomplete. As others have persuasively argued, markets are social institutions shaped by various levels of state and private control. Choices and preferences made in the "market" domain are, as Cass Sunstein explains, "endogenous rather than exogenous"—a function of current information, consumption patterns, existing legal rules, social norms, and culture.[19] For instance, the historical and present reality of race discrimination in the housing market inevitably affects individual preferences and mobility in the housing arena. Given this history and present reality, the "free" nature of market choices must be called into question.

Proponents of the "market dynamics" theory of hazardous waste distribution do acknowledge the influence of well-documented housing discrimination on individual preferences and mobility in the market. Such racial discrimination in the sale and rental of housing, one proponent notes, "relegates people of color (especially African Americans) to the least desirable neighborhoods, regardless of their income level."[20] Moreover, even after a neighborhood becomes predominantly composed of people of color, market dynamics proponents recognize that "racial discrimination in the promulgation and enforcement of zoning and environmental protection laws, the provision of municipal services, and the lending practices of banks, may cause neighborhood quality to decline further" and that the "additional decline . . . will induce those who can leave the neighborhood—the least poor and those least subject to discrimination—to do so."[21] Nevertheless, by continuing to describe the forces that underlie racially disparate environmental distributions as "free market" dynamics, the explanation tends to subsume social practices of racial discrimination into rational economic processes and choices. The collapse of social practices of racial discrimination into economic processes subtly expands the domain of the "free market" to include, and hence to obscure, racially biased social practices.

The "market dynamics" explanation, like the "lifestyle" explanation, thus rests on a descriptive, rather than a normative, causal account of the racial disparities in environmental justice research. It is important not to confuse the two accounts. Undoubtedly the dynamics of the housing market, broadly construed to include discriminatory practices, can theoretically explain some of the racially disparate outcomes in environmental hazard distribution. As Regina Austin and Michael Schill have pointed out, given the combination of poverty and racially discriminatory practices, there might be a number of developmental patterns that would result in poor people of color either moving to, or being trapped in, neighborhoods with a disproportionate number of hazardous waste sites.[22] For instance, in one pattern, communities where poor people of color now live may have originally been homes to whites who "worked in the facilities that generate toxic emissions." In those communities, Austin and Schill explain, the housing and industry may have "sprang up roughly simultaneously," and whites may have "vacated the housing (but not necessarily the jobs) for better shelter as their socioeconomic status improved." In turn, poorer Latinos and African Americans "who enjoy much less residential mobility" may have taken their place. In another pattern, housing for African Americans and Latinos may have been built in the vicinity of existing industrial operations because "the land was cheap and the people were poor." In still another pattern, sources of toxic pollution may have been placed in existing minority communities. Determining the various factors that contribute to the distributive outcomes is indeed an important epistemological inquiry.

The "chicken-or-egg" question posed by commentators does not, however, answer the more fundamental inquiry posed by environmental justice research. The question underlying environmental justice research is normative; it asks, "What do we mean when we call an outcome racist or evidence of injustice?" The chicken-or-egg inquiry posed by these commentators is empirical; it asks, "Which came first, the waste facilities or the poor people of color?" Answering the second question does not necessarily answer the first. That is, the normative claim embedded in environmental justice research is not answered simply by a descriptive analysis of the forces that underlie a particular distributional pattern. Uncovering the patterns and processes underlying the distributive outcomes is an important first step; a normative evaluation of these patterns and processes is the next crucial step.

The post-siting market dynamics analysis employed is certainly useful in determining whether it is more descriptively correct to attribute environmental disparities to one set of social and/or economic processes than to another. However, even if one could establish that "market dynamics," and not the siting process itself, produce racially disparate outcomes, this would not tell us whether such market forces are just or illicit. Similarly, even if "lifestyle" factors accurately describe the forces that underlie exposure to a particular environmental hazard, further analysis is needed to evaluate whether those forces themselves are attributable to unjust social practices or norms or to some other benign explanation.

Structural Racism versus Judicially Constructed "Racism"

As Gerald Torres reminds us, in order to make sense of the term "environmental racism," one "must have a clear idea of what it means to call a particular activity racist."[23] Similarly, in order to determine whether the processes underlying particular distributions are racist, we must be clear on what that term means. On the one hand, as Torres explains, "the term racism draws its contemporary moral strength by being clearly identified with the history of the structural oppression of African Americans and other people of color in this society." On the other hand, judicial constructions of racism have severely narrowed the concept in recent years. The disparate impact of governmental or private action on a historically oppressed group, such as African Americans, is no longer sufficient to establish an actionable claim of race discrimination under the U.S. Constitution and most civil rights laws. Since 1976, the U.S. Supreme Court has construed "race discrimination" to mean intentional or purposeful conduct on the basis of race, or at least some consciousness of race as a factor motivating conduct.[24] This construction requires that the intent be attached to an individual actor. Hence, labeling the outcomes that correlate race and exposure to environmental hazards as "racist" invites the demand for evidence of an overt race-conscious impetus and a "single bad actor."[25]

Not surprisingly, claims of environmental racism have not fit into the existing judicial construction of racism. The invariable judicial response has been to reject environmental racism claims for failure to prove the requisite discriminatory intent attached to an identifiable perpetrator, notwithstanding demonstrations of disparate impact and discriminatory outcomes. For example, in *R.I.S.E., Inc. v. Kay,* a federal district court found no discrimination in the siting of a landfill in a predominantly African American area of a county despite evidence that, during the past twenty years, the County Board of Supervisors had approved three other landfills that were placed within one mile of neighborhoods that were respectively 100 percent, 95 percent, and 100 percent African American.[26] The proposed landfill in *R.I.S.E.* would have been placed within half a mile of a population that was 64 percent African American and 36 percent white. The population of the County was 50 percent African American and 50 percent white. Moreover, in the one instance where the County Board of Supervisors had opposed a landfill in the County, the surrounding community was predominantly white.

The *R.I.S.E.* court reasoned that, although the placement of the proposed facility would have a disproportionate impact on African American residents, "the Equal Protection Clause does not impose an affirmative duty to equalize the impact of official decisions on different racial groups." Instead, the clause "merely prohibits government officials from intentionally discriminating on the basis of race." The plaintiffs, in spite of the facts of the case, failed to meet their burden of proving intentional discrimination. The Court accepted, instead, the County's facially neutral explanation that it was motivated not by racial bias but by other factors. Despite the fact that residents opposed the facility, the Court found that the County Board had been motivated by the economic, environmental, and cultural needs of the African American community.[27]

This prevailing understanding of "racism," molded by judicial constructions, is myopic in its failure to accommodate for the fact that the nature of racism has become appreciably more subtle and structural. Historically, disparate racial treatment and impacts were easily traceable to overt, racially motivated actions. However, partly as a result of laws that punish and forbid such overt behavior, decision makers rarely openly and intentionally seek a discriminatory outcome. As Charles Lawrence argues, requiring conscious intent before characterizing an outcome as racist ignores "the fact that decisions about racial matters are influenced in large part by factors that can be characterized as neither intentional— in the sense that certain outcomes are self-consciously sought—nor unintentional—in the sense that outcomes are random, fortuitous, and uninfluenced by the decision maker's beliefs, desires and wishes."[28] Understanding racism thus requires a broader analysis, beyond legal understandings of this complex social phenomenon.

Judicial notions of "racism" may be necessary for various jurisprudential reasons—for instance, an intent requirement arguably reinforces the separation of powers between courts and political branches by making it difficult for courts to intervene in more democratic processes.[29] However, our definitions of racism and injustice need not be confined to juridical notions. As we have written elsewhere, and as illustrated by the Chester case study, the struggle for environmental justice is primarily a political and economic struggle, with law one facet of that struggle.[30] Understanding environmental racism thus requires a conceptual framework that (1) retains a structural view of economic and social forces as they influence discriminatory outcomes, (2) isolates the dynamics within environmental decision-making processes that further contribute to such outcomes, and (3) normatively evaluates social forces and environmental decision-making processes which contribute to disparities in environmental hazard distribution.[31]

The Social Structure of Environmental Racism: The Role of Race and Space

Let us assume that the current physical distribution of hazardous waste facilities could be attributed to the location of older facilities in neighborhoods that subsequently became populated by poor people of color—that "market dynamics" produced the racially disparate outcomes found in some communities. Even accepting that the siting process is not responsible for all racially disparate outcomes in environmental hazard distribution and that instead the demographics of a given community with a waste facility have changed over time, it is not easy to dismiss the notion that racism or injustice produced the results. If existing racially discriminatory processes in the housing market, for example, contribute to the distribution of environmental hazards, or of people of color, then it is entirely appropriate to call such outcomes unjust, and even racist.[32] In this sense, "environmental racism" is not a separate phenomenon at all. Environmental outcomes are instead a manifestation of racially discriminatory practices that continue to exist in our society.

The inequitable distribution of environmental hazards, particularly commercial waste facilities, can be traced historically to the patterns of residential segregation and its resulting structural inequalities. Spatial segregation and isolation are key features of racial inequality in our society. Racial segregation, in turn, shapes how groups are viewed and what type of resources they get. This spatial inequality creates a vicious, self-perpetuating circle of causation, resulting in uniquely disadvantaged communities. A brief look at the history of spatial segregation confirms that the construction of racial space, and its mechanisms, have had profound consequences in the distribution of social goods. Given this history, it is not difficult to conclude that the physical distribution of hazardous waste facilities is linked to the historical organization of racially identified space and its precipitating social processes and mechanisms—namely, discriminatory zoning, housing, and real estate practices.

In their book *American Apartheid: Segregation and the Making of the Underclass*, Douglas Massey and Nancy Denton chart the course of racially segregated space, beginning in the nineteenth century.[33] As they persuasively argue, residential segregation did not always exist, nor did it come about naturally. Segregation did not result from the "desires" of African Americans and other people of color (the "lifestyle" explanation), "impersonal market forces" (the "market dynamics" explanation), or as "a chance by-product of other socioeconomic processes," explain Massey and Denton. Before 1900, for instance, "blacks and whites lived side by side in American cities" in the north—in places like as Chicago, Detroit, and Philadelphia—as well as in the south in cities like Charleston, New Orleans, and Savannah. However, at critical points between the end of the Civil War in 1865 and the passage of the Fair Housing Act in 1968, "white America chose to strengthen the walls of the ghetto." During this time period, residential segregation was constructed and imposed through various public and private processes—discriminatory real estate practices, exclusionary and expulsive zoning, redlining, and white flight, among others—that both contained growing urban black populations and limited the mobility of blacks and other people of color. Some of these actions and decisions were individual, some were collective, and others reflected "the powers and prerogatives of government"; together, these practices effectively constructed and maintained the residential color line well into the twentieth century and up to the present.

Even if society were to purge itself of racism and become color-blind, and people were to behave purely as rational economic actors in their choices of mobility and residential location, racially segregated space would still persist today absent affirmative efforts to dismantle the vestiges of historical racism. As Richard Ford explains, "race-neutral policy could be expected to entrench segregation and socio-economic stratification in a society with a history of racism."[34] His conclusion rests on the fact that leaving historical residential segregation intact would affect virtually every aspect of social status, including employment opportunities and residential mobility. For instance, because the education system is financed through local taxes, segregated localities would inevitably offer vastly different levels of educational opportunity: "the poor, black cities would have poorer education facilities than the wealthy, white cities." In turn, "whites would be better equipped to obtain high-income employment than would blacks." Whites' increased economic status would likewise translate into an increased ability to buy into economically superior neighborhoods and would mean that the market value of white homes on average would be significantly higher than that of black homes. Thus, "blacks attempting to move into white neighborhoods would, on average, have less collateral with which to obtain new mortgages, or less equity to convert into cash."

Residential segregation would also result in closed social networks, which "form the basis of the ties and the communities of trust that open the doors of opportunity in the business world," and thus would decrease the likelihood that crucial social connections would be formed between members of different races. Without some intervention to dismantle historical racial segregation, racial stratification on all levels of society would likely perpetuate itself, explains Ford, even in the absence of current racism. Although "there is no racist actor or racist policy in this model," racially defined communities "perform the 'work' of segregation silently." Racially stratified space thus, as Ford concludes, becomes "the inert context in which individuals make rational choices" and "a controlling structure in which seemingly innocuous actions lead to racially detrimental consequences."

Unfortunately, we don't live in a color-blind world, nor one in which legal rules and social action have eliminated either the vestiges of historical racism or even all of the current manifestations of racism. Adding racist actors and current racism to historical patterns, Ford explains, further exacerbates the dynamic of racial stratification and makes possible a number of public activities and private practices that continue to entrench racial inequality. As Massey and Denton document, the systematic segregation and isolation of racial groups continues to this day as a result of exclusionary real estate practices, racial and cultural bias, and pervasive discrimination. Surveys indicate that whites continue to be very apprehensive about racial mixing, fearing declines in property values and other deleterious effect on neighborhood qualities. To a large extent, these fears are based on racial stereotypes about African Americans and other groups.[35] Nevertheless, for whatever reason, white demand decreases for neighborhoods that African Americans and Latinos, in particular, begin to integrate.[36]

Moreover, the cultural differences and socialization resulting from the history of racism and from racial segregation have produced a fear and distrust of whites, particularly by African Americans, who fear white hostility, rejection and/or violence, studies show. As a result, many of them are reluctant to live in white neighborhoods in the absence of a significant number of other African Americans. Thus, even when African Americans *are* able to move into white neighborhoods, "contemporary society imposes significant costs" on integration.[37] "The additional amenities and lower taxes of the white neighborhood [are] often outweighed by the intangible but real costs of living as an isolated minority in an alien and sometimes hostile environment."[38] These costs make it even more difficult for African Americans, and members of other racial groups, to move to predominantly white neighborhoods, regardless of class.

The attitudes and fears of both whites and people of color would not in and of themselves perpetuate racial segregation without discriminatory mechanisms to enforce them. As Massey and Denton have shown, the "segmentation of black and white housing demand" is encouraged and supported by pervasive discrimination in the housing and lending markets. Empirical evidence demonstrates that real estate agents often limit the likelihood of black entry into white neighborhoods "through a series of exclusionary tactics" and "channel black demand for housing into areas that are within or near existing ghettos." This discrimination by realtors is further enforced by the "allocation of mortgages and home improvement loans, which systematically channel money away from integrated areas." In essence, race remains the "dominant organizing principle" for housing and residential patterns in spite of the Fair Housing Act and other civil rights reforms.[39]

In addition to discriminatory real estate and lending practices and "white flight," a variety of facially neutral rules and decisions add to the creation and maintenance of racially identified, and subordinate, neighborhoods. For instance, the MIT economist Yale Rabin has demonstrated that, in communities across the country, many residential neighborhoods composed of people of color have been re-zoned as industrial by white planning boards, a process Rabin calls "expulsive zoning." While these zoning decisions are not made with reference to race, their impact, given racial segregation, has profound racial implications. As Rabin explains, "[b]ecause it appears that [the re-zoned] areas were mainly black, and because whites who may have been similarly displaced were not subject to racially determined limitations in seeking alternative housing, the adverse impacts of expulsive zoning on blacks were far more severe and included, in addition to accelerated blight, increases in overcrowding and racial segregation." These types of zoning decisions allowed heavy industry to locate in African American residential neighborhoods and also led banks to stop loaning money for home improvement and maintenance because of improper zoning.[40] As we saw in Chester, one of the common attributes of communities that are experiencing a disproportionate influx of waste facilities is their status as former industrial towns, now abandoned by industry and desperate for new economic development. Indeed, as we shall see, waste facility developers affirmatively select sites in heavy industrial areas that have little or no commercial activity.

Physical segregation and isolation thus have intense political and economic consequences, particularly for poor African Americans and Latinos living in inner cities. Segregation not only concentrates poverty but also economically dislocates people.[41] This racialization of space "reaches to the societal processes in which people participate and to the structures and institutions that people produce."[42] Residential location, for instance, is seen as an indication of the attitudes, values, and behavioral inclinations of the types of people who are assumed to live there.[43] Segregated communities are isolated not only geographically and economically, but also socially and culturally; this isolation, in turn, leads to political marginalization.[44] Accordingly, the concerns of such communities are rarely taken seriously in the political process, and are often ignored altogether by decision makers.[45] This observation is borne out graphically in the experiences of the residents of Kettleman City and Chester, chronicled in previous chapters, and those of Buttonwillow residents, detailed in chapter 4.

Social Structure and the Siting Process

The preceding assessment of post-siting market dynamics is still an incomplete causal account of environmental injustice in communities such as Chester. Post-siting market dynamics may explain how communities like Chester became predominantly poor and/or of color *after* the influx of older industrial and waste facilities. Post-siting market dynamics does not, however, explain the *current* siting pattern in Chester, nor the wave of environmental disputes arising in many communities across the country. Empirical studies continue to document that new waste facilities are disproportionately sited in low-income communities of color. Moreover, anecdotal accounts of current siting disputes paint a troublesome picture of disproportionate siting patterns in poor communities of color. The Chester experience illustrates one such account. The *R.I.S.E.* case, discussed earlier, illustrates another. There are countless other examples across the country.

Examining the structured inequalities embedded in post-siting "market dynamics" does help one understand and evaluate current siting processes within their social context. Although the siting process does not produce the structured inequalities created in part by racially discriminatory processes, as we have detailed, it is heavily dependent upon them. Conventional industry wisdom counsels private companies to target sites that are in neighborhoods "least likely to express opposition"—those with poorly educated residents of low socioeconomic status. Not surprisingly, many communities that host toxic waste sites possess these characteristics. State permitting laws remain neutral, or blind, toward these inequalities; they therefore perpetuate, and indeed exacerbate, distributional inequalities.[46]

In most states, the hazardous waste siting process begins when the private sector chooses a site for the location of a proposed facility. Because the proposed location of a hazardous waste facility near, particularly, a neighborhood of white people of high socioeconomic status often faces strong public opposition, there is a limited supply of land on which to site such facilities.[47] Inevitably, the siting process focuses on industrial, or rural, communities, many of which are populated predominantly by people of color. Because land values are lower in heavily industrial and rural communities than in white suburbs, these areas are attractive to industries that are seeking to reduce the cost of doing business.[48] Furthermore, these communities are presumed to pose little threat of political resistance because of their subordinate socioeconomic, and often racial, status.[49]

Rarely does a "smoking gun"—explicit racial criteria or motivation—exist behind the decision to locate a toxic waste facility in a community of color. The reasons frequently given by companies for siting facilities are that such communities have low-cost land, sparse populations, and desirable geological attributes.[50] Notably, however, there is evidence that portions of the waste industry target neighborhoods that possess the attributes of many poor communities of color, using "race-neutral criteria." In 1984, the California Waste Management Board commissioned a study on how to site waste incinerators. The report, written by the political consulting firm Cerrell Associates of Los Angeles and entitled *Political Difficulties Facing Waste-to-Energy Conversion Plant Siting* (popularly known as the Cerrell Report), set out "to assist in selecting a site that offers the least potential of generating public opposition."[51] The report acknowledged that "since the 1970s, political criteria have become every bit as important in determining the outcome of a project as engineering factors." The Cerrell Report suggests that companies target small, rural communities whose residents are low income, older people, or people with a high school education or less; communities with a high proportion of Catholic residents; and communities whose residents are engaged in resource extractive industries such as agriculture, mining, and forestry. Ideally, the report states, "officials and companies should look for lower socioeconomic neighborhoods that are also in a heavy industrial area with little, if any, commercial activity."

While corporations were quick to disavow the use of the study, this community profile just happens to fit all three of the California communities that host the state's commercial toxic waste dumps—Buttonwillow (chronicled in chapter 4), Kettleman City (chronicled in the Preface) and Westmorland. Each of these small, rural communities has a high percentage of residents who live below the poverty line. Each community is predominantly Latino and Catholic, with many farm-workers, and most residents have few years of formal education. Additionally, the Cerrell profile fits another community profiled in this book: Chester, Pennsylvania, is a heavy-industrial inner city with little commercial activity, populated predominantly by working-class and poor people of color.

Likewise, even the "race-neutral" criteria used by government and industry for siting waste facilities—such as the presence of cheap land values, appropriate zoning, low population densities, proximity to transportation routes, and the absence of proximity to institutions such as hospitals and schools—turn out not to be "race neutral" after all, when seen in their social and historical context. Race potentially plays a factor in almost every "neutral" siting criterion used. "Cheap land values" is, understandably, a key siting criteria for the waste industry and other developers. However, because of historical segregation and racism, land values in the United States are integrally tied to race. In urban areas across the United States, this is starkly clear: an acre of land in the San Fernando Valley of Los Angeles has roughly the same physical characteristics as an acre of land in South Central Los Angeles, but people are willing to pay a premium to live in all-white neighborhoods. In rural areas, the pattern is similar: low land values tend to be found in poor areas, and people of color are overrepresented among the rural poverty population.

The land value cycle is vicious, too: once a neighborhood becomes host to industry, land values typically fall or do not increase as quickly as those in purely residential neighborhoods. Thus, a community that initially has low land values because it is home to people of color becomes a community that has low land values because it has a preponderance of industry, which in turn attracts more industry, creating a cumulative effect on land values. As we noted earlier, calling these changes "market driven" naturalizes the underlying racism in the valuation of the land.

Thus, when a company makes a siting decision on the basis of land values in urban areas, far from being "race neutral," it is focusing on land more likely to be in proximity to people of color.

Zoning is inextricably linked with race, as well. As we noted earlier, Yale Rabin's studies of historical zoning decisions have documented numerous instances where stable African American residential communities were "down-zoned" to industrial status by biased decision makers, allowing inappropriate land uses near residents and ruining the social fabric of the neighborhoods. Rabin found that local zoning bodies in the early part of the century routinely zoned as "industrial" many residential African American communities, even as they zoned as "residential" similar white areas. These zoning practices permitted the intrusion of disruptive, incompatible uses and generally undermined the character, quality, and stability of the black residential areas. Such "expulsive zoning," as Rabin calls it, permanently alters the character of a neighborhood, often depressing property values and causing community blight.[52] The lower property values and the zoning status are then easily invoked as "neutral" criteria upon which siting decisions are made.

"Low population density" translates to the siting of facilities in rural areas. In a major region of the country—the U.S. South—rural areas have populations that are disproportionately African American because of the historical influence of slavery on population settlement and distribution patterns.[53] In fact, a study of Mississippi discovered that population density was inversely correlated with race; that is, the less dense the population was, the more African American it became.[54] In other areas such as Texas and California, where historical settlement patterns and the current agricultural economy result in a rural population that is increasingly Latino, low population densities lead to the siting of facilities near farm-worker communities.

Proximity to major transportation routes may also skew the siting process toward communities of color, as freeways appear to be disproportionately sited in such communities.[55] Similarly, locational criteria—prohibitions against the siting of waste facilities near neighborhood amenities like hospitals and schools—skew the process toward underdeveloped communities of color, since such communities are less likely to have hospitals and schools. Hence, siting criteria that prohibit the siting of waste facilities close to such facilities perpetuate the historical lack of such amenities in these communities.

The sociologist Robert Bullard documented this underlying racial discrimination in an otherwise "neutral" siting process. Bullard's documentation was recognized in a 1997 decision by the Nuclear Regulatory Commission's Atomic Safety and Licensing Board, which overturned a facility's permit. In an administrative appeal to block the siting of a uranium enrichment facility in a poor and African American area of Louisiana, Professor Bullard successfully argued that racism more than likely played a significant part in the selection process. Bullard demonstrated (through a statistical analysis) that at each progressively narrower stage of the company's site selection process, the level of poverty and African Americans in the local population rose dramatically until it culminated in the selection of a site whose a local population is extremely poor and 97 percent African American. The race-neutral siting criteria— including the criteria of low population and the need to site the facility five miles from institutions such as schools, hospitals, and nursing homes—operated in conjunction with the current racial segregation and the resulting inferior infrastructure (e.g., lack of adequate schools, road paving, water supply) to ensure that the location selected would be a poor community of color. The NRC's licensing board, on the basis of Bullard's evidence, overturned the facility's permit and directed the NRC staff to conduct a "thorough and in-depth investigation" of the site selection process and to determine whether "the selection process was tainted by racial bias." In doing so, it ordered the staff to "lift some rocks and look under them" because racial discrimination is "rarely, if ever, admitted" and is "often rationalized under some other seemingly racially neutral guise, making it difficult to ferret out," and "direct evidence of racial discrimination is rarely found."[56]

The Structure of State Environmental Decision Making: Waste Permitting Processes

Permitting laws and policies both mediate and legitimize the dependence of private decision makers on structural inequalities in choosing facility sites. An important starting point for understanding the structure of environmental decision making with regard to siting waste facilities is the respective roles of the federal and state governments. Simply put, the federal government has relinquished the siting of waste facilities to the states. The Resource Conservation and Recovery Act (RCRA) comprehensively regulates solid and hazardous wastes from "cradle to grave"—from waste creation through disposal—but essentially delegates responsibilities for locating and permitting waste processing facilities to state environmental agencies.[57] The United States Environmental Protection Agency has provided some guidance to states in constructing permitting and siting programs. The EPA counsels states to execute a technical evaluation of proposed sites before any single site is selected, to select sites through a process that provides for public participation, and to ensure that site selection processes are not encumbered by blanket local vetoes, which would permit local governments to outlaw the siting of any unwanted facility within their jurisdictions.[58] On the whole, state programs follow this broad outline in permitting waste facilities. Aside from these guidelines, however, states are free to regulate siting, including the permitting of waste facilities, as they please. State permitting processes vary widely.

Though state siting regulations vary, some common themes illustrate the complicit role of these laws in inequitably distributing toxic waste facilities. Even though private decision makers must seek permits from official decision makers, such as state agencies, there are often no formal criteria that take into account the siting processes' reliance on structural inequalities; indeed, too often state agencies passively acquiesce to industry siting decisions. Aside from technical siting criteria and (often weak) public notice requirements, the permitting decision is almost entirely in the discretion of administrative agencies. Unfortunately, these agencies, in determining a proposed facility's "suitability" for a community, rarely look beyond the geological and environmental characteristics of the proposed site. Most agencies would argue that current permitting laws do not allow them to do so. This is true. Permitting laws generally do not specify evaluation criteria that allow for a formal assessment of the demographics, health problems, quality of life, and infrastructure of the surrounding community, or of the cumulative environmental or health effects of other facilities in the area.

There are two main ways states regulate or take part in waste facility siting, which we call the *passive* and *active* approaches.[59] Most states take a passive or *ad hoc* approach to siting, allowing private companies to initiate the process by seeking a permit to construct a facility at a specific location chosen by the private entity. Far fewer states take an active or *"advance site designation"* approach, in which a state siting committee initiates the siting process by identifying suitable sites around the state for future waste facilities. The state then solicits private-sector proposals for developing facilities on those sites or simply maintains the inventory of sites until project proposals are submitted by developers.

Under the majority, passive, approach to siting, private developers identify the sites for waste facilities, using a variety of criteria, including land values, zoning, access to major transportation routes, political considerations, and other characteristics of the host community. Although most of these criteria appear neutral on their face, as we have explained, many actually have profound racial implications, being based on historical racially based decisions and thus perpetuating the disproportionate siting of waste facilities in communities of color. Land values and zoning, for example, as explained earlier, may be based on racially premised historical land use patterns and expulsive zoning. Political considerations, such as the degree of expected community opposition, also lead to racially biased outcomes.

After the prospective waste facility developer initiates the process by choosing a potential site location, it applies for a permit from the state environmental agency. The agency evaluates the application, then approves or rejects the permit application according to whether the applicant has met all the legal criteria for receiving a permit. In assessing the suitability of a proposed waste facility site, decision makers rely primarily on technical criteria and an environmental assessment of the facility. Decision makers generally do not consider the cumulative impact of the new facility and the preexisting facilities or land uses, the potential for disproportionate location of facilities in the host community, or the demographics of the targeted community. Instead, each permit is considered in a vacuum, requiring only that the individual facility at issue comply with applicable environmental regulations and other environmental assessments (e.g., avoiding a certain degree of proximity to wells, surface waters, residences, recreational areas, wetlands, and endangered species habitat).[60]

There are exceptions to this socioeconomic myopia in assessing the suitability of a facility in a particular community. Some states have incorporated "soft criteria" into their site suitability assessment, considering such nonenvironmental factors as the demographics of the community, community perceptions and opposition, psychological costs, the potential for change in property values, the presence of other facilities in the community, and the cumulative health risks presented by other sources in the host community.[61] Some states mandate a formal environmental impact statement for hazardous waste facilities, often requiring the consideration of the social and economic impacts resulting from the proposed facilities.[62] Still other states control the distribution of waste facilities by prohibiting them in areas already burdened by the presence of one or more facilities.[63]

Nevertheless, despite the increasing use of "soft" environmental assessment criteria, it is not clear how much weight socioeconomic factors are given in the decision-making process. State administrators retain considerable discretion in applying nontechnical criteria, allowing for the possibility that these criteria will ultimately be ignored in the final decision. Likewise, even where state law mandates an environmental impact report that analyzes socioeconomic impacts, there is no assurance that the environmental assessment will acknowledge severely disadvantaged communities, let alone study them for potential impact; even if an impact is *recognized,* few states require that it be mitigated before a project is approved.[64]

Some socioeconomic studies determine that a community will benefit from the proposed facility, on the theory that the development will bring jobs or tax revenues to the area. However, developers' proffers of increased employment opportunities and host fees are often called "environmental extortion" by residents faced with the trade-off between jobs and health.[65] Furthermore, the economic development promises are rarely realized. The reality is that industrial development of the sort challenged in environmental justice struggles such as those in Chester provides few, if any, jobs for the residents around a facility and in fact can cost the community jobs immediately and in the long term, as well as burden all residents with higher taxes.

Nowhere is this more apparent than in Cancer Alley, the industrial corridor along the Mississippi River between Baton Rouge and New Orleans, Louisiana.[66] Convent, Louisiana, a predominantly poor, African American community, is host to the largest number of industrial facilities of any town along Cancer Alley. Convent also has the highest unemployment rate of any community along Cancer Alley. The Shintech Corporation proposed to build yet another plant in the community and promised that the plant would foster economic development. But many community residents were rightly skeptical, contending that such jobs had been promised at nine other industrial facilities that were operating in Convent, yet those companies had hired few if any local residents. Had they done so, Convent would not have had the highest unemployment of all the towns in Cancer Alley. Instead, many community residents reasonably concluded that they would get only Shintech's toxic emissions, not its jobs. Eventually, corporate officials were forced to admit that almost none of the labor for the plant would come from the local community, because the educational background of local residents did not meet the company requirements.

One Michigan court recently recognized that there is often a gap between the promise and the reality of economic benefits in vulnerable communities that host waste facilities. In a case in which a community group challenged a waste incinerator, the Genesee Power Station in Flint, Michigan, the court took note of the fact that the newly constructed $80 million plant failed to employ one person of color in its construction. The court further noted that only one of thirty permanent positions at the plant was occupied by a person of color, and that person was hired at minimum wage. The court concluded, as have many communities, that "the people who will benefit from the profits of the plant do not reside in the neighborhood. However, those who will bear the brunt of the pollution cannot even obtain employment in the plant."[67] In Kettleman City, the revenues from the proposed waste incinerator were to go to the adjacent white community in the county, not to the Latino community in which the facility was to be located and its effects most intensely felt. Other communities, such as Chester, have seen enough waste facilities proliferate around them, and have observed often enough the resulting lack of economic development, to realize the hollowness of promises of economic "benefits."

Beyond the Distributive Paradigm

The studies that chart the disproportionate distribution of environmental hazards have been a wake up call for those in this country who care about social justice. However, in a sense, the studies are just a beginning in fully understanding the phenomenon of environmental injustice or racism. As we have demonstrated, focusing on distributional results alone obscures the social structure and institutional context in which environmental decisions are made. Absent a deeper focus on the processes that lead to racially disparate outcomes, the studies provide only an incomplete understanding of environmental racism.

This is not to say that distributive patterns are not crucial to the environmental justice inquiry, even when it focuses on environmental decision making. Distributional patterns and decision-making processes are intricately intertwined in important ways. As we have said, distributive patterns are a crucial entry point for exploring the justice of the social processes that underlie those patterns, including environmental decision-making processes. Evaluating decision-making processes, in turn, also requires an evaluation of distributions. For instance, a legitimate decision-making process often depends upon an adequate distribution of various social goods, or rights, that are crucial to participation in that process.[68] In the environmental justice context, for instance, some social groups approach environmental decision-making processes with fewer social goods (e.g., time, money, education, information, specialized knowledge, access, and influence) than more privileged groups. Not surprisingly, these same groups remain disadvantaged in the distribution of goods by those processes.

As we began to explore in this chapter, and will continue to explore in the next two chapters, environmental decision-making processes are a location of contestation by, and reform through, grassroots struggles. However, formal decision-making processes are not the only area where ordinary citizens are taking control of the decisions that affect their lives. Through direct protests, litigation, and other strategies, environmental justice advocates are questioning the justice of existing decision-making processes and at the same time creating their own organizations and networks to affect the way in which environmental decisions get made.

FOUR

Buttonwillow

Resistance and Disillusion in Rural California

It was a hot summer afternoon in Buttonwillow, California, when someone knocked on Rosa Solorio-Garcia's front door to tell her that her friend and babysitter, Juanita Fernandez, had fainted in a neighbor's front yard. Rosa, worried because Juanita was pregnant, rushed out the door. By the time she got to the sidewalk, Juanita was coming down the street screaming. "She came into the house screaming, and I really didn't know what was going on," recalls Rosa. "It was hard to calm her down. I finally calmed her down, and she told me that the doctor said her baby had anencephaly"—that is, the baby did not have a brain. "The doctor just cold-bloodedly told her that she was going to have a baby that was going to be deformed. So she freaked out. And she fainted along the way home, I guess, from the heat and the stress and everything."

Juanita Fernandez and Rosa Solorio-Garcia are among the many Buttonwillow residents who will never forget that day, which changed their lives forever. The discovery that Juanita was to have a child with a severe birth defect galvanized their tiny community and raised the stakes considerably in a local struggle that was just beginning—the struggle by the residents of Buttonwillow to stop the expansion of a nearby toxic waste dump run by Laidlaw, a Canadian toxic waste giant.

Juanita carried the child to term, five months later, in September 1992; when young Alberto was born, he lived just forty minutes. The child's funeral brought the community group together in an agonizing fashion. "The funeral was devastating," remembers Luke Cole. "It was really tough seeing this little tiny coffin lowered into the ground." That same month, another child in the community—the son of Maria and Cheto Rodriguez—was born with a severe birth defect, spina bifida, in which the spinal column is not completely formed. Coming at the same time as Juanita's child, the Rodriguez child helped community residents put two and two together. In their minds, Laidlaw had to be the culprit.

> Those cases were then linked to Laidlaw. It was linked. I mean, we couldn't prove it, right? But, in everybody's mind it was because of what was going on with Laidlaw. Myself, I thought, the community is surrounded by agriculture, so you may have all kinds of things. It might not just be Laidlaw in itself. You know, pesticides sprayed for cotton, all these other things, all these chemicals that are around them. But, then, because Laidlaw is there, it became also linked to Laidlaw. It had an impact. The first impact kind of weighed everybody down. But then, the more that we got into it, I think it made them angry, very angry.
>
> —Lupe Martinez, organizer

The Community Awakens

Buttonwillow is a working-class town of 1,500 residents in the southern end of California's San Joaquin Valley. Its residents work primarily in the two main industries of the area—agriculture and oil production. Just over 50 percent of the residents are Latino; most are farm-workers employed on nearby ranches.

Buttonwillow is also the host to one of California's three toxic waste dumps, the Lokern facility, run by the Canadian toxic waste dumping company Laidlaw, which is eight miles west of the tiny town. Highway 58, until recently the main route for trucks filled with toxic waste bound for the dump, runs through the middle of town and past the local elementary school. At times, more than 200 trucks a day would whiz by the school, carrying their toxic load. "The trucks carrying toxic waste come through town, and they park at the local restaurant, and we can smell the stuff coming out," says a Buttonwillow resident, Saul Moreno.

Fernandez, a recent immigrant from Mexico, was living with the Garcias and taking care of their three children while Rosa and her husband, Lorenzo, were at work. She was four months pregnant with her first child, and Rosa had taken her to the local clinic, a block away, for a checkup. The doctor had determined that Juanita's child would be born without a brain. While it is impossible to determine the cause of the child's anencephaly, residents sincerely believe it was the toxic dump.

The residents of Buttonwillow almost didn't learn about the toxic dump expansion. Juanita and Rosa discovered the permitting process by accident, by running into some neighbors at a meeting about educational issues. The neighbors had heard about a meeting concerning the dump. Some days later, as Rosa and Juanita were driving by the local school one evening in January 1992, they saw a number of cars parked there, and Solorio-Garcia remembered the dump meeting. Fernandez urged her to check it out, and they found that what was going on was a presentation on the dump. Laidlaw was proposing to dramatically expand the existing dump; it wanted to double the dump's capacity to make it the largest capacity dump in the United States and to change the types of chemicals it took from strictly petroleum waste to more than 450 types of highly toxic substances.

The women also found that those in attendance were almost entirely white. "It was just people in suits," says Solorio-Garcia. There were only three Latinos at the entire meeting. As Fernandez remembers, the presentation was highly technical. "Rosa did not understand, although she speaks fluent English, and I understood even less. And Rosa said, 'Let's go, we can't even understand anything.' And we left." One of the Latinos followed Fernandez and Solorio-Garcia out of the meeting and introduced himself as Lupe Martinez, a community organizer with California Rural Legal Assistance Foundation. Martinez informed the women about the toxic waste disposal site near their town. As Fernandez notes, "that was the first time that we took notice of the dump." Solorio-Garcia and Fernandez, and some of their neighbors, formed a community organization to fight the dump expansion and called it *Padres Hacia una Vida Mejor*, Spanish for "Parents for Better Living."

The Permitting Process: Opportunities for Organizing

The meeting that Fernandez and Solorio-Garcia had stumbled upon was that of the Local Assessment Committee (LAC), a group appointed by the Kern County Board of Supervisors under a California State Law known as the Tanner Act. The Act, passed during the 1980s, was an attempt to give local residents some say in the toxic waste facility permitting process. In enacting the Act, the state legislature found that the then existing "procedures for approving hazardous waste facilities do not provide meaningful opportunities for public involvement and are not suitably structured to allow the public to make its concerns known and to cause these concerns to be taken into consideration."[1]

The LAC had been appointed before Buttonwillow residents knew about it, and no residents of Buttonwillow sat on the committee. Dennis Palla, a former resident of Buttonwillow who still farmed nearby, was a member, and many white Buttonwillow residents considered him their representative. Latino Buttonwillow residents who attended the meeting felt wholly unrepresented.

Martinez and members of Padres used the LAC meetings as a focus for their organizing. By the third meeting of the LAC, recalls Martinez, "we got really prepared, and we did a lot of organizing, we did some visiting, house meetings, personal visits, they did the phone calling, and I guess the first time we got something like 200 people there from the community." Martinez used the local farm-worker radio station to publicize the LAC meetings, in Spanish, to nearby residents. Buttonwillow residents, driven by the fear of the toxic waste dump that many had just learned existed nearby, came together to protect their community. "They knew that it used to smell, and once in a while they would get these drifts. They knew that something was going on. A lot of people were having all kinds of problems, health problems, within the community, for being such a small community," says Martinez.

The LAC was unprepared for an active audience. When Buttonwillow residents began attending the LAC meetings, their requests for information were met with indifference or even outright hostility. Questions were never answered, and it appeared to these residents who were trying to take part that their concerns were not being taken seriously. This treatment infuriated audience members, whose initial fear of the dump turned to anger at the County and at Laidlaw. A Buttonwillow resident, Eduardo Montoya, explains that what "motivated the community very much was the LAC, where you would ask questions but get no answers. It would anger you and motivate you to keep coming back."

Montoya notes that much of the residents' anger would have dissipated if they had been able to participate and get genuine answers to their questions. "If in these things they would have given us any kind of an answer—granted, we still did not know anything—we would have thought, 'Oh, okay, it's all right.' And perhaps we would not have returned. Or we would not have opposed it."

While the LAC itself was not responsive, County officials' response to residents' demands added fuel to the fire: when those present at the LAC meeting got angry, the County officials called in the Sheriff to "restore order." "They never responded to the people," says Fernandez bitterly. "They called the police. They thought we were going to attack them, or I don't know what." Other times the County officials laughed at residents' comments. Kern County's actions galvanized the community residents who came to the meetings, uniting them.

The turnout at the LAC meetings, sparked by Padres' organizing, consisted almost entirely of Latino Buttonwillow residents. Padres initially tried to reach out to the whole Buttonwillow community. "We would make fliers for meetings of the committee, or meetings of the LAC, or meetings at the school of the community, we would make them in English and Spanish. We never defined ourselves, we never specified ourselves as a strictly Latino group. It's just that whites and blacks do not go," says Montoya. The lack of participation by whites and blacks—almost 50 percent of Buttonwillow residents—would later prove to be significant.

The Community Comes to Its Voice

Because the town is heavily Latino, and many of its farm-worker residents do not speak English well, if at all, community residents repeatedly asked Kern County and Laidlaw for Spanish translation of public meetings and environmental review documents. As Juanita Fernandez comments, "There were a lot more Mexican people than white people. Everything was in English, and we could not understand." An organizer, Lupe Martinez, remembers that, when Latinos first requested that documents and discussions be translated, the County "refused to bring in an interpreter. So it became a challenge. And, by God, we were going to get one, one way or another."

The Spanish translation issue dominated each monthly meeting of the LAC, with almost every public comment addressing it. Lupe Martinez was a catalyst for Padres' effort. "When Lupe came, he lit the match," recalls Montoya. "And, in one meeting, when the council did not want to listen, when they did not want to translate, then Lupe told everyone to go outside." The entire audience, 90 percent of whom spoke only Spanish, got up and left the meeting. The press, sensing a story, followed—as Montoya remembers, "it had a strong impact on the press. That was when the attention of the press was captured for the first time." Padres organized protests at the meetings, and the controversy kept the level of attendance at LAC meetings high.

Taking part in the meetings was also an important education for those who did it. "One thing that happened was that feeling the support of the Buttonwillow people is what empowered me," explains Rosa Solorio-Garcia. "When you stand in front of the LAC and you say, 'We're not going to let these people come to Buttonwillow and dump on us, right?' And to hear the people say 'no!'—You feel that people are supporting you."

At about this time, Rosa Solorio-Garcia got the opportunity to attend a workshop in Alabama sponsored by the Highlander Institute, which transformed the way she saw the struggle.

It was just being there. All the role playing that they did there. And all the stuff that they did there. And talking to other people from all over the nation that had gone through the same thing. And I kept thinking. It took almost to the last day because they didn't just say government officials are crooked. Because if they said it, I don't think anyone would believe them. But it's like, from their experiences and their conversations, and their role playing, they show you what they had gone through. And then, it was like, "Oh my God!" You know they're saying that the County is not there to listen to us, and EPA doesn't care whether the air is contaminated, the water, whatever. And it's just a big realization, and frightening. To me it was very, very frightening. Because now I knew all that stuff, and I didn't know what to do about it. That was scary, because then I had to come back and I had to tell people in Buttonwillow that we had to count on us and what we can do. . . . and they couldn't believe that I was telling them that we couldn't count on EPA. I remember Paco, he was the hardest to convince. Because he came from Mexico and . . . Well, they all did. And it's like, the U.S. is a better country, and there's no corruption—like in Mexico you see it outright in front of you, but here it's more subtle. And it was very hard for him to accept the fact that the U.S. was just as crooked as Mexico.

—Rosa Solorio-Garcia

Solorio-Garcia's experience in Alabama gave her the conceptual framework to understand the reality the group had been experiencing in Buttonwillow—that of an unresponsive government agency apparently in league with the toxic dump company. This new consciousness helped Padres understand better the power dynamics the group faced.[2]

Victories and Setbacks

Padres Hacia una Vida Mejor scored a major victory when Laidlaw agreed, in May, to provide oral translation of the proceedings of the Local Assessment Committee. "I think one of the biggest victories that we had was getting the translator," says Solorio-Garcia. "Because those people, if you had seen them, were adamant, they were like insulted because we were asking for the meetings to be translated and for all the paperwork coming out of the County to be translated. And they said 'no, no, no, and no.' People felt empowered, that they had . . . convinced the County to translate. And it was being there that had made that happen."

That victory was short-lived, however. Unbeknownst to Padres, the County unilaterally suspended meetings of the LAC in June. With the LAC meetings stopped, there was little focus for the community's anger. Padres, Martinez, and outside supporters planned a major rally and march to bring attention to the struggle over the dump. The idea was to march to the dump site to focus Kern County's attention on the expansion proposal.

The march was a major success for the group. Local farmers allowed their massive tractors to be used to lead the march, the eight huge machines boldly demonstrating that "big ag" in Kern County opposed the dump expansion. Greenpeace arranged to bring in activists from another major environmental justice struggle then taking place, in East Liverpool, Ohio. Close to one thousand Padres members and supporters took part, marching four miles in blistering August heat, chanting and singing.

After the march, activism quieted down. Without the monthly LAC meetings as a catalyst, attendance at Padres's own meetings dwindled, and the group became unfocused. There was also a change in the nature of the support the community received from outside. Lupe Martinez, the sparkplug of the early organizing drive, went back to work for the United Farm Workers. "My fear," says Martinez, "when it came down that I had mixed feelings of whether I was going to leave or not, was that it was going to die. That's the organizer's nightmare. That everything that you did might not be there at all. Maybe what you did was not what you thought you had done. And so when I left, when I was about to leave, I felt that 'What if I didn't do it right? What if all of the sudden I'm gone and it's dead, and nothing is going to happen? So, everything that I did was for nothing, then.' And that's probably the biggest fear that an organizer has." His replacement, CRLA Foundation's new organizer in the Central Valley, Mario Madrid, was more laid back and low key in his style than the effervescent Martinez, which made Madrid's transition into and acceptance by the Buttonwillow community difficult.

The Process Restarts, and the Struggle Continues . . .

The next official action on the dump did not come for eighteen months, until the County issued an Environmental Impact Report (EIR) in January 1994. The EIR, required by the California Environmental Quality Act (CEQA), examines the potential environmental impacts of major projects such as toxic waste dumps. Padres used the EIR as an organizing tool, holding house meetings at which community leaders described the struggle against the dump expansion and talked about the EIR. The house meetings started at Rosa's home. "And from that house we had another meeting. And from that house another meeting. And from that house another meeting. And, we just kept going," says Solorio-Garcia. Padres would use flip charts to write down each concern raised by those in the meetings, and to spur discussions on each issue. Relying on a provision in CEQA that required the County to respond to each comment on the EIR, Padres tried to generate as many comments as possible. Group leaders brought paper and pencils to the house meetings and had people write their concerns in a letter of comment on the EIR. People who could not write dictated their letters to others. "You're talking about a lot of people who are illiterate or do not feel comfortable with writing, period, much less a letter to an official from the County," says Solorio-Garcia. At the end of the meeting, participants were asked to host their own house meeting with other friends. "We went full blast for a few weeks, where every night there was a meeting in somebody's house," says Solorio-Garcia.

The letter-writing strategy was directly copied from CRLA's experiences in Kettleman City—in Buttonwillow, however, the organizing drive netted more than 270 letters of comment on the EIR, far surpassing the 119 in the Kettleman struggle. "Luke said he needed some letters," says Solorio-Garcia. "And he said he wanted 100 letters, or something like that. And we said, 'No way! We'll get you 200 letters.'" Most of the letters were in Spanish—another part of the strategy growing out of the Kettleman struggle.[3]

During the spring of 1994, the County began to take steps to revive the LAC. In the nearly two years since the LAC had last met, two of the members had resigned, and one had died. The County sent out notices of the vacancies. Three Buttonwillow residents, leaders of Padres—Eduardo Montoya, Saul Moreno, and Francisco Beltran—applied for seats on the LAC. Montoya thought he fit the profile for an LAC member perfectly. "I was a reflection of the community because I did not speak English well. The community did not speak English well. I was the perfect representative of the community. I am like the majority of the community of Buttonwillow," he says. But, when the new appointees where announced, the County had named three new members of the LAC—none from Buttonwillow, and none Latino.

Another opportunity arose when one of the new members turned out to have a conflict of interest and resigned from the LAC in June. Latino Buttonwillow residents petitioned the Board of Supervisors to appoint a Latino candidate, and more than forty residents appeared at a Board meeting to press their cause. The Board then chose a new LAC member—a white Buttonwillow resident who had not even applied for the LAC position until two months after the formal application process closed. Padres members, many of whom had attended almost every LAC meeting held to date, were dismayed and felt the decisions were racially motivated. So did one LAC member who was supportive of Padres; he resigned, telling the County to replace him with "one of the interested minority persons from Buttonwillow who *ally* have been denied full participation in the process thus far." After further pressure from Padres, the Board named Eduardo Montoya to the LAC in early September 1994.

The County restarted the LAC meetings almost twenty-seven months after suspending them, late in September 1994. It was difficult for the Latino residents of Buttonwillow to organize amid the political atmosphere in Kern County in the fall of 1994. Proposition 187, a statewide ballot initiative to deny undocumented immigrants access to medical care and public schools, was on the November ballot, and the debate over it was stirring up anti-immigrant hysteria throughout the conservative Central Valley. Protests against the Proposition by the Latino community, including demonstrations in which Latino high school students marched out of school, polarized the issue further. More than 73 percent of Kern County voters ended up voting for the proposition, which passed with 59 percent of the vote statewide.

When the County resuscitated the LAC process late in September, the Spanish-language issue again dominated the LAC meeting. While Laidlaw provided interpreters for Spanish speakers, the focus of contention quickly shifted to the Environmental Impact Report (EIR), the thousand-page technical document that was supposed to form the basis for the LAC's deliberations. Eduardo Montoya, the newest member of the LAC, told his fellow members that he could not understand the document in English. Over strenuous objections from County officials, the LAC voted to hold a special meeting on whether to request translation of the EIR.

Before the special meeting on translation, the Board of Supervisors sent a letter to the LAC, instructing it that it could not request translation. At the October meeting, the LAC voted overwhelmingly to request such translation. "I gotta hand it to the LAC. They basically believed in the principle that there should be full communication for everyone, as far as all the process of this," says Mario Madrid. "And they backed up the request that the EIR report be translated into Spanish."

After the LAC vote on translation, the County staff conveyed the LAC's request to the Board of Supervisors and recommended that the Board deny it, which the Board did. The LAC members, and active members of the Buttonwillow community who were looking forward to the translation, were angry. At the next meeting of the LAC, LAC members and the public took out their anger on County staff.

Kern County was personified at the LAC meetings by County Planning Director Ted James, who antagonized the community from the very start. James made an appealing villain: a frog-like bureaucrat who seemed incapable of understanding or responding to the community, he became the focus of Buttonwillow residents' ire. And James responded, but not in the way the community would have liked. Each time the LAC voted to request something from the Board of Supervisors, James, theoretically the emissary from the LAC to the Board, presented the LAC's request and recommended that the Board deny it. The Board routinely followed James's advice. This duplicity reinforced the community's, and the LAC's, distrust of James.

At the next LAC meeting, on November 22, the LAC voted to request a grant for an independent consultant to advise the LAC on earthquake safety and landfills. County staff representative James told the LAC that the request was "premature" and recommended to the Board that they deny the request. The Board summarily denied the LAC's request for a consultant.

 Montoya was incredulous when the Board rejected the LAC's requests for consultants. "That money was not going to be paid by the county. The applicant, Laidlaw, was going to pay it. And yet, the county denied our requests again, and again, and again, and again."

The Board of Supervisors instructed the LAC to complete its work by the beginning of December, and the LAC met repeatedly in the weeks coming up to the deadline. It again requested a technical consultant, this time on the longevity of landfill liners, a key issue that had been raised by the public. County officials delayed taking this request to the Board of Supervisors for two weeks and then placed it on the agenda after the Board's consideration of the waste facility permit itself, making it a moot issue.

Power Struggles

Two incidents at the Board of Supervisors demonstrated both the potential and the limitations of pressing the boundaries of power relationships in Kern County.

At one Board hearing, held to consider the selection of new members for the Local Assessment Committee, about forty Buttonwillow residents, accompanied by Greenpeace organizer Bradley Angel and by Padres' attorney, Luke Cole, moved to the well of the Board Chambers to speak. When they were done, the Chair of the Board asked them to return to their seats. Cole and Angel quietly urged the group to stay put, and, after a moment of indecision, all stayed standing at the front of the room. The Chair of the Board, Ben Austin, then repeatedly ordered them to sit down. They remained standing. After a tense stand-off, Board Chair Austin, himself a retired sheriff, realized that short of ordering the Sheriff to clear the room, he could do nothing about the residents, and the Board meeting continued.

This incident was an important event in the deconstruction (and consequent reconstruction) of power relations during the struggle. Before this event, Buttonwillow residents did not question the Board Chair's power and their own powerlessness. When Buttonwillow residents refused to sit down during the Supervisors' hearing, they had the experience of feeling their own power, and also experiencing the powerlessness of the Chair of the Board.[4] They understood the contingency of the Board Chair's power in that situation. They reconstructed the power relations of the situation—albeit slightly—to give themselves more power.

The limits to this reconstruction of power relations were made painfully apparent just months later, on December 12, 1994, at the Board of Supervisors' hearing on whether to grant the dump expansion permit. The hearing was attended by about seventy-five Buttonwillow residents, as well as by supporters such as Cole and Angel.

During the hearing, Angel began testifying, and Sonia Santana, another Greenpeace staffer, translated his remarks into Spanish for the benefit of the audience. Board Chair Austin quickly moved to stop Angel, stating that there would be "no translation."[5] When Angel continued to speak and to have his remarks translated, one of the members of the Board moved for a recess, and the Board quickly left the room. Before leaving, Austin instructed two sheriff's deputies to remove Angel from the room. The two deputies physically lifted the somewhat diminutive Angel and carried him from the room to a police car waiting outside at the curb, followed by several TV cameras and a horde of onlookers. After handcuffing Angel, the deputies roughly thrust him into the back of the car and took him off to the County jail, some fifteen miles outside of town, where he spent the night before being released at 6:00 the following morning. Buttonwillow residents who came to testify against the dump were intimidated, and some did not testify after all. Many did, however. "The possibility of going to jail did scare me," says Juanita Fernandez, "but the dump scares me more."

The Board, after hearing more testimony, approved the dump expansion proposal and disbanded the LAC.

Thus, Buttonwillow residents' initial experiences in taking some power from the Board were met with serious retribution—by the Board's physically retaking its space through the intimidating tactic of arresting a speaker (for the crime of requesting Spanish translation; no charges were ever filed) and by its exercise of political power in approving the dump over the opposition of the community.

Laidlaw also painted all opponents of the dump expansion as "outsiders" and continually stressed the home-grown roots of its employees. Padres was amazed that a Canadian company, with its U.S. headquarters in South Carolina, could paint the opposition spearheaded by Buttonwillow residents as the work of "outsiders," but the high visibility of Cole and Angel helped the charge stick where it counted, with local decision makers. "Unfortunately," says Dennis Palla, "the way it was framed by Laidlaw and the County—they were very successful in doing this—was that it was outside agitation. It was CRLA coming in. It was Greenpeace."

The effect of this perception was to limit participation by people outside the Latino community. Conservative, white rural residents wanted nothing to do with CRLA—long a nemesis of agribusiness interests in the Valley—and Greenpeace, which they perceived as a radical extremist group. Farmers already in the struggle against the dump, like Dennis Palla, had moments of cognitive dissonance and, sometimes, raised consciousness.

> The sentiment would be for most people that, 'well, gee, I don't even have to think about it now. I don't want to be associated with them.' So, it puts me in kind of a strange position because everybody knows that my politics are conservative. At least everybody that knows me knows that. And yet they see that well Dennis is over here and he's dealing with the people, so

what's the deal? It's like a paradox. A really difficult time making the two equate. But I've told them my own personal feeling, from the very beginning, is that I'm willing to take help from anybody who's willing to help me . . . as long as they're willing to be an ally and be on the same side I am and go towards the same goal, I don't care what their politics are. It's like, to use this as an analogy, but when you're being faced with a gigantic gun and it's pointing you right in the face, you don't take the time to ask the person, this person's willing to come on and help you out, you're not going to ask them well are you Democrat or are you Republican, are you Greenpeace, or are you whatever? You know, can you help me out here? When you both perceive it as a danger, as the enemy if you want to say that, you work through the differences.

—Dennis Palla, local farmer

Spanish Translation: Organizing Issue or Wedge?

The fight over the translation issue, in retrospect, may have hurt Padres more than it helped at this point in the struggle. In the beginning, the language issue was a major asset; it galvanized members of the Latino community around an issue and brought them out to meeting after meeting. It fit squarely with the group's ambition to fully take part in the permitting process. The group and the lawyer also saw it, on the basis of the Kettleman City experience, as a potentially successful legal hook. "It was a part of the strategy. It was something that we were going to jam the County with," says organizer Martinez. "Did it have an effect in keeping us from organizing the rest of the community? I don't know. I would think so."

Madrid, Martinez' replacement, thought that the language issue limited the organization's overall appeal in the Buttonwillow community. "Because language became the issue, the blacks didn't get involved and the whites didn't get involved. And it became an issue of racism," notes Madrid. "The whites didn't want to get involved because what they were fighting for was Spanish translation, something they didn't support. Having to translate for all these people who don't speak English, who should if they want to live in our country. And simultaneously this was going on during Prop. 187. So that this heightened awareness of the issues of translation that divided the community."

Martinez, on the other hand, sees it as a failure to communicate to the other residents how the translation issue fit into the broader strategy to stop the dump. "Maybe that's where we failed . . . maybe it did become a whole racial issue, or racism, right? Where the blacks felt that, you know, how could they go to the meetings if there's nothing but Latinos there? And maybe it did happen. And maybe it wasn't a failure, maybe it was more of a lack of educating the whole community."

Madrid was against the prominent place the Spanish translation issue played in the local struggle; he wanted to focus on Laidlaw's spotty compliance record at facilities around the country. In retrospect, Madrid may have been correct, but his coolness toward the community's primary strategy eroded his community support. "I would have played the Spanish really low," Madrid explains. "Because here is what happened: look at the newspapers during that period of September through December of 1994. The newspapers, the *Californian*, which is the Bakersfield newspaper, the largest newspaper in Kern County, when they would report on the meetings, they would always highlight the Spanish question, with these reactionary-type headlines." While the substance of the dump and Laidlaw's record were being discussed at the meetings, the press was reporting only on the Spanish-translation conflict. "It was translation, they really built up the translation issue," says Palla. "So, really all you heard about was a group of Mexicans are upset because something is not being spoken in Spanish, and most of the sentiment was, 'Well, they can learn English.'"

> The real issues of the dump, in terms of the business of the dump, were never really heard in the public hearing because the whole Spanish thing always dominated. And, if you're kind of hip to the politics of Kern County, this is kind of the last of the good ol' boys counties. It's politically correct in Kern County to be anti-Spanish. The biggest industries here are oil and agriculture. And, so, it was popular to take the position on the Spanish thing. The Board, I feel, were very crafty in their move to just put all their attention on the Spanish question. Because, if on our side we were using the translation as a tactic basically to derail the process and give us more time, they used the Spanish question to waste time. And, so, in other words, who lost but the public? The public never got the hearings that were basically going to discuss what this dump expansion thing was all about.
> —Mario Madrid, community organizer

The Legal Strategy: The Long Road to Nowhere

Ironically, the legal strategy behind the Buttonwillow struggle was sparked by a white local farmer, Dennis Palla. During the first few months of the permitting process, Palla contacted Luke Cole, an environmental justice lawyer in San Francisco, for advice. Cole and his colleague Ralph Abascal, with California Rural Legal Assistance, had recently won a case against another toxic waste dumper, Chemical Waste Management, when the company had tried to build an incinerator at its dump near Kettleman City, about an hour north of Buttonwillow in Kings County. Part of the case had turned on whether the County was required to translate environmental review documents into Spanish to make them accessible to the 95 percent of Kettleman City residents who were Latino; a Sacramento Superior Court judge had ruled that the County should have provided such translation.[6] That success had rested heavily on the fact pattern that Cole had developed through a community organizing strategy in Kettleman City, encouraging Spanish-speaking residents to take part in the environmental review process.[7]

Fresh from victory in Kettleman City, Cole was excited to try his model in an almost identical situation: again, a major toxic waste dumper wanted a new permit to expand the dump near a Latino farm-worker town. Abascal had a few pet legal theories he was interested in trying out as well: he was searching for a compelling fact situation in which to try to litigate an environmental justice claim using Title VIII of the Fair Housing Act of 1968, which he believed could provide a tool to challenge the increased segregation that appeared to him to invariably follow the siting of toxic waste dumps.[8] They hoped to become involved in the Buttonwillow fight but told Palla that, as poverty lawyers, they could not represent a wealthy farmer.

Cole sent community organizer Lupe Martinez to a meeting being held in Buttonwillow to get the lay of the land. Martinez met several Buttonwillow residents, including Rosa Solorio-Garcia, and CRLA Foundation was invited into the community. Martinez worked with the community so that it understood that the struggle would have to be waged by community residents.

My struggle was to make them understand that they're the ones who have
to make everything happen. It was not him [the lawyer] who was going to
be able to come in, it was not me who was going to be there to come and
save them. I mean, we're not coming in on a horse and here's a knight in
shining armor, coming in and saving the community. And I had prepared
them for that. My whole thing was: it's yours, it's all of us, and it's not having an attorney come in and he's going to run and do everything for you,
and so on. They knew that. But we also knew that we needed technical assistance, we needed the legal advice, we needed all these other things that
the community didn't have.

—Lupe Martinez, organizer

Cole helped guide the strategy of the community group throughout
the administrative process, pushing Padres to run the organizing drive
around comment letters in Spanish on the EIR.

Sensing that the Board of Supervisors would approve the project,
Padres began preparing the next phase of its attack on the facility's permit—the legal strategy—even before the Board acted. The week before
the Board of Supervisors' vote, Padres unveiled the first thrust of its legal
strategy. The group gathered in San Francisco to announce the filing of
an administrative complaint under Title VI of the Civil Rights Act of
1964 against Kern County, Laidlaw, and the State Department of Toxic
Substances Control. The timing of the event was chosen to maximize
publicity about the Buttonwillow struggle; Padres held a press conference on December 9, just three days before the Board hearing.

Title VI, the federal law that bars discrimination on the basis of race,
color or national origin by agencies that receive federal financial assistance, had been used by civil rights groups for years, but rarely in the environmental justice context. Cole was excited about its possibilities after
major media attention to a similar complaint filed in Louisiana. Under
the direction of cocounsel Anne Simon, students at the Environmental
Law Community Clinic in Berkeley succeeded in tracking federal money
from the U.S. Environmental Protection Agency to DTSC, and from the
U.S. Department of Housing and Urban Development to Kern County;
the complaint was thus filed with those two federal agencies. The complaint alleged that the County, the State, and Laidlaw had taken actions
that had the effect of discriminating against Latino residents of Buttonwillow, who were being forced to bear the impact of the dump. To

strengthen the complaint, Cole contacted his client groups in Kettleman City and Westmorland, the two other California communities that host toxic waste dumps, and had them sign onto the effort. All three communities are similar: small, rural, farm-worker communities with high percentages of Latino residents.

The complaint had its initial desired effect: it generated statewide press coverage, including extensive articles in the *San Francisco Chronicle*, the *San Francisco Examiner*, and the *Los Angeles Times.* Buttonwillow residents were, on a statewide basis, defining the terms of the struggle as a civil rights, not an environmental, fight. The filing of the complaint did not influence the Supervisors, however, who approved the permit 4-1 on December 12, 1994.

After the Board of Supervisor's vote, Padres launched its second legal attack—a suit, filed in Superior Court, challenging the County's decision on a variety of environmental and civil rights grounds. The idea behind combining both environmental and civil rights theories in one lawsuit was to paint as complete a picture for the judge as possible; the attorneys thought that by talking about the racial discrimination that members of Padres had suffered, they could persuade the judge to rule for Padres on environmental grounds.

The case was assigned to Judge Roger Randall, a Yale-educated, no-nonsense judge known for his careful preparation. Randall's first action in the case was to announce to all parties that he belonged to the Rotary Club with Larry Moxley, Laidlaw's vice president. Randall then ruled against Padres on a series of motions that eviscerated its legal case: he threw out the Spanish translation claim as unsupported by California law and also dismissed Abascal's cherished Title VIII claim. Padres's attorneys plodded forward on the remaining parts of the case.

Randall's decision on the merits, issued on April 29, 1996, surprised everyone: he ruled for Padres and set aside Laidlaw's permit. He agreed with Padres that the County had not followed the Tanner Act when it unilaterally suspended the LAC, when it denied the LAC technical assistance grants, and when it prematurely disbanded the LAC. He also ruled that the County had violated its own General Plan by approving the dump without determining whether there was a local need for it. Randall also suspended the dump's permit because of violations of the California Environmental Quality Act.

The lawyers were overjoyed—they had taken on Kern County in its own conservative court and won. Buttonwillow residents were more subdued; in the sixteen months since the lawsuit had been filed, the community group had become largely dormant.

Laidlaw filed an appeal days later, and the battleground shifted to the Fifth District Court of Appeal, based in Fresno. The Court of Appeal ruled on July 23, 1997, overturning the Superior Court and reinstating Laidlaw's permit. The seventy-four page opinion dispatched every legal argument Padres had raised, ruling for Kern County on every major point. Further galling to the group, the names of members of Padres were repeatedly misspelled in the opinion. The only positive aspect of the case that Padres's legal team could find was that the Court had ordered that the decision not be published in the official reports, meaning that it had no precedential value and could not be cited in other cases or used against other community groups.

After the defeat in the Court of Appeal, Cole was seriously demoralized. He had made a simple mistake: he hadn't listened to his own teachings about not putting faith in the legal system.[9] Padres had won the case in front of a conservative, white male Kern County Superior Court judge, he had figured; surely, the Court of Appeal would see the case the same way.

During the almost three years it took the case to wind its way through the Superior Court and Court of Appeal (from January 1995 to August 1997), the community group had largely relaxed and become dormant. Intermittent efforts by Cole to spur the group to action had met with little success. With their struggle tied up in the courts, Padres's leaders had moved on to more pressing things. Rosa and Lorenzo Garcia had a new home built in nearby Shafter. Juan Reyes and Juanita Fernandez had a second child, Mireda. Paco and Lydia Beltran watched their oldest son, Gabriel, apply to and be accepted at California Polytechnic University at San Luis Obispo. Children grew older, plantings and harvests came and went. The struggle against the dump seemed far away.

With the loss in the Court of Appeal, the struggle returned home. The core group of Padres met but was disheartened. Rosa Solorio-Garcia tried to be optimistic. "I see it as, you know it's taken them at least two more years, three more years for Laidlaw to be allowed to start dumping more stuff in there. But, it's very hard to keep the momentum going.

And if people aren't informed regularly and constantly of what's going on, then they sort of 'get cold,' and they think it's gone away. And I think that's what we're dealing with right now."

Because the Court of Appeal's ruling had taken away the legal foundation for their civil rights claims—that the County and Laidlaw had illegally run the permitting process in a way that excluded Latinos from participating—Padres dismissed their civil rights claims in December 1997. They were shocked when in February 1998, Laidlaw and the County filed a motion with the Superior Court, asking the Court to grant them $300,000 in attorneys fees from Padres and the individual plaintiffs.

Padres saw the move as a Strategic Lawsuit Against Public Participation, or SLAPP suit. "It was clearly a SLAPP, suit, designed to intimidate Padres," says Richard Pearl, an attorney who specializes in attorneys' fees cases who agreed to represent Padres on a pro bono basis. Pearl, Cole and Padres itself were shocked when Judge Randall, who had ruled for Padres on closely related environmental questions, determined that three of the arguments made by Padres were "frivolous" and that Laidlaw and the County were entitled to attorneys' fees. While Laidlaw and the County had asked for $300,000, Randall determined that, because the Padres plaintiffs were low-income farm-workers, they had to pay $4,000—$1,000 to the County and $3,000 to Laidlaw. The Court also awarded Laidlaw and the County costs of $4,900.

Stunned, and facing the possibility of a huge debt ($8,900 was a significant amount to a group of farm-workers, who as an occupational class make roughly $8,000 a year), Padres decided to try to settle the case. In the midst of settlement discussions, Padres did not even oppose the final permit for the dump expansion Laidlaw needed, and received in October 1998, from the Air District. Laidlaw refused to settle, however, and the Court of Appeal ultimately vindicated Padres and overturned two of the Superior Court's three findings of "frivolousness."

The Title VI complaint ended up providing no support for the community. EPA took more than six months just to accept the complaint for investigation, although its regulations require it to act within twenty days; it accepted the complaint against the state DTSC only, dismissing Laidlaw. HUD accepted the complaint against Kern County but never seriously investigated. What the lawyer and community had hoped would be a tool to raise civil rights issues and put pressure on the County and state[10] turned out to have little utility in the long run because of the inability or unwillingness of the federal agencies, EPA and HUD, to mount serious investigations.

Conclusion

If Laidlaw does win this struggle, Buttonwillow residents believe it is only because the company has more resources than the community. "They have the power of money," says Juanita Fernandez. "They have the power to perhaps control everything, right?" chimes in her husband, Juan Reyes. "In this sense, I notice similarities to Mexico. In Mexico anyone with money can control things. And here, it is just a little bit more discreet, but it amounts to the same thing. That is the way it seems to me here. Because it is a large company, it can pay off everything, it can pay the lawyers and everything."

Taking part in the struggle has transformed members of Padres and their community. On the individual level, leaders of Padres have become empowered and learned new skills. Eduardo Montoya had never been involved with a community group before the dump struggle; he is now a community leader and served on the LAC. Eduardo and his wife, Dora, and four other Padres members also became U.S. citizens as a result of the dump fight. Sylvia Moreno and other Spanish-speaking women in the community used to take an English-speaking friend to translate for them at the doctor's office or the Department of Motor Vehicles; now Sylvia and others are taking English as a Second Language classes and are applying to become U.S. citizens. "I think CRLA and the struggle and everybody who's helped has empowered these people to want to do this," says Rosa Solorio-Garcia. "Their self-confidence has really grown, and I see it as everything that they've done here."

"Maldijo el dia que I got involved," laughs Solorio-Garcia. "I was a happy housewife and teacher till I got involved." By being put in situations she had never imagined being in, such as having to speak in front of a room full of people, Solorio-Garcia realized that she could in fact do more than she thought. "I guess I'm a leader, but I didn't know I was a leader until this thing with the dump," says Solorio-Garcia, who is using skills she learned in the dump struggle, such as how to write press releases and work with the media, in her activism around bilingual education in her new home town of Shafter.

The struggle has also been a radicalizing event for some. Local farmer Dennis Palla, a self-described "white, conservative Republican," illustrates this phenomenon.

> There is an element, there definitely is a very conservative element. And I'm part of that. . . . When I first got involved in this thing in '85, we were confronted with the idea of protesting and going out with signs, what have you. We felt no, that's not the thing to do. We need to make sure to stay on the good side of the supervisors. Well, you know, since then we've learned that that's been pretty futile. So we've been open to a lot more radical viewpoints. But still, you're dealing with the reality that we're in a very conservative area.
> —Dennis Palla, local farmer

Part of this radicalization comes from the fact that the struggle has made many participants skeptical of their government. For some, the process was slow and triggered by small events—noticing a lie by a government official, for example. Eduardo Montoya first realized that government officials were lying to the people of Buttonwillow when, in a meeting of the LAC, a State environmental official claimed to have never heard of a notorious toxic waste dump at Casmalia in nearby Santa Barbara County that had been closed down by the State because it was leaking and causing serious health consequences to the community. "It was impossible for a high-ranking EPA official not to know where Casmalia was," says Montoya. This realization, compounded by other, similar events, made Montoya a skeptic. "More than anything, I was disillusioned. Because I really believed that the United States government was different than the Mexican government," says Montoya. "The only difference is that, in Mexico they do what they do outside of the law. And in the U.S. they want to make the laws legitimate what they do. In other words, they want to make things appear legal."

These individual transformations also had an impact on the community of Buttonwillow, as personal skepticism became community skepticism and outright hostility to government. The process of the struggle gave participants, collectively, an understanding of political reality: that, in the words of Lupe Martinez, "the government is there not to protect the community, but to make sure these things go through and they do get permitted."

The community also came together as a community around the struggle, building deep bonds of friendship in some cases, forged by the tragedies along the way. "Because Juanita was pregnant and she was going to have this baby born like this, it made us even bond more," explains Solorio-Garcia. "We needed to keep on fighting for Juanita and other women who might have babies in Buttonwillow being born like that."

In some senses, then, the community's struggle against the dump has been successful regardless of the ultimate outcome: people have come together to realize, and exercise, their collective power. New friendships have been made, new coalitions built, new skills learned. The residents' experiences have had and will have a lasting impact on them and on Buttonwillow.

On another level, however, the struggle has been a failure: not only is the dump expansion moving forward, but many Padres members have been demoralized by the seven-year struggle. "I feel like I'm throwing rocks at the moon," sighs Paco Beltran, "and catching them on my head." The residents were forced to rely on litigation when all other avenues to achieving community victory had been closed off. The loss of momentum in Padres during the late stages of litigation was palpable; people saw the lawsuit as the only way to beat the county. The reliance on the law, and on outsiders, came at the expense of the self-reliant, cohesive, and dynamic group of just a few years before. While the lawsuit failed, time will tell whether the group comes back together, perhaps around the next community issue.

FIVE

Processes of Struggle

Grassroots Resistance and the Structure of
Environmental Decision Making

Grassroots struggles for environmental justice do not take place in a vacuum. Such struggles exist in the context of, and are shaped by, environmental laws that greatly influence both the process and the outcomes of siting disputes. The activism of community groups like the Padres in Buttonwillow often begins as a reaction to the impact of increasing numbers of polluting facilities on the community residents' health and quality of life. However, their activism quickly becomes a struggle over the legitimacy of decision-making processes, the exclusion from and the marginalization of disaffected residents during those processes, and the structural forces that constrain individuals in these communities from fully participating in decisions that fundamentally affect their lives. Grassroots environmental justice groups, such as the Padres organization in Buttonwillow, come to recognize the limits of formal environmental decision-making processes, even those designed for their participation. Eventually, community groups are forced to look outside these processes to ensure that their concerns and expertise about problems in their community are represented in the ultimate decision.

In this chapter, we continue to examine the legal and regulatory context in which local grassroots struggles take place. In particular, we discuss the environmental decision-making processes embedded in hazardous waste facility permitting laws. However, as we have previously stressed, our analysis is applicable to a variety of siting and other environmental justice struggles. While permitting laws have undergone significant transformation to provide for more community participation, these transformations have simply left intact the underlying power disparities in the relationships of the participants. By examining the dynamics of legal and regulatory reform, we hope to shift the focus away from individual actors and the fruitless search for clearly identified perpetrators and victims toward a focus on the structured nature of decision-making power.

While many environmental laws promise public participation, to varying degrees, in decision-making processes, they leave in place, as do many formal administrative processes, the underlying social relationships of its participants. For instance, recall that in chapter 3 we discussed the forces and mechanisms that construct racially identified space, with its devastating social, economic, and political consequences for poor people of color. These forces, as we explained, undoubtedly constrain the choices and mobility of these individuals. The constraints imposed on individuals in poor communities of color result not only from social phenomena or forces such as racial bias, in the housing market for instance, but also from institutional mechanisms that operationalize the social constraints. That is, one participant has power over another in a decision-making process because of a network of rules and practices that both structure the relationship of participants in that process.[1] However, regardless of the type of participatory process employed, environmental decision-making processes replicate, and facilitate, the constraints imposed by others in the social structure.

Grassroots struggles frequently pit low-income communities and communities of color against the facility owners and state environmental agencies. By virtue of their social status, individuals in these communities are vulnerable to more powerful interests in environmental decision-making processes. A local group's struggle may begin as an effort to obtain information about a proposal it has recently discovered, to build a waste or other facility in its community. Community residents may be frustrated that this is the first time they have heard of such a proposal, even though the decision-making process has been under way for months, or often years. Nevertheless, many community groups begin by trying to work through formal administrative permitting processes. They may seek out a meeting with the state agency or other decision maker responsible for the permitting decision, or they may meet with the company that is proposing the facility to learn more about its plans. Too often these encounters turn into struggles with state decision makers and industry representatives. Concerned residents become intimidated and deterred (temporarily) by the deluge of technical information and terminology used by those in the system.

Many community groups do attempt to work "through the system," by becoming conversant with the technical aspects of the development proposed for their neighborhood. Most often, however, concerned residents become frustrated at their inability to penetrate the wall of indifference, disinformation, and lack of respect they encounter from government agencies and facility proponents. Increasingly, communities around the country are filing lawsuits as part of their struggles to influence both the structure of, and their inclusion in, environmental decision-making processes. Communities such as Kettleman City and Buttonwillow have petitioned the courts to enforce the participatory promise embodied in environmental laws. Other communities, like Chester, invoke civil rights laws to enforce basic notions of equity in environmental decision-making processes. Some communities bring lawsuits on both environmental and civil rights grounds, partly as a way to frame their political struggle in terms that highlight the social dynamics that underlie the shortcomings in environmental decision making. As we discuss in this chapter, however, litigation is limited in its ability to transform the way in which environmental decisions are made.

We attribute the success of grassroots environmental justice struggles, ultimately, to strong community organizations and regional networks. As we explain at the end of this chapter, and as the next chapter illustrates, the grassroots organizations created in the midst of struggles for environmental justice are crucial in creating an ongoing role for community participation in all decisions that fundamentally affect the participants' lives. When local groups are able to link their victories in the environmental realm to broader political and economic struggles, the potential exists to redefine existing power relations, to unsettle cultural assumptions about race and class, and to create new political possibilities for historically marginalized communities in local decision-making processes.

The Participatory Promise (and Failure) of Environmental Decision Making

Environmental decision making, like much administrative decision making, gains its legitimacy, in part, from the democratic norm embedded in much of environmental law, particularly public participation provisions. Congress and state legislatures over the past twenty years have thus included opportunities for public participation in a number of environmental laws.[2] These provisions generally have several features in common: public input during the environmental decision-making process, a requirement that agencies respond to that public input, and provisions that allow lawsuits by the public to enforce the law (known as "citizens' suits").

Not all public participation laws are the same, however. State hazardous waste permitting laws vary from the barebones public notice and comment requirement to local citizen advisory groups like that in the Buttonwillow case study to the intricate impact review processes modeled after the federal National Environmental Policy Act (NEPA). Depending upon the mechanisms for citizen input in the decision-making process, the process can be an exercise in democratic deliberation with the proposed host community, an aggregation of pluralistic viewpoints on the proposed siting, or a vehicle for exclusion of citizens most affected by the proposed land use. State law thus greatly structures the agency of grassroots participants, including the opportunity to influence the outcome of the environmental decision and, ultimately, to shape the future of their communities.

The question of exactly what type of participation environmental laws should embody, and what rules best exemplify that participation, has gone largely unresolved. The Environmental Justice Movement, however, has answered the participation question clearly and decisively. The Movement's principles and practice have focused on the idea that communities should speak for themselves, that those who must bear the brunt of a decision should have an equal and influential role in making the decision.[3] Given current social and structural inequalities, however, problems of accountability and special interest influence are likely to render traditional participatory processes problematic in disadvantaged communities. This is true regardless of the political norm that underlies participatory processes in environmental law.

Pluralistic Pitfalls

Legal pluralism is the model that best describes the idea behind the participatory decision-making processes in much of environmental law. Pluralist decision making resembles something akin to a political marketplace, where different interest groups struggle and compete for scarce social resources and political victories.[4] Implicit in the pluralist model is the requirement that the decision-making process provide a forum for exchange and bargaining among the different interests. In a well-functioning pluralistic process, the decision maker would aggregate the preferences of all interest groups. The decision-making outcome would reflect, on balance, a mix of predominating preferences. Hence, in an ideal pluralistic process, a wide range of interests would be represented, no single interest would dominate, and the identities of the participants would not determine the outcome. However, if the decision maker has been "captured" by a single interest, or by a coalition of interests, then the process is illegitimate. Such capture may result from the different capacities and resources of certain interests in relation to others or from the lack of adequate representation of key interests in the process.

In the environmental context, basic notice and comment rules exemplify the pluralistic model of decision making. Most states' permitting processes for waste facilities are modeled after the federal permitting regulations.[5] That is, all states require, at a minimum, that an applicant or agency provide notice to the public and that there be a reasonable period to receive written or oral comments on the proposed waste facility. Public notice is typically provided for in state statutes by newspaper publication prior to a hearing and, less often, by broadcast on local radio stations. In some states, an "information repository," theoretically accessible to the public and intended to provide the public with documents relating to a permit, is required or allowed at the agency's discretion. Most states also provide for special notice and comment procedures for local officials and property owners near the site.

Most states also allow for a public hearing on the proposed permit. The earliest opportunity for public input is at the pre-application stage.

Only a handful of states require that before a company applies for a waste permit, it send a letter of intent to the local agency and hold a public hearing. The majority of states either mandate a public hearing on the permit application itself or allow such a hearing at the decision makers' discretion. Under the latter provisions, a public hearing is held only when the decision maker determines that there is "significant public interest" or when a hearing is otherwise deemed "appropriate" or in the public interest. These subjective determinations are left entirely to agency discretion, and it is not uncommon for the community and the agency to disagree on the merits of such determinations. Recall that in Chester, Pennsylvania, the state environmental agency declined to hold a hearing on a proposed infectious medical waste sterilization facility despite the 500 signatures in opposition to the project that were delivered to the State and to the City Council.

State laws based on the National Environmental Policy Act (NEPA) also reflect a pluralistic model of decision making.[6] NEPA requires an environmental impact review for federal actions with a significant impact on the environment. In this review, decision makers are required to document—and, ideally, to consider—a range of possible impacts, including ecological, aesthetic, historic, cultural, economic, social, and health impacts, whether direct, indirect, or cumulative. Currently, sixteen states, the District of Columbia, and Puerto Rico have "mini-NEPA" statutes, while another five states require environmental analysis for specific types of projects.[7] These statutes complement, rather than replace, other procedures for public participation in state permitting laws.

In a nutshell, the process under state mini-NEPA statutes looks like this: once the company files a formal application with the agency, the agency evaluates the project for its potential effect on the environment, usually using an "Environmental Assessment," or EA. If the project will have a potentially significant effect on the environment, state law directs the agency to prepare an Environmental Impact Statement, or EIS. The local agency holds a meeting to determine the scope of the EIS. This scoping meeting is open to the public, but it is often attended only by officials from other government agencies. The agency then prepares the environmental impact review document detailing the potential effects of the project or contracts with a consultant to produce the report. The EIS is circulated for public comment to anyone who requests it. Thereafter, the local agency prepares a response to the public comments. Local agencies often hold public hearings on the EIS. Finally, the local agency decides whether to permit the project, theoretically basing its decision on the EIS and on the public comments.

Notice and comment procedures, including public hearings and NEPA-like processes, reflect the prevailing pluralistic structure in that they are, according to one commentator, "generic institutional mechanisms intended to promote access and equal footing among, in agency parlance, 'stakeholders.'"[8] Public hearings provide an opportunity for the community to come out in force and express itself to the decision makers, face to face. Public hearings also provide an opportunity for industry, local officials, and local businesses to express their support or opposition to the facility. Theoretically, the various organized interests in the process operate in a free and unfettered marketplace of bargaining influence. At the close of the comment period, the permitting agency reviews and responds to all significant comments submitted, usually explaining how those comments are addressed in its final permit decision.

A closer look at the operation of pluralist-inspired environmental decision-making processes reveals that what most commentators have established is merely theory, not reality. Pluralism, in practice, tends to exclude those lacking the material prerequisites to equal participation.[9] Certain preexisting social disadvantages interact with formal pluralistic processes in a way that reproduces unequal influence in the decision-making process. Bureaucrats in state and local environmental agencies respond to pressure, and, when deciding between the desires of a community and those of a company, they often favor the interest that puts the most pressure on them. Low-income and communities of color enter the decision-making process with fewer resources than other interests in the decision-making process. These communities have less time, less information, and less specialized knowledge about the legal, technical, and economic issues involved. A communities' lack of access to such information and knowledge creates severe barriers to its full participation in a pluralistic process. As democratic theorists have recognized, information and knowledge are a form of political power in pluralistic processes; only when access to them is relatively equal among parties to a conflict can the parties truly understand their own interests and dialogue proceed toward the democratic ideal.[10]

Pluralistic decision-making processes also favor the waste facility developer's interests, allowing those interests to "capture" the decision-making process by virtue of their superior economic power, knowledge, and opportunity to influence the process. As Christopher Foreman notes, one of the systematic hurdles to effective democratic empowerment of ordinary citizens in regulatory processes is the superior position of some interests in the decision-making process. He notes that "[o]ften before proposals are embodied in bills, Federal Register notices, or permit applications (and sometimes even before anything exists in written form), business representatives have had informal opportunities to telegraph their views. In many instances, business will have initiated proposals. Considerable information and influence easily flows to such participants. By contrast, channels of focused public involvement tend to be weaker and to be activated later."[11]

Foreman's analysis is certainly true of the waste permitting process. Despite basic notice and comment requirements, many communities do not receive adequate notice and knowledge about the process. In communities where literacy levels are low, it is unlikely that many citizens will become aware of or read the official notice.[12] In some communities, as in Chester, notices are printed in minuscule type in a small space at the back of the local newspaper, eluding even avid readers of the newspaper. In many Latino communities, like Kettleman City and Buttonwillow, notices in English may be overlooked or not understood. Even where the law requires information repositories in a local community, documents are often not translated into the community's language or are written in such technical language that they are inaccessible even to relatively educated people.[13]

Opportunities for public comment most often come only *after* the decision-making process has been going on for some time, often years. With the exception of a few states that require a pre-application hearing, the public enters only after the applicant has chosen a site and submitted its application and the decision maker has reviewed the application for completeness and deliberated with the waste facility developer/applicant on various technical matters. By the time an agency solicits comments from the public or holds a hearing, the decision maker has often made an initial decision on whether to grant the permit, without input from the interests of those (usually the community) who have not found a way into the decision-making process prior to the formal comment period. The decision maker has already expended considerable energy, resources, and expertise on the permit application and will most likely be reluctant to amend or change its judgments to reflect public concerns about the application. Since community participation comes so late in the process, the decision-making process becomes an "announce and defend" approach. Many communities conclude that the public participation process is designed not to hear and address their concerns but instead to manage, defuse, and ultimately coopt community opposition to projects. The decision maker has, in effect, been captured by the applicant.

A similar type of capture occurs in many NEPA and mini-NEPA processes. As the Counsel on Environmental Quality (CEQ) recently reported as part of its review of the first twenty-five years of NEPA, many communities feel that the process is often triggered too late to be fully effective.[14] Agency and private sector planning processes begin long before the NEPA or State mini-NEPA process. By the time the Environmental Impact Statement (EIS) process is started, the report notes, alternatives and strategic choices are foreclosed. Some communities view the EIS process, according to CEQ, as "largely a one-way communication track that does not use their input effectively." Others consider the whole NEPA or mini-NEPA process cooptive and view it as having been set up by industry to achieve predictability (i.e., permits) by effectively channeling public opposition against facilities into a manageable process; such activists approach environmental review processes with great skepticism.

More fundamentally, pluralism is not an ideal model by which to resolve highly contentious public issues in a way that lends legitimacy to the ultimate decision. Public hearings, even when they are held early in the process and when they are representative, simply allot a certain amount of time to hear testimony by the public and do not foster substantive opportunities for dialogue between decision makers and those most affected by a proposed project or development. As Eileen Gauna explains, "although in all proceedings there is a potential for dialogue, the 'step up to the microphone and have your say in less than fifteen minutes' approach of many [public] meetings resembles more of a crude preference tally rather than meaningful deliberation"; more often than not, "the commentator has her say and sits down without any indication that the decision maker has seriously considered the position."[15] Public hearings may be a good opportunity for decision makers to hear the views of the affected community and perhaps to engage in brief question-and-answer sessions; however, they are a poor forum for "extensive development of information, a shared baseline of understanding, and the development of a consensus" necessary for a legitimate decision-making process.[16]

Deliberative Leanings

A recent move away from the pluralist model of public participation is evident in many state permitting processes. Increasingly, permitting processes seek to involve more meaningful dialogue and consultation with local advisory committees, such as the LAC in Buttonwillow. In the permitting process for waste facilities, at least a dozen states mandate the formation of local advisory committees.[17] Advisory committees are usually active only for the period during which a specific permit is under consideration. The committees are generally appointed at the time of the filing of the notice of intent to file an application or a notice of application, thereby allowing for early public involvement in the process. Such committees are typically directed to assess the social, environmental, and economic impact of the proposed facility and to report their findings to the entity responsible for making the final permit decision. Equally important, local advisory committees offer the opportunity for a qualitatively deliberative process, one that creates an opportunity for lay and technical people to work together, have a dialogue, and reach consensus.

The core elements of dialogue and consensus about the common good are at the heart of the much heralded move toward deliberative democratic principles, as an alternative to interest-group pluralism.[18] A deliberative process often refers to a mode of decision making in which participants engage in rational discourse about what outcome(s) best serves the common good of the community involved. In contrast to pluralism, the common good does not reflect merely aggregated and bargained preferences of the participants. Instead, participants are expected to set aside and revise their own preferences in the interest of finding shared values. While participants are expected to, and do, express private pref-

erences, these preferences are subjected to critical examination and reasoned debate in a deliberative process. Such debate, it is hoped, moves
participants beyond their own self-interests toward consensus or, at the
least, brings forth alternative perspectives and additional information. In
a deliberative process, citizens thus *create* the common good through
discourse, as opposed to *discovering* it through preexisting preferences.

Deliberation works best where there is adequate representation, or inclusion, of affected interests and mutual respect among the participants.
Where material inequalities exist or where representation is flawed or
nominal, a deliberative process can suffer from illegitimacy in its outcomes as much as a pluralistic process can. Similarly, too much participation, or unwieldy and unorganized participation, can be as destructive to
deliberation as too little participation.[19] Moreover, deliberation depends
upon, and instills, "civic virtue" in its participants. That is, deliberation
both requires and enhances citizen participation in, and engagement
with, social and political issues. Not only do participants learn to think
critically and rationally about such issues, but they also must be respect-
ful to others in the process. Mutual respect is both necessary and fostered
when participants deliberate with others as equals, by offering rational
reasons for their actions and by respecting the reasons given by others. It
is only when participants respect and engage other viewpoints that they
can shape dialogue and move toward a consensus.

While deliberation requires "no particular set of institutional
arrangements,"[20] certain types of decision-making structures can address the problems inherent in pluralism—capture, inequality of political access/power, and lack of equal representation—and enhance deliberation. Theoretically, local advisory boards embrace a deliberative
ideal, "meaning that essential activities are learning about the issues,
candidly discussing reasons for and against various alternative solutions, and striving to reach a consensus resolution."[21] Advisory committees are legislatively directed to assess the socioeconomic benefits
and burdens of the facility, review all permit application materials, and
promote public participation and education about the permitting
process. Many states explicitly ask for recommendations about
whether the permit should be granted.[22] Ideally, advisory committee
discussions result in a consensus recommendation to the sponsoring

agency about whether permitting is in the best interest of the community. However, "even if consensus cannot be reached, a successful citizens advisory board can narrow areas of disagreement, help affected parties recognize others' concerns and their bona fides, bring forward alternatives that had not previously been considered, and (if nothing else) elucidate issues that remain to be resolved."[23]

Problems of capture and representation are theoretically minimized by the regulation of representation on the advisory committee. Generally, state laws aim for a diverse membership on advisory committees, mandating representation of the proposed host community, surrounding communities, affected business and industries, and environmental and other public interest groups. Members are generally appointed by either the chief executive officer, typically the mayor, or legislative body, typically the city or county council, of the host community. Additionally, many advisory committees are instructed to hold public hearings on the subject of the proposed facility permit. Public hearings serve a dual purpose. Such hearings expand the range of participation, and perhaps representation, without expanding the membership of the advisory committee or substantially impeding its deliberations. Public hearings also may give added legitimacy to the ultimate consensus and/or recommendation of the committee if it is seen as having considered the views of a fully representative cross-section of the community.

The material inequalities of participants in the decision-making process—lack of information and technical skills—similarly are reduced by advisory committee schemes. All advisory committee members have access to the same information and documents. Most advisory committees are eligible to receive technical assistance, usually in the form of grants for hiring consultants, lawyers, and other necessary personnel. Technical assistance provisions exist out of recognition that "local citizens might not always possess the knowledge and expertise to negotiate effectively with facility proponents."[24] Those committees that are not eligible for technical assistance run into a serious legitimacy problem, however. The sole source of technical expertise on such committees is often industry representatives. Where this is the case, the committee runs the risk of allowing one interest to dominate discussions about technical aspects of a project.

Deliberative Challenges

Despite the *ideal* of deliberation embraced by citizen advisory committees, implementation of the deliberative ideal can be severely hampered. As we've discussed, the key prerequisites to deliberation are broad representation, equalization of material resources, and mutual respect. However, as the Buttonwillow case study illustrates, some decision makers have empaneled unrepresentative deliberative bodies, bodies that exclude certain segments of a local community. Some decision makers have not acted to equalize access to resources and have denied needed resources to the deliberative bodies, despite the existence of laws that mandate the provision of technical assistance grants. Nevertheless, it is possible that stricter regulatory requirements could overcome problems of access and material inequalities.

Even if problems of representation and material resources can be attended to by tightening regulatory requirements, there are other social constraints on some individuals that even an ideal deliberative process does not address. Issues of mutual respect and status, in particular, are more impenetrable. Mutual respect among participants in a deliberative process can be difficult to establish because of what Lynn Sanders calls "the systematic disregard of ascriptively defined groups," such as Latinos and African Americans, which works to undermine the deliberative process.[25] The status inequalities that result from such systematic disregard, Sanders explains, undermine the possibilities of mutual respect among participants in a deliberative process, "so that participation [by disregarded groups] instills a sense of alienation rather than . . . community." Status inequalities resulting from prejudice and privilege are "sneaky, invisible, and pernicious" and are not "countered by good arguments" in a rational deliberative process.

Without mutual respect and attention to the structural and status vulnerabilities of the participants in the advisory process, the whole deliberative process breaks down: broad participation declines, certain interests are excluded, and a legitimate consensus is unattainable. Simply "distributing skills and resources," as Sanders explains, is "unlikely to ensure more egalitarian and democratic discussions." Something more fundamental is needed: attention to the "dynamics of deliberation"—who dominates, whose perspective is suppressed—and the ways in which those dynamics are consequential for the justice of the decision-making outcomes of even the most ideal deliberative processes.

The experiences of residents of Buttonwillow, California, illuminate some of the pitfalls of the deliberative process model. While we chronicled the overall struggle of Buttonwillow residents in chapter 4, we focus here on the residents' encounters with a citizens' advisory committee. Recall that the deliberative process broke down in Buttonwillow because of difficulties of representation, inadequate access to material goods, and status and power inequalities. When the process began, there were no representatives of Buttonwillow on the Local Assessment Committee (LAC), though the meetings were physically held in Buttonwillow. Although more than 50 percent of the population of Buttonwillow is Latino, and that of Kern County as a whole is some 28 percent Latino, not a single Latino was appointed by the County to the LAC. Dozens of community residents, primarily Spanish-speaking Latinos, attended the LAC meetings held once a month for six months until July 1992. At the first six meetings, residents pressed the County to provide Spanish translation for the majority of attendees who spoke no English. The facility proponent, Laidlaw—not the County—finally agreed to provide such translation in June 1992. Kern County then unilaterally suspended the LAC in July 1992.

During that suspension, the draft and the final Environmental Impact Reports (EIRs) on the facility expansion were completed, but not sent to LAC members. In the twenty-seven months that the LAC did not meet, two members resigned, and one died. Despite applications from Latino Buttonwillow residents, the County selected two people from outside the community, both white, as replacements. One white Buttonwillow resident, whose application had not been submitted during the LAC application process (as the Latinos' applications had) was also selected, in a move that confirmed to Buttonwillow residents the illegitimacy of the process. When one white member of the LAC resigned in protest and said that a Latino from Buttonwillow should be appointed, the Board finally appointed Eduardo Montoya, a farm-worker foreman from Buttonwillow, to the LAC in September 1994.

The County reconvened the LAC late in September 1994 and gave it ten weeks to complete its business. The LAC requested technical assistance grants for translation of documents into Spanish for one of its members, for independent advice on seismic issues, and for independent advice on landfill liners. County staff actively opposed every request, and the Board of Supervisors turned down every request. The LAC received no technical assistance grants.

The LAC also battled County staff about control of the LAC meetings, from setting the agenda to conducting the meetings to hiring outside consultants. Piqued by the County staff's continuing opposition to the LAC's requests for independent consultants, the LAC tried unsuccessfully to set its own agenda. "We spent our time arguing with the County," says LAC member Montoya. "When finally the LAC tried to run the meeting, the County Planning Department blocked the LAC completely. We never got a chance to run the meetings ourselves."

The LAC's frustration was shared by the public attendees, who watched as the LAC meetings were taken up with conflict between LAC members and the County staff, while opportunities for public comment dwindled. "The public could see the LAC was trying to do something and the County was blocking them. The public didn't have input," says Montoya. "The County didn't want the public to know what was going on."

Not surprisingly, the LAC was unable to arrive at any consensus in the short time given it. At its December 1994 hearing on the waste facility expansion project, the Board of Supervisors disbanded the LAC over the protests of Buttonwillow residents and LAC members. "The Board knew beforehand that they would approve the dump," says LAC member Montoya. With the LAC, "they were just going through the motions." Residents felt personally insulted and betrayed by the Board's action. Particularly hurt were those who had devoted countless hours to preparing for, attending, and testifying at the thirteen LAC meetings that were held over the thirty-six month permitting process. "If I had to do it again, I wouldn't go through a process like that," says Rosa Solorio-Garcia, who attended every LAC meeting. "It was a real slap in the face."

Beyond eliminating any role for the community in the siting decision, the County's actions in disregarding and disbanding the LAC had the (perhaps intended) outcome of stifling *future* public participation in County decisions by Buttonwillow residents. "If something comes up in Buttonwillow again, people are not going to take part, they're not going to become involved," says Solorio-Garcia. This negative long-term impact on civic participation is the exact opposite of the outcome envisioned by the ideally deliberative process embraced by local advisory committees. Indeed, in cases like Buttonwillow, local advisory groups can limit public participation, "functioning as a gatekeeper and filters."[26]

Contrast the LAC process in Buttonwillow with that followed in another California community. In Martinez, California, a local advisory committee was empaneled by the Martinez City Council to review a proposal by Rhone-Poulenc, an operating sulfuric acid recycling plant in the town, to expand the plant into a commercial toxic waste incinerator, the largest such incinerator in the western United States.[27] The LAC was "very technically skilled," according to Paul Craig, a member; among its seven members were a biochemist, an engineer, an expert on environmental policy, and a staffer of the local utilities district. Active and engaged members took part in the four-year LAC process, educated themselves, and were educated by the LAC's consultants. The LAC hired several consultants, one of which produced a well-researched 150-page study for the LAC on the impact of the proposed toxic waste incinerator on property values. The study fed the already strong community opposition to the facility.

Martinez's elected officials strongly supported the LAC, giving it such latitude and so many technical assistance grants that Rhone-Poulenc at one point protested and refused to pay any further fees. The City Council remained officially neutral throughout the LAC process but did indicate a hostility to incineration in general when it passed, unanimously, a resolution stating that it was illegal to import any toxic waste from outside Martinez for incineration. The Martinez LAC process was interrupted in June 1992 by a spectacular, and deadly, accident at the Rhone-Poulenc plant, in which one worker was killed and another critically injured during normal maintenance operations. "Their facility and credibility were badly damaged," says Cathy Ivers, a Martinez resident who attended most of the LAC meetings. Just months later, under increased community pressure, Rhone-Poulenc agreed to drop the incinerator proposal. The company set up a foundation to contribute to the Martinez community, a foundation that operates to this day.

Did the Martinez LAC live up to its deliberative promise? LAC member Craig summarizes his evaluation: "On balance, the [process] seems to me to be lending a significant element of rationality and public expo-sure to the siting process. The process is slow, cumbersome, and very time consuming, but it does meet all other reasonable tests for opening the decision process to detailed public scrutiny." In Martinez, partici-pants in the LAC process felt empowered, felt that they had as much right to speak as anyone else. In Buttonwillow, on the other hand, the residents felt silenced. In Martinez, both the decision makers and the public were committed to the LAC process, and it worked as designed. In Buttonwillow, the County Board of Supervisors actively attacked the LAC, although members of the public tried diligently to participate, and the process wound up with the LAC—and two other community groups—suing the Board.

What, then, is the difference between these two cases, and what do they teach us about why the deliberative ideal became reality in Mar-tinez, but not in Buttonwillow? Perhaps the demographics of the com-munities in question, of the LAC, and of the decision makers influenced the dynamics of the deliberative process. When we examine the relative homogeneity of Martinez and the reflection of Martinez's population in both the LAC and the decision makers, a contrast between it and the Buttonwillow situation emerges. Buttonwillow is overwhelmingly a community of color and Martinez is white, while the LACs and the de-cision makers in both cases were overwhelmingly white. In some situa-tions, this disparity might not matter; in Buttonwillow it appears to have greatly influenced the failure of the LAC process.

The adequacy of representation and the access to resources also dis-tinguish the Martinez situation from Buttonwillow. As we pointed out earlier, advisory committee members are not chosen by the populace but are instead appointed by local officials, who normally support incoming waste facilities touting economic benefits. As a result, community groups likely to oppose additional waste facilities may easily be left out of the de-liberative process, as happened in Buttonwillow. The City Council strongly supported the LAC in Martinez in its wide-ranging investiga-tion of the impacts of the proposed incinerator; in Buttonwillow, the Board of Supervisors denied every request from the LAC for technical assistance grants. The Martinez LAC, because it involved only a city, drew members from a more compact geographic area than the Button-willow LAC, which drew members from across Kern County (which is larger than Connecticut). This may have increased the Martinez LAC's effectiveness and responsiveness to public input. One of the major complaints growing out of the Buttonwillow LAC process was that the LAC was not representative of the local community; this led to tension and distrust between the public and the LAC.

Even a truly deliberative process, one unencumbered by problems of mutual respect, representation, or access to material goods, will suffer from problems of legitimacy if its members feel coopted by the process. That is, while formerly excluded groups may gain access to decision makers and obtain some of the material tools necessary to level the dialogue among participants in the decision-making process, the decision-making power relations may not change in some advisory committee processes. As Bruce Williams and Albert Matheny have pointed out, "[t]he structure of [advisory committees] creates a threat to continuing mobilization of citizens around toxic issues because opponents of such mobilization can now point to [these committees] as a sufficient substitute for independent citizen action. If, in fact, [advisory committees] are dominated by industry, their broadly representative composition may be used to pit a 'consensual' [advisory committee] understanding of toxics policy against the 'radical' one advocated by a local grassroots group, thus discrediting the latter."[28]

A community group may also feel disempowered by advisory committees because of their very nature. Advisory committees have no formal power and influence. Because these committees are "advisory" only, it is not clear how much weight their analysis is given in the final decision. Government decision makers are, to be sure, counseled to consider the recommendations of the advisory committee, but in the end they retain the discretion to dismiss or discount the committee's recommendations in making their final decision. Absent any real decision-making influence and power, advisory committee participation may actually sap the power of a vibrant community group and coopt the fundamental challenges it poses to the status quo.

Another drawback to community advisory committees is, ironically, the processes' relative informality (as compared to, say, the structure of a formal lawsuit). Critical Race Theorists posit that people of color and poor people fare less well in informal situations.[29] "[I]nformality increases power differentials," explains Richard Delgado.

It's not simply because of the greater discretion the decision-maker wields, although this does open the door for prejudice even wider than it is in court. Rather, it's because all the hallmarks of formality you find in the courtroom—the flags, the robes, the judge sitting on high, the codes of evidence and procedure—all of these remind everyone present that the values that are to prevail are those of the American Creed: fairness, equal treatment, a day in court for everyone.[30]

Thus, the informality of advisory committees' deliberations may exacerbate power imbalances brought to the table.

In sum, creation of site-specific advisory committees is an important, if flawed, step toward providing meaningful decision-making access to vulnerable communities on issues that fundamentally affect their lives. Such committees offer opportunities for a deliberative process, potentially overcoming the shortcomings that plague pluralistic decision-making processes. However, without a substantive commitment to take seriously social and institutional constraints on vulnerable communities, to neutralize those constraints in the decision-making process, and to share decision-making influence, even deliberatively-oriented advisory committees fall short of providing a legitimate decision-making process for communities asked to bear the burdens of hazardous waste (and other) facilities. Many communities continue to feel that the "system is stacked and that no amount of participation by itself will change the relations of power that give rise to environmental degradation."[31]

The Limits of Litigation

Given the barriers to meaningful participation and influence in formal decision-making processes, it is not surprising that many community groups turn to litigation as part of their struggle. As we have seen in Kettleman City and in Buttonwillow, litigation has prompted certain changes in permitting processes, such as the translation of documents into the communities' language. Nevertheless, in spite of the successes in cases like Kettleman City, attempts to transform permitting processes to account for social disparities through litigation have been largely unsuccessful. Moreover, as we explain in this section, the legal and political costs of resorting to certain litigation strategies outweigh the limited successes of cases like Kettleman City. Litigation can be inappropriate for, or unavailable to, communities struggling for environmental justice. Because environmental justice struggles are political and economic struggles, legal responses have fallen woefully short of aiding communities and in some cases have hurt their struggles.

Using Environmental Law to Change Environmental Decision-Making Norms

Litigation on behalf of poor communities and communities of color that are fighting environmental dangers dates at least to the 1960s, although those who brought the suits did not see themselves as part of the Environmental Justice Movement. Legal services attorneys brought suits on behalf of farm-workers to ban dangerous pesticides[32] and on behalf of poor rural residents to stop strip mining. Since the 1960s, legal services and other attorneys have brought dozens of suits on behalf of low-income communities, many of them communities of color, in environmental justice struggles. Most of these suits, which were often successful, were based on environmental, rather than civil rights, laws. Environmental law challenges in the context of environmental justice struggles have a proven track record of success.

The crux of successful lawsuits based on environmental law is the focus on procedure. Many state and federal environmental laws, especially those related to permitting facilities, are procedurally oriented: they set out a series of procedural hoops to be jumped through; once an applicant has successfully jumped through the hoops, the applicant receives a permit. For example, lawyers using this approach filed suit on behalf of Mothers of East Los Angeles to point out flaws in the environmental review of a proposed toxic waste incinerator. When the community group won the lawsuit, the incinerator company withdrew its application rather than complete a full environmental review.

There is also some latitude for pushing the boundaries of the public participation requirement in most environmental laws. Again, this strategy relies on attacks on the procedure of permitting, rather than the substance or the outcome. Recall the lawsuit in Kettleman City, profiled in the Preface, involving the community group *El Pueblo para el Aire y Agua Limpio*. The dispute in El Pueblo involved the siting of a hazardous waste incinerator near Kettleman City, California, where 95 percent of the population is Latino, with a 40 percent of the population monolingual Spanish-speaking. When the permitting agency, Kings County, provided the community with the required documents—the hearing notices, public testimony, and three versions of the EIR—it had not translated them into Spanish. Moreover, the EIR was difficult to read in English, because it used highly technical language and obscure scientific terms.[33] In response to eighty-one written requests for translation of notices and of the draft EIR, the County Planning Commission informed the community that "it is the policy of Kings County to publish environmental documents in English." At the only public hearing on the proposed facility, the Planning Commission refused to provide translation or to allow private interpreters for Spanish-speaking attendees. Nor were Spanish statements translated for English speakers in the audience, except for the Commissioners, who could listen through earphones to their own interpreter.

After the Planning Commission approved the permit, a group of Kettleman City residents brought a lawsuit under, among other statutes, the California Environmental Quality Act (CEQA), its mini-NEPA, to invalidate the permit and to enjoin construction of the incinerator. The residents argued that the failure to translate crucial documents and meetings had effectively excluded many citizens from exercising their statutory right to participate in the decision-making process. The California Superior Court agreed, ruling that "meaningful involvement in the CEQA process was effectively precluded by the absence of Spanish translation."

The Kettleman City case influenced President Clinton's Executive Order on Environmental Justice, particularly its recommendation that crucial documents be translated into a community's language. Similarly, the Council on Environmental Quality recognizes that vulnerable communities may require "adaptive" or "innovative" approaches to overcome "linguistic, institutional, cultural, economic, historical, or other potential barriers" to effective participation in environmental decision-making processes. These barriers may range from an agency's failure to provide "translations of documents" to the scheduling of meetings at times and in places that are "not convenient to working families."[34] To this extent, litigation enforcing the procedural guarantees of environmental laws has been successful in ensuring socially and economically disadvantaged communities equal access to the environmental decision-making processes.

Nevertheless, litigation based on environmental laws has been unsuccessful in transforming decision-making processes beyond basic "access" requirements. Courts have not been responsive to complaints that status inequalities and lack of mutual respect preclude some environmental decision-making processes from being "meaningful" for individuals in vulnerable communities. When courts have been willing to look beyond "access" guarantees to ensure that communities have an influential voice in the process, such victories are usually short-lived.

For instance, consider a recent case that challenged a permit issued to the Genesee Power Station, a wood waste–fired steam electric generation plant, by the Michigan Department of Environmental Quality (MDEQ).[35] African Americans constitute the majority of the population living within three miles of the Genesee Power Station. Many residents in the community opposed the permit because it would allow the facility to emit significant levels of lead in an already environmentally burdened community. Among other bases, the community challenged the issuance of the permit on the basis that opportunities for public participation were inadequate. The public comment period for the permit lasted forty-two days, more than the required thirty days. Two separate public hearings were held, although none is required unless the permit issuer determines that there is strong public interest, in which case only one hearing is required. Nevertheless, community members asserted that they were made to sit for hours while the committee conducted other business. According to the community group, the decision makers delivered a revised draft permit to the group during the public hearing, leaving no time for review by experts. When the group finally got a chance to testify, the decision makers talked among themselves, laughed, and paid little attention. Moreover, the hearing took place at a location more than an hour from the proposed site, forcing concerned residents to rent a bus. The decision maker, MDEQ, did not contradict the community's assertions about the public hearing, thus "lending credence to those assertions," according to the reviewing panel.

An Environmental Appeals Board (EAB) disagreed with the challengers, ruling that the community did have a "meaningful opportunity" to have its views heard during the course of the permitting process. The

EAB ruled that it would have been better to reschedule the meeting but that, while insensitive, the Commission's behavior was not so serious that the Commission should be required to go through the whole process again. An important factor in the EAB's decision was the fact that there had been a public hearing prior to the one at issue in which members of the public were allowed to make their views known. Moreover, the EAB noted, the final draft permit reflected changes based on comments received at the first hearing and during the public comment period.

The community group took the matter to court, and a Michigan Circuit Court (in an unpublished opinion) disagreed with the EAB's assessment. Basing its decision in part on the Michigan Constitution, the court issued an injunction prohibiting the State of Michigan from granting any more permits until it had reformed its system of environmental protection—including a requirement that the State perform risk assessments and reform its public hearing process, which the court found was not "meaningful." The court found specifically that "the opportunity to make public comment without the power to apply political pressure on the decision makers does not constitute a situation where people who are affected have a real voice in the decision." Unfortunately, a Michigan Appeals Court soon reversed the Circuit Court's decision.[36]

Using Civil Rights to Affect Environmental Decision Making

The movement for environmental justice owes much in history, inspiration, and tactics to the Civil Rights Movement, and it is thus no surprise that the legal activity growing out of the movement should try to use civil rights laws. Many people view a civil rights case out of Texas in the late 1970s as the parent of environmental justice litigation. That case, brought in 1979 by Linda McKeever Bullard on behalf of residents of Houston's Northwood Manor, was the first suit in the country to challenge the siting of an unwanted waste facility on civil rights grounds.[37] The suit charged that the City of Houston and Browning Ferris Industries were discriminating against the residents of that neighborhood, most of whom were African American, by placing the garbage dump there. This ground-breaking lawsuit was the inspiration for the legal piece to the Environmental Justice Movement, a movement which was in its infancy when the suit was brought.

Lawsuits that allege violations of civil rights laws, or that are based upon civil rights constitutional norms, are one tool that communities have tried to use to influence environmental decision-making processes. Adding civil rights claims as part of an environmental law suit or administrative complaint allows a community group to paint a fuller picture of the nature of the problem in a community.[38] Alleging civil rights claims, especially as part of a lawsuit that also uses environmental laws, can be very useful in building morale, raising the profile of a community's struggle, and educating the public about environmental racism.

However, civil rights claims, particularly those based on constitutional principles of equal protection, have not been successful in transforming environmental decision-making processes to take into account the social, political, and economic vulnerability of poor communities of color. Courts have significantly watered down civil rights laws in the past twenty years, so what appears to the average person to be a clear civil rights violation might not fit the narrow legal definition of such a violation. As we discussed in chapter 3, courts have ruled that a government action that might have a discriminatory impact is not unconstitutional unless the decision maker had a discriminatory *intent*, something that is very hard to prove. Consequently, no plaintiff has prevailed in alleging a federal constitutional violation in an environmental justice suit, although this strategy has been tried in numerous jurisdictions around the country.[39]

The civil rights claims that promise the best avenue of relief are those based upon civil rights statutes, particularly those statutes that allow proof of a violation on the basis of discriminatory *impact* rather than discriminatory *intent*. Two central civil rights statutes that contain an impact standard and that are potentially available and appropriate in environmental justice struggles are Title VI of the Civil Rights Act of 1964 and Title VIII of the Civil Rights Act of 1968. Title VI prohibits discrimination on the grounds of race, color, and national origin by "any program or activity receiving Federal financial assistance." While litigants under Title VI itself must prove that a defendant intentionally discriminated, the regulations implementing Title

VI across the federal government generally state that discriminatory effect (or disparate impact) alone is enough to show unlawful discrimination.[40] Because of these differing standards, environmental justice cases have relied on the regulations that are used to implement Title VI, rather than on the statute itself.

The discriminatory effect standard is codified in the regulations of most federal agencies, including the Environmental Protection Agency and the Departments of Agriculture, Defense, Energy, and Interior.[41] Because many state agencies receive federal funding (often channeled through particular federal agencies), and because Title VI broadly defines "program or activity receiving Federal financial assistance," Title VI may be applied against state and local agencies. Title VI applies to an entire state agency if even one part of that agency receives federal funding; because of this broad coverage, most state agencies likely to be encountered in an environmental justice suit are probably also subject to Title VI.[42]

Strategies for employing Title VI in environmental justice and other cases have been well discussed in legal literature,[43] and the approach has been used in a series of cases. In one case, residents of the African American Crest Street neighborhood in Durham, North Carolina, intervened in the siting process for a freeway that was to be built through their community. The Crest Street Community Council, represented by the local legal services office, North Central Legal Assistance Program, used Title VI in a complaint to the U.S. Department of Transportation (DOT) to challenge the state's freeway construction plans. After investigation, DOT informed the state that there was "reasonable cause to believe that the construction of the expressway along the alignment proposed in the Draft [Environmental Impact Statement] would constitute a prima facie violation of Title VI[.]" In a negotiated settlement, the state agreed to reroute the proposed freeway and to modify an interchange to preserve the community church and park.[44]

A recent Supreme Court action in the Chester case has led some to question the continuing viability of lawsuits under Title VI regulations, as the Court appeared poised to abolish citizens' rights to sue under such regulations.[45] Recall that a group of Chester citizens sued the Pennsylvania Department of Environmental Protection (DEP), alleging that its permitting policies had concentrated a disproportionate share of pollution in Chester. Over a ten-year period, the lawsuit alleged, the Pennsylvania DEP issued seven permits for commercial waste facilities in the overwhelmingly white county, five of which were in the predominantly low-income, African American City of Chester. The case centered around the most recent permit issued by DEP, for a plant to burn contaminated soil. The federal District Court threw out the case on the grounds that the community group had no right to sue under EPA's Title VI regulations. The Chester group appealed to the Third Circuit, which ruled that citizens such as those in Chester did have a "private right of action" under EPA's Title VI regulations. The U.S. Supreme Court took the case after the State of Pennsylvania appealed, but when the developer of the soil burning plant in question failed to secure local permits and abandoned the project, the Supreme Court declared the case moot and vacated the Third Circuit's decision. Several other cases have raised the same issue of whether a private right of action exists, and the question may yet again reach the Supreme Court.[46]

Title VIII offers environmental justice attorneys another possible statutory base for a civil rights claim. Title VIII, also known as the Fair Housing Act, bars discrimination "against any person in the . . . sale or rental of a dwelling, or in the provision of services or facilities in connection therewith, because of race, color, religion, sex, familial status or national origin."[47] Although there has yet to be a reported case involving an environmental justice dispute, it is an intriguing statute for several reasons.

First, the statute does not require a proof of intentional discrimination to establish a prima facie case of discrimination—a plaintiff need only prove that the conduct of the defendant actually or predictably results in racial discrimination, that is, that it has discriminatory impact.[48] To rebut a prima facie case, a defendant must then prove that its conduct is justified in theory and practice by a legitimate interest and that no alternative course of action could be taken that would serve the interest with less discriminatory impact. Second, the statute does not require that the alleged violator receive federal financial assistance. It thus applies to private companies engaged in discriminatory conduct. It also applies to local government agencies and, more importantly, to those agencies' zoning decisions. This offers environmental justice advocates a tool with which to challenge government rezoning of residential neighborhoods in communities of color to allow noxious facilities or other inappropriate land uses—a historical practice that Yale Rabin calls "expulsive zoning."[49]

Third, although the statute is written to narrowly apply to fair housing cases, it has been used to challenge the "segregative effect" of government decisions—that is, decisions that have the impact of increasing segregation. Title VIII might be implicated if a community can successfully demonstrate that zoning changes that allow inappropriate land uses in residential communities are closely enough related to the "provision of services or facilities" for sale or rental of housing and that they have segregative effect. These two hurdles—the nexus to housing and the actual segregative effect of a proposed land use—may be high but in the right case may be surmountable.[50] Nevertheless, even if a plaintiff group can make a prima facie case of discrimination, a defendant can overcome this finding by showing that the siting or zoning decision is based on a legitimate interest and that no alternative course of action could be taken that would serve the interest with less discriminatory impact.

The Politics of Law

Because environmental justice struggles are at heart political and economic struggles, a legal response is often inappropriate or unavailable. In fact, bringing a lawsuit may ensure certain loss of the struggle at hand or cause significant disempowerment of community residents. Tactically, taking environmental problems out of the streets and into the courts has proven, in many instances, to be a mistake. In struggles between private industry and a host community, there are two types of power: the power of money and the power of people. Private industry has the money, while communities have the people; this disparity in resources is evident in many environmental justice cases, such as those litigated in Buttonwillow and in Chester. In court, industry has access to the best lawyers, scientists, and government officials money can buy; to have a chance, a community group must often hire expensive experts. Relying on lawyers, rather than on a community's own actions, necessarily involves having just one or two people speaking for the community. On the other hand, a community-based political organizing strategy can be broad and participatory and can include all members of the community.

An important footnote to the warning against reliance on litigation in environmental justice struggles is the following: there may be some political benefits in bringing civil rights suits as part of a local fight. First, bringing a civil rights suit against local government officials can be very satisfying for the community group involved, because it calls the problem what it is: a violation of civil rights. This "naming names" has many advantages.[51] It is one high-profile way of saying that the official being sued is engaging in unjust practices. This act alone makes such suits worth it to some groups with long-term experiences with decision makers—filing a suit allows a community to say "officially" what has existed for a long time and builds morale within the group. Additionally, by calling an environmental dispute by a different name—a civil rights dispute—a community group can educate its members, politicians, and other communities. It may help local residents, decision makers, and company officials see the problem differently. More importantly, renaming the problem raises the consciousness of the general public about the issue of environmental racism. By calling a dispute a civil rights struggle, a group may also find allies in more traditional civil rights groups in its region that may not have recognized the civil rights implications of the struggle for environmental justice. At the same time, the group may lose allies who are squeamish about talking about race issues.

Second, civil rights lawsuits in environmental struggles are still relatively new and thus command media attention, especially if a corporate giant is being sued. In the Kettleman City incinerator struggle, the civil rights and environmental suit the community brought was written about in national publications such as *The Wall Street Journal* and the *Christian Science Monitor*. The publicity was important in drawing even more attention to the community's struggle and in building grassroots momentum. As part of its story about the suit, *Business Week* did a chart titled "Did Chem Waste Discriminate?" The chart listed all of Chem Waste's incinerator facilities around the country, each of which is in a neighborhood with populations that are 80 percent or more people of color.[52] That chart said it all, and was an incredibly effective educational tool.

Influencing Decision Makers by Building Power Within: Coalition Building and Networking

The success of grassroots environmental justice groups in local struggles to control their environment reflects the degree to which such groups have built a movement largely outside of formal decision-making structures and litigation avenues. The locus and style of environmental justice advocacy will be increasingly determined by a group's access to power; if a group cannot influence decision making within the system, it will wield its influence from outside the system. It must influence decision makers—or, better, be the decision makers. The groups portrayed in this book recognize that the key to building sustainable communities in the twenty-first century will be building power from within their communities.

One of the ways in which power is being built within communities is through the development of coalitions and networks. At some point, a community group usually finds it necessary to expand its base. Grassroots environmental justice groups have often formed partnerships with other local institutions, such as churches, medical centers, and schools, to broaden the group's appeal and reach. Such expansion helps to send a stronger message to decision makers and also takes the focus and pressure off groups that have so many other "first-order" concerns—work, school, children, and everyday survival. Recall that in Chester, for instance, the community group CRCQL held a regional environmental justice retreat at a nearby college to educate a broader constituency about its struggle. The retreat resulted in the formation of Campus Coalition Concerning Chester (dubbed C4 by participants), a group of students from more than fifteen college campuses across four states. The coalition has been invaluable in educating many people across racial, class, and geographic lines about Chester's struggle for environmental justice, and involving them into it.

Many groups also form networks with organizations outside their communities, usually in other parts of the region or country. These networks allow local groups to support each other, share strategies, and bring their combined power and resources to bear on local issues. They provide information and technical expertise to grassroots constituencies

| 131 |

to build local power, influence policy decisions, and create more opportunities for input into the spectrum of decision making that affects disenfranchised communities. The Indigenous Environmental Network, profiled in the chapter 6, is a national coalition of Native American groups dedicated to environmental justice. There are many other networks: the Asian Pacific Environmental Network, the Military Production Network, and the Southwest Network for Environmental and Economic Justice all unite local environmental justice organizations into broad, regional coalitions to build greater power.

Most grassroots environmental justice advocates are more concerned with building viable community organizations and regional networks than with winning any particular environmental battle. They recognize that communities must take ownership of the struggle and "ultimately their own communities."[53] Community fights over particular facilities will come and go, but redlining, racism, unemployment, and crime will remain in low-income communities long after; it is hoped that strategies that address environmental justice problems by building local power will have an impact on longer-term problems, as well.

Indeed, many community organizations and networks created during the heat of local environmental fights have gone on to be creative, contributing community forces for social and economic justice. For example, Concerned Citizens of South Central Los Angeles, formed to fight a garbage incinerator, now develops low-income housing. *Madres del Este de Los Angeles-Santa Isabel* grew out of the struggle against a prison in East Los Angeles and now runs job training and conservation programs. West Harlem Environmental Action, which sprang up around a sewage treatment plant controversy, plans to produce a cable television show and run an environmental education program for inner-city youth. Similarly, the SouthWest Organizing Project has grown from focusing on discrete campaigns into a multiracial, multi-issue, community-based organization whose mission is to empower the disenfranchised in the Southwest to realize social, racial, and economic justice.

The establishment of broad-based social justice networks dispels the notion that the Environmental Justice Movement is simply another example of "NIMBYism"—an acronym for "not in my back yard." The Environmental Justice Movement is engaged in something much more transformative. Communities have organized to resist toxic intrusions, created and strengthened networks to support each others' struggles, begun to elect their own sympathetic state and local officials, pushed legal and environmental groups to increase their activity in the field, and acquired the tools they need to stop decision makers from taking advantage of communities' historical lack of political and economic power. As the next two chapters illustrate, the grassroots movement for environmental justice has transformed not only individuals and communities but also the very nature of environmental politics.

SIX

In Defense of Mother Earth

The Indigenous Environmental Network

The Indigenous Environmental Network, an international coalition of more than forty grassroots Indian environmental justice groups based in Bemidji, Minnesota, began in a humble spot: Lori Goodman's kitchen table in Dilkon, a small, isolated Navajo town of 285 people in northeast Arizona. It was around that table that Goodman and other activists first strategized on how to beat a toxic waste incinerator proposed for their community—a struggle that would lead them to initiate the broad-based effort focused on Native American environmental issues that evolved into the network.

It sounded like a great idea to Tribal officials on the Navajo reservation: a $40 million recycling plant that would bring 200 desperately needed jobs to the isolated Navajo community of Dilkon, Arizona, where unemployment hovered around 75 percent. Waste-Tech Services promised the community of Dilkon $200,000 a year, with an additional $600,000 a year to be paid to the Navajo Nation in rent and lease funds. Company officials pledged that 95 percent of the jobs would go to Navajo workers and that they would set up a scholarship fund for Navajo students interested in coming back to work as chemists or technicians at the plant.[1] On the basis of these representations by the company, the Tribal chair (similar to a state governor of the reservation) approved the plant in August 1988, and Waste-Tech began plans to set up shop in the remote town.

Then local residents heard about the proposal. When an article appeared in a local newspaper, in December 1988, Dilkon residents began to organize and to find out about the proposal.[2] They formed Citizens

Against Ruining our Environment (CARE) and began meeting regularly to figure out what the proposed project was all about.

The "great idea" began to fade as the community discovered more details of the proposed facility. The "recycling facility" turned out to be a toxic waste incinerator, designed to burn chemicals and industrial solvents from oil fields, lumber yards, and hospitals.[3] The toxic waste would be trucked in from California, Nevada, Colorado, and even Puerto Rico.[4] Tons of incinerator ash would be left over from the process.

Waste-Tech had assured the community that the ash would be safe.[5] But CARE's investigations, and information supplied by Greenpeace, revealed that ash left over from toxic waste incineration is itself toxic. Each previously undisclosed fact revealed by CARE reduced the project's credibility in Dilkon.

Early in 1989, the incinerator proposal ran into even bigger problems. Public outrage against the incinerator was building throughout the Navajo reservation. News articles revealed that Waste-Tech's parent company, Blaze Construction, had hired Navajo Nation Tribal Chair Peter MacDonald's son—for $6,000 a month—to help the company get the necessary permits from the Navajo Nation,[6] in what looked to CARE and others like an attempt to buy approval of the project over local opposition.

Community outrage rose to a crescendo when residents discovered that the incinerator would also burn medical waste, including human body parts and amputated limbs. "That's what really turned the stomachs of the Elders," explained CARE cofounder Abe Plummer. "We have a belief that you respect the dead, and if you have to cut off a part of the body you put it in the Earth with respect—with prayers, not just throw it in the trash."[7]

CARE both created and stoked this outrage. The small group meeting around the kitchen table quickly grew into an eighty-member organization that prepared residents to testify at the upcoming public hearings on the project. CARE moved its planning meetings to the local school.

In an effort to build public support for their now controversial proposal, Waste-Tech Services, Inc., and High-Tech Recycling, Inc., brought a panel of engineering experts to a public hearing held by the Tribe in Dilkon on February 25, 1989, to discuss the project. At the end of the hearing, a vote was taken of those residents present: ninety-nine opposed the project, while six supported it.[8] Tribal decision makers saw the writing on the wall, and at the next council meeting, on March 6, they unanimously rescinded the earlier approval and requested further that "the toxic waste site not be located anywhere within the Navajo reservation."[9]

Waste-Tech pulled out of the project. The facility's other major backer, High-Tech Recycling, tried again the following month with a proposal for a "treatment, storage, and disposal facility"—a fancy name for a toxic waste dump. The Dilkon community was not impressed. Things came to a head on April 11, at a community meeting at which company officials presented the dump proposal. CARE had invited a Greenpeace staffer, Bradley Angel, to the meeting, and Angel made a presentation on the dangers of toxic dumps and pointed out how other Tribes throughout the West were being similarly targeted for unwanted waste facilities. Tribal Elders asked the company, "If it is so safe, if it is such a good idea, if it makes so much money, why aren't the white people grabbing at it in L.A. and San Francisco?"[10] By the end of the meeting, the company's representative announced that he was forced to abandon the dump proposal at Dilkon.[11] CARE's victories over the incinerator and the dump projects, with their beginnings at Lori Goodman's kitchen table, would come to have national implications.

Beyond Dilkon

Native Americans have a tie to the land that is different from that of other U.S. residents, and this tie informs the grassroots environmental activism in Indian communities. Spiritually and legally, Indians have a unique relationship with the land: spiritually, many Indians worship their ancestral lands, which figure in different Tribes' creation stories. The birds and animals that inhabit the land are sacred, messengers for the spirits or even spirits themselves. "The spirit of the broader indigenous movement," explains Jackie Warledo, a founder of the Indigenous Environmental Network and for many years the Native Lands Campaigner for Greenpeace, "is that integral understanding that you're a part of everything—you're not set apart, you're a part *of*."[12] For tens of thousands of years, Indian nations have had a relationship with their surroundings, and in today's Environmental Justice Movement activists are defending that relationship by defending Mother Earth. The degradation of natural resources has a distinct impact on Native peoples.

These issues are very hard to deal with. It's even hard for some of our communities to deal with things that are causing death in our communities. It's really hard to talk about PCB contamination along the St. Lawrence River corridor in New York when you know that your sisters are there, that their breastmilk is contaminated with PCB. It's hard to deal with when you're talking with people that still maintain a fishing culture living along the Columbia River, who show us photographs of contaminated fish tissue, fish you see were mutated. They know that there already has been radioactive impacts to the fish. And they know that as long as they continue to eat the fish that the health of their people is going to be impacted. But they also know too that it's not as simple as issuing a fish advisory notification; it's not as simple as telling a mother not to breastfeed. Because the original instructions are not man made. These are original instructions that are part of our spiritual being. We have a relationship, deeper than a brother-sister relationship, with these creations, with the fish nation. These people along the Columbia are the river people, they've been living there for thousands of years. That fish is their brother. And the fish says, "Take of me, take of me, eat of me, I'm here for you and you are here for me. I need you. We need each other." So if you stop eating the fish, that affects the whole balance of things. A lot of the people we've been talking with and we meet are part of subsistence cultures, land-based cultures, that still live off the land, even though we've done what we can to notify them on what the impacts are, they make their decision to continue to eat those things in the food web. Even knowing that the food web is contaminated.

—Tom Goldtooth[13]

Legally, Native Americans have a different relationship with the land as well. They are the only group of U.S. citizens who have prescribed areas to live on, in the form of reservations, pueblos, and rancherias. Because of their historical, spiritual, and legal ties to the land, Native Americans do not have the same mobility that others facing environmental hazards might have. "Because we're still here in our original lands, we still have the memory of particular spots, we still have the connection and the relationship to particular places on this land," says Warledo.

In the late 1980s, many Native communities were approached by outside companies with proposals for toxic waste dumps, incinerators, and other industrial facilities. The companies were seeking jurisdictions with less regulation, and less environmental oversight and enforcement, than were imposed by state governments. The companies sought to capitalize on the confusion over environmental regulatory authority on Indian lands: state law does not apply to Indian lands if it is preempted by federal law or if its imposition would interfere with a Tribe's ability to regulate and govern its own affairs, so Native lands are not subject to the more stringent environmental requirements imposed under state law. Federal environmental laws do apply to Indian lands (with the prominent exception of the Resource Conservation and Recovery Act, which covers the disposal of hazardous waste), but the U.S. Environmental Protection Agency has almost no enforcement presence on reservations. The Tribes involved, many of which did not have environmental protection departments or Tribal environmental laws, often looked at the proposals as economic development opportunities. It was only when Tribal residents began to investigate the proposals that their true nature became evident. "In the late '80s, people began to ask questions and want to know more about these facilities and these activities," explains Jackie Warledo. "In the early '90s, as people began to communicate with each other and reach out to larger environmental organizations for information on these kinds of facilities, for community people, there was caution and concern, and, in some cases, there was community opposition to these facilities being sited."

It was in this context that CARE beat the Dilkon incinerator and established a link to other, similarly-situated Native communities with their own environmental struggles. When other Native groups began to hear about CARE's success, CARE received phone calls from around the country requesting help in other environmental struggles on Indian reservations. One of CARE's outside supporters, Bradley Angel of Greenpeace, had been working with several other grassroots Indian groups and was also flooded with calls. At the victory celebration in Dilkon, CARE leader Abe Plummer suggested that CARE host a conference of Indian people who were fighting waste facilities, to network and share information. Plummer turned to Angel, who was attending the celebration, and said, "And Greenpeace will pay for the conference, right?" Angel lobbied his Washington, D.C.–based superiors, explaining the burgeoning number of proposals for toxic facilities on Indian lands, and when CARE decided to convene a gathering, Greenpeace, together with Chris Peters of the Seventh Generation Fund, provided financial backing. More than 200 people from twenty-five different Tribes attended the gathering that resulted, which convened in Dilkon in June 1990 and which was billed the "Protecting Mother Earth Conference."

At the Dilkon gathering, a moment of realization took place in some participants' minds. CARE members were aware of the United Church of Christ's *Toxic Wastes and Race* report, and they connected the national pattern of unequal distribution of toxic waste facilities to the targeting of their community for the toxic waste incinerator.[14] Nevertheless, they and others were surprised to see the same issues—outside interests seeking to place undesirable land uses on Indian reservations—arise in a variety of guises, from nuclear waste storage facilities to toxic waste landfills to garbage dumps. "These companies seem to feel that it's just Indian land—and who cares about one more dead Indian? It's the same mentality from way back," said Abe Plummer of CARE.[15]

Nor could tribal members depend on their elected leaders. "Corporations seemed to be lining the pocketbooks of a lot of tribal leaders, especially if it involved natural resources and environment," explains Tom Goldtooth, coordinator of IEN. "What was emerging was a grassroots movement, of grassroots people, speaking out from the grassroots level."

At the Dilkon gathering leaders also realized that grassroots tribal groups needed to remain in contact. "People began to realize that there was a lot of communication and networking that was needed," says Warledo, who helped organize the first meeting. "People felt that we needed some kind of a mechanism or an entity that would connect the communities," she notes, adding that grassroots tribal groups wanted "places that you could get information on, 'what is an incinerator?' 'what is a landfill?' 'what are the regulations on them?'" People at the first gathering had a host of unanswered questions.

No concrete organization grew out of the Dilkon gathering. Instead, there was a strong sense that people should communicate among themselves. Several of the core activists who had met and networked at the Dilkon conference kept in contact and soon decided that a second conference should be planned for the following summer.

The second gathering was held near Bear Butte, South Dakota, the following June. At Bear Butte, those who gathered physically demonstrated their solidarity with two local Lakota groups, the Good Road Coalition and the Native Resource Coalition, which were fighting massive garbage dumps proposed for the nearby Pine Ridge and Rosebud reservations. At Bear Butte, the debate around the formation of a national network also came to a head. "People wanted coverage," says Warledo, but "people didn't want another national organization."

A Network of Indigenous People Working on Environmental Issues: IEN Is Born

The loose group of people exchanging phone calls became more solidified after Bear Butte. "Early on, we asked ourselves, 'what is this?'" remembers Jackie Warledo. "It was a network, and it was focused on environmental issues, and it was an entity that would do this work by and for indigenous people—it was an indigenous environmental network." Thus, the Indigenous Environmental Network was born.

The ten or twelve Native American activists who formed the loose group and who ultimately founded IEN didn't want just another national organization; they wanted a real network, a body that would share information among its members. During the year after Bear Butte, several organizational meetings were held to develop by-laws and an organizational structure. "It was a little slow," says Goldtooth, "because people said 'yes, these are by-laws, but we want to have our own language, where we will be able put together something that we can say reflects traditional values. And there was no other model at the time—most of the things that were developed were based upon white folks' hierarchy systems: board of directors, structures, and this is something that the constituents of IEN did not want." These meetings did not take place in a vacuum: the First National People of Color Environmental Leadership Summit took place in October 1991, and many of the early organizers of IEN took part in the summit. Other networks, particularly the Southwest Network for Environmental and Economic Justice, were also organizing at the time. But IEN was different: it was not a geographically-based network but was made up of grassroots Indian groups around the United States. It was an activist group, but, unlike the other environmental justice networks that were developing at the time, it had a strong spiritual component to its work and identity. Goldtooth calls IEN "a form of de-programming."

> The Indigenous Environmental Network came out of the fire, our sacred fire. Everyone I've talked to who were the founders, and those other people who have come to the gatherings, believe that there is a spiritual foundation to our Network, that we were brought together from many different tribes and cultures and languages but that we have something in common that brought us together, and that's faith, a spiritualness in our cultures and our spiritual belief that no matter what we do, we have to continue to pray and respect the Mother Earth.
>
> —Tom Goldtooth

At the third annual gathering, at Celilo, Oregon, IEN created the National Task Force, which soon evolved into IEN's governing body, the national council. The national council is made up of grassroots Indian groups, such as CARE and the Columbia River Economic and Education Alliance, as well as several national groups such as the International Indian Treaty Council and the Indigenous Women's Network. The groups have institutional seats on the national council, a structure designed so that individuals who serve are selected by and accountable to their organizations. There are also three "regional" seats on the national council, one each from Oklahoma, Alaska, and the Great Lakes; these representatives are chosen by grassroots groups in their region. Because many of the struggles in Indian county are between Tribal governments and grassroots Indian groups, Tribal nations are not represented on the national council. "We are all members of our own nations and IEN has working relationships now with many tribal Nations, of course," says Warledo, "but IEN is for the grassroots."

The national council's decision making is by consensus, a style drawn from Native American traditions. Such a decision-making style—in which everyone must agree on a particular course of action before it is undertaken—is not always easy, admit IEN leaders. "The thing that keeps us working at it, at getting us through the complications, is the commitment to the common spiritual foundation," explains Warledo. "Not any one person or one Tribe's spiritual ways, but a common foundation that is reflected in our guiding documents."

Walking the Walk: IEN in Action

In the early years, IEN carried out its work through the national council; this sharing of responsibility was not only a political statement but a practical necessity: IEN had no employees. The national council organized the annual "Protecting Mother Earth" gathering and fielded questions from grassroots Indian groups around the country. "Every year that we've had a gathering, we get more phone calls," explains Goldtooth, "and it started to create a bottleneck because we didn't have any staff."

Fundraising by council members paid off in 1995: after working as IEN's volunteer coordinator, Tom Goldtooth was hired as IEN's first staff person. Goldtooth, who had come of age in an era of Indian activism and had been involved with IEN since 1991, was at the time the environmental director of the Red Lakes Band of Chippewa. Through his work he had come to the realization that the chronic underfunding of Indian environmental programs by the federal government occurred not by accident but by design. "I started to look at this as another colonial action of the government," he explains. "I've always had this feeling that the government is in cahoots with corporations, and that it's the corporations that want to take advantage of our resources. Surely, corporations don't want tribes to have strong environmental protection infrastructures; they don't want tribes to be exercising full sovereignty to implement their own enforcement laws, because if the tribes did do that, it may limit or fully restrict the ability of these corporations to continue to tap the tender resources, the water resources, the mineral resources."

Goldtooth's hiring gave IEN new capacity to serve grassroots groups. He brought both technical expertise as a Tribal environmental manager and strategic expertise from his years of experience as an activist. He has expanded the work of IEN significantly, and today IEN's work takes place on a variety of levels: the group provides education and training, technical assistance, strategic advice, and networking. A primary focus of IEN, and one of its key strategies, has remained the annual gathering.

Gatherings as Political Strategy and Spiritual Sustenance

IEN's yearly Protecting Mother Earth conferences are central to its mission, helping to bring together Native American activists and their allies to network and strategize, rededicate themselves to the struggle, celebrate victories, educate one another and learn from homegrown experts, support local struggles, and see old friends. There are dozens of panel workshops with Native leaders and outside technical experts that provide both substantive information and strategic advice. Many activists find that other attendees from other communities are fighting similar struggles, and informal caucusing is a common event.

A typical day at the 1999 conference, for example, began with a sunrise prayer ceremony, followed by a morning plenary session on "Uranium and Indigenous People," which featured speakers from Native American pueblos in New Mexico as well as an Indian activist from Canada and an aboriginal mining activist from Australia. At lunch, advocacy groups such as Health Care without Harm gave brief presentations on their work. After lunch, there were a variety of concurrent workshops with titles like "Uranium Mining/Milling Radiation Victims Compensation Payment," "Introduction to Federal and Indigenous Environmental Laws," "Biological Diversity and the Impact of Globalism," "Nuclear Colonialism," and "Landfills, Incineration, and Municipal Solid Waste." Some of the workshops were technical in nature—subjects included how to file radiation illness claims and what the technical flaws are in landfills—while others were aimed at describing different struggles or policies. There were also training sessions (e.g., "Basic Media Skills and Tactics" and "Air Testing"), as well as training in traditional Indian ways such as adobe building and the use of medicinal herbs and plants. In the evening, those gathered took part in cultural performances such as dances and drumming displays.

Each conference creates hundreds of new experts on local issues, who take their newly learned knowledge back to their communities and struggles. "We have our gatherings at different places throughout the country, so we have different faces," explains Goldtooth. In this way, IEN builds both the capacity and the consciousness of conference attendees.

The location of each Protecting Mother Earth conference serves to highlight local struggles, bringing together activists at environmental justice flashpoints around the country. "The role of the conference is to express physical solidarity with the host community. When you have five hundred people there, then it's a major morale boost to whoever's living there," says Goldtooth. "And it spreads the word about that particular struggle back to these hundred of places where all the participants have come from." The Third Annual Gathering, in 1992 at Celilo, Oregon, on the banks of the Columbia River, drew attention to the Hanford federal nuclear site and its impact on Columbia River tribes. Native anti-nuclear activists who met at the conference later formed a smaller network to work solely on nuclear issues.

The June 1993 conference, held at the Sac and Fox Nation in central Oklahoma, celebrated that Nation's recent rejection of a proposal to build a high-level radioactive waste disposal facility on the reservation, as well as called attention to the impacts of energy resource development on Oklahoma tribes. Exxon's proposed Crandon zinc and copper sulfide mine near five Wisconsin Indian reservations was the target of the June 1994 conference, hosted by the Mole Lake Sokaogon Chippewa community. The mine threatened to contaminate surface waters—and thus wild rice beds—in Central Wisconsin. The June 1995 conference, near Chickaloon Village, Alaska, focused attention on the legion of environmental problems faced by Alaska Native nations, including cleanup of oil production contamination, forestry, nuclear waste, and the repeated attempts to open up the Arctic National Wildlife Refuge—home of the porcupine caribou, sacred to the Gwiichin people—for oil drilling. In 1996, the Eastern Cherokee Defense League hosted the conference in Cherokee, North Carolina, raising consciousness about dioxin from a local paper mill, acid rain and deforestation issues, and the impact of tourism on the Cherokee. The massive cyanide heap leach gold mine above the Fort Belknap reservation was the focal point of 1997's conference, hosted by the Gros Ventre and Assiniboine Tribes of Montana. And sacred sites threatened by geothermal energy development and a ski resort were the issues highlighted by the 1998 gathering, held in Northern California on the Pitt River Tribe's ancestral lands.

There is also a deep spiritual component to each conference: the conference begins with the lighting of the sacred fire, which is kept burning throughout the gathering. Sunrise prayer ceremonies kick off most mornings, and many participate in sweat lodges in the evenings after the day's proceedings. Dances and drumming are the highlight of each evening, as the different Tribes represented share their cultural traditions with the group.

To be a so-called "environmentalist" you're talking about spiritual things. So that's why at our gatherings it's just natural that we have a sacred fire. We light a sacred fire at every one of our gatherings for four days. We start out at sunrise, and we burn that fire continuously, it has never gone out during those four days in eight years. We let it die out at the conclusion of the summit. . . . We feel from the deepest of our hearts in our Network that this fire guides us throughout the whole year. It guides all the people that come to the gathering and those that haven't come to the gatherings that are dealing with these very serious issues involving the sacredness of the earth and the sacredness of creation. And what that fire symbolizes is understanding and protection, and it represents the light that we all seek in our own life from the great spirit, from some higher power, however people perceive that.

—Tom Goldtooth

The conferences can be empowering for those who attend. "As people take on and learn and link up with others, they're empowered, they're encouraged—they can be creative; they can think of several options to anything that they must cover and have other people that they can turn to for strategy," says Warledo. "It gives them that experience—they become experts and they can take on their struggle or issue so that as their lands and their health are faced with another assault, they are not looking for someone else to come in and do anything for them."

IEN in Action

IEN's work goes far beyond its annual gatherings. It extends to sharing information, providing training and technical assistance, developing policy, and offering strategic advice.

For IEN, information is power. "If you look at our community members that live way out in the bush, that live way out in the prairie, the desert, and plateaus—that are working on issues from mining issues to water diversion, water rights, to air pollution to timber, a number of different issues—they don't have information at the community level," says Goldtooth. "A lot of them don't have phones, and for a lot of them, the roads are impassable at times of weather." To get its constituents the information they need, IEN acts like the hub of a wheel, providing a common place through which individuals and communities can communicate. In a clearinghouse fashion, it shares information gathered from one community with other communities that are facing similar struggles. Going beyond being simply a library of resources, however, is the key to IEN's networking: "When there's something impacting a community, it may be an issue where we know another community doing the same thing, and we will facilitate the communication between those two groups," explains Jackie Warledo. "IEN will try to put communities in touch with the source for themselves, and if they want us to help them walk through that or guide them, we will, but they don't have to come through us—they can take those next steps themselves."

> The network started at a time when toxic waste dumping was a big issue, and I think we've been effective since then on educating our communities that toxic dumping on Indian land is not an option for discussion, that it was not respectful of our spiritual beliefs as Native people. We learned that the technology behind landfilling and incineration was still a beginning technology; we learned that there is no engineer that would sign the dotted line that the liner would not leak; we learned that there's still a lot of air pollution with incineration and that you still have the landfill with incinerators. We started learning all these things through the network, just basically talking to people from the grassroots level, with common language. I guess that's one of the things that came out of our network, was deciphering all of this technology and these terms into language that our people understand.
>
> —Tom Goldtooth

IEN encourages grassroots Indian groups to work with their own tribes to resolve environmental problems. "In a lot of the cases, their own tribal leaders who make the decisions are not provided adequate information," says Goldtooth. "If they are provided information, it usually comes from the company that wants to come in. We find that usually the leaders have been open to information and that we've been able to turn some decisions around." In cases where local tribal authorities are unresponsive, IEN helps groups take their struggle to a different forum.

IEN's recent work with the Yankton Sioux illustrates its complementary approaches of offering organizing help, technical assistance, and education. When the local county in which the Yankton Sioux Reservation is located formed a solid waste compact with four surrounding counties to develop a garbage dump at the reservation boundary, activists contacted IEN. IEN provided tribal leaders and its environmental director with information on the hazards of landfills; this included technical studies of the reasons landfills fail. Tom Goldtooth worked with local activists to organize resistance to the landfill, publicizing some of the conclusions of the technical studies as well as sharing experiences from other reservations that had faced similar projects. Goldtooth also met with the Tribal Council to explain the landfill proposal and to support the Tribal members' opposition to it. The strategy that emerged from these meetings called for the Tribe to set up its own Tribal solid waste management program, building the capacity of the Tribe to handle its own environmental affairs.

In a similar manner, IEN worked with activist members of the Cahuilla Band of Mission Indians to determine effective responses to illegal dumping on the reservation. Part of IEN's work was concrete: it helped bring in a soil scientist, who was able to perform soil and water testing to determine what contaminants were present at the illegal dumpsite. Perhaps a more important part of its work was developing the capacity of tribal leaders to direct the outside expert's work; IEN helped these leaders develop the questions to be asked and to understand the answers to them. Tribal activists used the same approach for dealing with the legal resources provided by IEN, going over legal questions and strategies before bringing in the lawyer.

IEN also arranged for a fly-over of the reservation by environmental activists and tribal members to take aerial photographs of the dumping. "That was the first time that the community members have ever seen the bird's-eye view of what they were dealing with," says Goldtooth, noting that Tribal members then used the photographs as an organizing tool on the reservation. "Now they've got some evidence, reports, and they've got aerial photographs, and now they're able to respond on a local level."

At Fort Belknap, Montana, Tribal officials of the Gros Ventre and Assiniboine Tribes contacted IEN for assistance in challenging the expansion of the Pegasus cyanide heap leach gold mine directly adjacent to the reservation. IEN was able to put tribal officials in touch with a pro bono geologist, a retired EPA employee, who was able to point out a number of flaws in the Environmental Impact Statement for the Pegasus mine expansion. This advice also influenced the Tribes' posture in approving a consent decree EPA had negotiated with Pegasus.

IEN as a Policy Voice for the Grassroots

IEN now serves as a national voice on environmental justice for scattered grassroots tribal groups. In this role, IEN brings to the attention of decision makers the issues that affect indigenous people in their communities and leverages its access to those decision makers to bring resolution to local problems.

Tom Goldtooth, national coordinator of IEN, sits on the U.S. EPA's National Environmental Justice Advisory Council, the body appointed to give input to the agency on environmental justice matters, and chairs the NEJAC's Indigenous Subcommittee. Through that forum, IEN has consistently been able to present crucial local issues to decision makers in Washington, D.C.; the bundling of local issues also helps demonstrate the national policy implications of EPA's actions in any particular situation.

At a recent NEJAC meeting, for example, Goldtooth was able to present testimony on behalf of the Fort Mojave Tribe of California, the Klickitat Band of Washington State, the Walpole Island First Nation of Ontario, Canada, and the Mattaponi of Virginia. By educating NEJAC members about local issues, Goldtooth has been able to build coalitions of NEJAC members; as a result, the council has consistently passed resolutions requesting that the EPA pay attention to Tribal struggles.

Partnerships with Outside Resources

IEN's creation led the national environmental group Greenpeace USA to rethink its policies and focus more on Native American issues.[16] Greenpeace staff, after being contacted by Native American activists from a number of reservations throughout the West, convinced the organization's leaders that Indian lands were becoming a toxic dumping ground and should be the focus of increased attention. To meet the challenge from Native American activists and its own staff, Greenpeace,

which offered significant financial help to the first three IEN conferences, hired a full-time organizer on Indian issues, Jackie Warledo, a respected activist from Oklahoma. "Greenpeace accepted the challenge,"
says Warledo, noting that Greenpeace ultimately hired several Indian activists and named a national Indian leader, Winona LaDuke, to its five-
member Board of Directors. "Greenpeace made a public commitment to
support the work of Native people in protecting the environment." This
commitment was crucial for getting the organization off the ground, but
IEN was quick to stand on its own. "Greenpeace gave momentum and
resources to the leadership that we had within IEN," says Goldtooth,
noting that Greenpeace staffers "solved a need for IEN and supported
the creation of IEN, but soon IEN developed its own strength, [and] its
own financial capacity." IEN worked in partnership with Greenpeace for
many years, until the late 1990s, when budget woes at Greenpeace led
the organization to rethink its policy priorities and close its Native lands
campaign.

IEN has also developed partnerships with other traditional environmental groups; it and Clean Water Action have a mercury project that focuses on the Great Lakes, and it has teamed up with the Institute for
Agricultural Policy and International Issues on biological diversity issues.
"As we further developed IEN, we found that there is some validity to
developing partnerships between us and nonnative groups," says Goldtooth, to develop capacity and knowledge on a particular issue with the
idea of ultimately developing a native organization around that issue.
Goldtooth chooses the description "partnership" carefully to emphasize
a coming together of two equal players to solve a common task, rather
than a dependent relationship.

Conclusion

Warledo notes that IEN is still a work-in-progress. "This is uncharted
territory—trying to do a network, working on consensus, covering a
large territory geographically, being inter-Tribal, with various issues,"
she points out. But she, Goldtooth, and other IEN veterans see the international network as key for moving the struggle for environmental
justice forward. IEN's goal, says Warledo, is "not to always have one
unit or one entity that is always the central one, but have IEN as more

SEVEN

Transformative Politics

The emergence of environmental justice networks such as the Indigenous Environmental Network represents a transformation of national environmental advocacy. Such networks reflect a move from the centralized, top-down approach taken by traditional environmental groups to a decentralized, geographically scattered but highly organized and mutually self-conscious approach—in other words, from a pyramid to a web in terms of organizational structure. Because of this transformation, it is possible to operate an effective national organization out of Bemidji, Minnesota, a locale far from the "power centers" of New York and Washington, D.C., where other environmental groups have located.

The changes in advocacy strategies that we have charted in the chapter on the IEN represent just one of the many ways in which environmental justice activism has transformed individuals, communities, institutions, and national policy over the past two decades. These transformations are sometimes subtle, sometimes dramatic, sometimes ephemeral, sometimes permanent; taken together, they may be the most important legacy of the grassroots movement for environmental justice in the United States. In this chapter we describe and analyze the transformative nature of the movement.

Individual Transformations: Power and Agency in Grassroots Struggles

On a personal level, thousands of people across the United States have experienced the transformation that takes place when one moves from being a bystander to being a participant in a struggle. This transformation has occurred through the creation of spaces for people to come together and take power over their lives. Environmental justice activism has created what Harry Boyte and Sara Evans call *free spaces,* "settings which create new opportunities for self-definition, for the development of public and leadership skills, for a new confidence in the possibilities of participation, and for wider mappings of the connections between movement members and other groups and institutions."[1] Part of what sustains these free spaces—in which ordinary people move from victims of to participants in the processes that govern their lives—is the realization that power relationships within a decision-making structure are fluid, contestable, and mutually transformative.

Many people who become involved in community struggles for environmental justice have never been active in their communities before and do not have, or perceive themselves as not having, the courage and skill it takes to be a community leader. Robert Bullard notes that the decision to either take action or tolerate a particular situation "often depends on how individuals perceive their ability to do something about or have an impact on the stressful situation."[2] However, through the process of the struggle—becoming aware of environmental threats in the community and then becoming involved in ameliorating those threats—countless individuals have come to realize that they can speak out and take action, perhaps even become leaders.

There comes a moment in many activists' lives when the feeling "I could never do that" is replaced with the realization—called by some the "aha! moment"—that "I can do that!" In the Buttonwillow struggle, discussed in chapter 4, community leader Rosa Solorio-Garcia came to this realization at a large rally in a neighboring town. At the rally, a woman from the community was exhorting the crowd, shouting from the stage. Solorio-Garcia turned to Lupe Martinez, the community organizer, and said, "God, how can you do that? I'm never going to do that. Don't you expect me to ever do that." Martinez responded by putting Solorio-Garcia next on the agenda to speak to the crowd. "Just like that. And here I was at the rally yelling at everybody and telling them about all the stuff in Buttonwillow. It's made me a totally different person. More outgoing, more positive about a lot of things."

> I would take something on because it had to be done, and then you learn how to do that. . . . I think that some of those were empowerment pieces

along the way—you accomplish something you never thought you could do. It gives you something inside that says—when a new challenge comes on—"confidence." It gives you the confidence to say, "I don't know how it will be, but I'll give it my best shot," and then you get through that, you overcome that and you have the confidence again to go on.

—Jackie Warledo, Indigenous Environmental Network

Achieving confidence is an often intangible outcome of taking part in an environmental justice struggle. On a more tangible level, participants in local struggles acquire skills and information that increase their capacity, or "personal efficacy,"[3] to become active in crucial decisions that affect their lives. Many individuals, through environmental justice struggles, gain expertise on several levels. On a skills-building level, for example, they may learn how to hold a press conference or speak in public. On a substantive level, they often become sophisticated about the process or industry they are challenging, emerging as "citizen experts" on hazardous waste incineration, sludge dumping, or pesticide spraying, for example.

These two elements—self-confidence and increased capacity—dialectically build on each other in a way that transforms the personal and collective experiences of power relations by ordinary residents in otherwise disenfranchised communities. The experiences of grassroots environmental justice activists hint at a much more complex view of agency and power than has generally been offered in the social justice context.[4] The traditional dominant-subordinate model of power relations is ill suited to environmental justice activism. It is true that grassroots environmental justice struggles pit low-income communities and communities of color against private developers, facility owners, and state environmental agencies. By virtue of their social status, low-income persons of color, in particular, are vulnerable to more powerful interests in the decision-making process. Nevertheless, grassroots successes have demonstrated to many individuals in embattled communities that they are not powerless in the sense of having no ability to affect change. Indeed, individuals in many vulnerable communities come to wield some degree of power, as is illustrated by the countless examples of overburdened communities that have successfully defeated siting efforts by private and public interests.

As Steven Winter has written, power should be viewed within a system of social relations, as a shared resource that can be activated from many different positions within that system.[5] Once power is understood as relational, "it becomes apparent that at least some of what the dominant 'have' must already be available to the subordinated." Hence, as Winter explains, "[t]o the exact degree that this understanding of power diminishes the agency of the dominant, it amplifies the agency of the subordinated. What it subtracts from one part of the network it necessarily redistributes to the other."

Feminist legal scholars have recently articulated a view of power and agency that goes beyond the traditional dominant-subordinate model and that is more applicable to grassroots environmental justice struggles. Collective resistance in the communities profiled in this book, amid social and structural constraints, reflects individuals operating with what Kathryn Abrams terms "incomplete agency."[6] Poor people of color's agency under oppression "is necessarily partial or constrained" because of "structures and practices that operate to deny or mitigate that capacity." Nevertheless, such agency reveals itself in the efforts by vulnerable individuals to resist those structures and practices. Hence, the choices and actions of individuals in grassroots struggles are "neither fully free nor completely determined."[7] Instead, they are influenced by independent self-conceptions, or internal agency, and by the reality of broader patterns of oppression.[8]

What accounts for the resistance to seemingly dominant social structures and practices by some of the most vulnerable members in our society? Sometimes the catalyst is merely seeing someone in a similar social situation take an action that is, for the individual observer, both unthinkable and immediately possible; this was the case for Rosa Solorio-Garcia at the rally. Taking action by itself may change the consciousness of those taking the action. As John Gaventa notes in the context of actions taken by previously disenfranchised residents of rural Appalachia, "[t]heir conceptions of themselves and their situation seemed to change with increased participation. . . . [Their] success, in turn, led to broader ideas for action."[9]

Other times, by coming together as a group and networking with others, vulnerable individuals feel less isolated, and more empowered. Individuals begin to understand their problem as a common problem, one that affects dozens or hundreds in their community (and, perhaps, thousands nationally and internationally). The individual realizes that the obstacles she is facing are not the result of her own behavior or station but the result of a system or structure of society. In Kettleman City, profiled in the Preface, this realization occurred when residents met in one anothers' homes to discuss the proposed toxic waste incinerator and discovered, through their conversations, that they had many concerns in common; their isolation in, and in some cases shame about, having a particular fear dissolved in the understanding that others had identical fears.[10] Coming together as a group not only develops a new consciousness among those gathering; the group itself finds that it has more power as a collective than the individuals who make it up.[11]

Seeing firsthand how, and why, environmental decisions are made is an eye-opening experience for many, who come to distrust the government or solidify a healthy skepticism toward it. The idea that "the government is on our side" is a strong one, with deep roots in the American psyche; it is a myth, however, that is debunked through the process of struggle for environmental justice.[12] In Buttonwillow, the experience of a local farmer, Dennis Palla, a self-described "white, conservative Republican," illustrates the phenomenon. When he first began opposing the toxic waste dump, in 1985, he made sure not to ruffle any feathers at the Board of Supervisors. "We were confronted with the idea of protesting and going out with [picket] signs," he explains. "We felt no, that's not the thing to do. We need to make sure to stay on the good side of the supervisors." Through taking part in the latest fight against the dump expansion, Palla came to a different understanding. "Well, you know, since then we've learned that that's been pretty futile. So we've been open to a lot more radical viewpoints." This included, in Palla's case, embracing the progressive environmental group Greenpeace, something heretofore unheard of in the farming community of rural Kern County.

Understanding their own community struggle as part of a larger movement, and as part of a larger social and economic structure, can (and often does) lead community residents to an *institutional understanding* of pollution and environmental laws, one that posits that the normal functioning of the social political economy generates not only environmental hazards but an unequal distribution of such hazards.[13] This institutional understanding provides the groundwork for making broader connections to environmental issues beyond the community that is the locus of the immediate struggle, and to other social justice issues. When individuals begin to make these connections, this often leads to a shift in the community's consciousness as well.

Community Transformation: Breaking the Cycle of Quiescence

When many people have individual epiphanies through a common experience, the result can be community transformation, as well—a collective emergence of solidarity, action and rebelliousness that builds on itself in an organic manner. John Gaventa has chronicled the shifting consciousness of Appalachian residents who fought powerful coal-mining interests that had stifled all change in their rural Tennessee community. For decades, the residents had been docile and uncomplaining in the face of severe oppression and deprivation, including "loss of homeplace, the contamination of streams, the drain of wealth [and] the destruction from the strip mining all around."[14] After several incidents—and an organizer—sparked their community into action, the residents began to exert their own collective power. This shift is what we describe here as *community transformation*. Gaventa describes the transformation in action:

> In the space of about five years, through a process of deciding upon and carrying out actions, definitions of interests shifted from those involving little conflict against the existing order (garbage collection) to the development of alternatives to that order (a factory, clinics) to the notion of challenging the order itself (land demands).[15]

As R. Gregory Roberts notes, "[b]y its nature, community empowerment transforms personal efficacy into group efficacy, which enables communities to take charge of the struggle, and eventually take charge of their respective communities."[16]

A community may come to be quiescent when its residents repeatedly experience individual or group oppression, or lose local struggles, as illustrated by Gaventa in his path-breaking studies of Appalachian mining communities.[17] Quiescence is the feeling among community residents that they are powerless to address perceived injustices, a "sense of inevitability, a prevailing belief that nothing can be done."[18] In many ways, this very quiescence is historically what has drawn industry to powerless communities, as the path of least resistance; industry's powerful presence then serves to perpetuate the powerlessness felt by residents. Feelings of powerlessness are common in disenfranchised communities, from urban enclaves to rural towns. "Colonialism has been very effective in our communities, to the point that a lot of our community members feel disempowered; they feel that they don't have the strength to make their own decisions," says Tom Goldtooth, of the Indigenous Environmental Network, of his experience on Indian reservations. "Very often, we give that power over to the government agencies that are in our communities, whether that's Indian Health Service or Bureau of Indian Affairs or the school systems."

As with the struggle of Appalachian mining communities, a successful environmental justice grassroots campaign or struggle may break the cycle of quiescence and transform a community's mood from a feeling of hopelessness to one of empowerment. For example, environmental struggles in the 1980s changed the political disengagement of many individuals in the Ironbound community of Newark, New Jersey.[19] An industrial magnet and once a thriving urban area, Ironbound has hosted iron forges, plastic and jewelry production factories, machine shops, and chemical manufacturing and waste disposal facilities.[20] Years of industrial occupation, the threat of incoming waste facilities, and other sources of environmental degradation slowly led to a decline in the quality of life in the Ironbound community and fostered a general attitude that "you can't fight City Hall."[21]

Two early struggles helped to break the Ironbound community's state of quiescence in taking on environmental threats. The community's first major public action on an environmental issue began in 1980, when community residents organized in response to noise pollution caused by caused by airplanes flying overhead. The flight paths of many aircraft, including the Concorde, brought them directly over Ironbound on their way to landing at John F. Kennedy International Airport in New York. The community's goal was clear: the airport must change the flight paths. In a battle that lasted almost a year, residents became a common, and vocal, presence at the airport. The Ironbound residents succeeded in getting the flight patterns changed to redirect the bulk of the flights so that they avoided Ironbound entirely. Though the rules were never completely obeyed, and the noise continues, that struggle became the impetus for the establishment of a base of citizen action in Ironbound to address quality of life issues.

In 1981, using the momentum gained from its battle against the airport, as well as from other efforts in areas such as housing and elderly rights, the community formed the Ironbound Committee against Toxic Wastes (ICATW). ICATW solidified the newfound political engagement of many individuals in the Ironbound community in a struggle against what was popularly referred to in the 1980s as "ocean incineration" of toxic waste. Under the ocean incineration plan, incinerator ships would dock and fill their holds with waste, then transport the waste offshore, where the ships would burn it a "safe" distance from land. The company, At-Sea Incineration, proposed constructing containment and transfer facilities, which would store the waste destined to be burned at sea, in the Port of Newark. At-Sea's proposed operations also involved having large trucks bring various toxic substances, such as dioxin, from neighboring states to be processed in the incinerator. The trucks would have to pass through densely populated areas of Newark, including the Ironbound neighborhood, on their way to the Port, where the wastes would be loaded onto two incineration ships to be carried out to sea for burning. Community residents worried about the health effects of the various hazardous chemicals that would be held on land, and those that would pass through their neighborhood.

Through coalition building and networking with local and national groups that were waging similar battles, concerned Ironbound residents discovered that they could influence decisions that affected their environment. Using the organizations' newsletter, *Ironbound Voices,* and the mainstream press, ICATW "got the word out" and intensified its efforts to organize the community and to voice its opposition to the proposed plan.

ICATW also built coalitions with other groups, locally and nationally, to increase the power of voices in opposition to ocean incineration, expanding the focus beyond the proposed Port Newark facility to ocean incineration nationally. ICATW quickly secured the involvement of a broad coalition of community and environmental groups[22] and ran a successful campaign to get nearby municipalities to oppose ocean incineration: "At one point we had every town inside of Essex and Hudson

Counties in a competition to pass resolutions opposing the facility," recalls ICATW member Arnold Cohen. Throughout ICATW's fight against incineration proposal, the government agency responsible for the permitting of the storage facility at the Port Newark site, the Newark Port Authority, refused to grant a permit to At-Sea, which ultimately withdrew the proposal in defeat.

The import of ICATW's victory over At-Sea was aptly summed up in an edition of the *Ironbound Voices*: "This victory over At-Sea is one of the greatest examples of people who saw a problem and then organized together to do something about it. The story of this victory should be put down in a book, as an inspiration to other people all over the United States to show them that they can do the same thing."[23]

Eight years after ICATW's initial involvement in the regional and national fight against ocean incineration, the waste industry ceased its efforts to make ocean incineration a reality in any community. ICATW's victory over At-Sea also had broader reverberations. ICATW's coalition-building and educational efforts helped to ensure that the banning of ocean incineration became a goal for international treaties.

"What we have learned from this fight is that we have power," concluded ICATW member Bob Cartwright, "As long as decisions get made by a small number of people behind closed doors, we lose. But when we force them to discuss their plans out in the open, and when people know the facts and can organize to do something about it, then we have power. And we can win!"[24]

Institutional Transformation

The community transformation that occurred in the Ironbound neighborhood had a ripple effect felt far beyond Newark, New Jersey: in part as a result of Ironbound residents' actions, national policy on ocean incineration shifted from full steam ahead to a complete abandonment of the idea. This type of impact of the Environmental Justice Movement—which has reached both the traditional environmental movement and national policy—is what we call *institutional transformation*. Institutional transformation takes several forms: institutions allied with the movement have been significantly changed, and institutions hostile to the movement have also changed. Here, we note the institutional transformation

of a major environmental group and of national environmental policy as
a result of environmental justice activism.

The Traditional Environmental Movement

Some traditional environmental groups, most notably Greenpeace USA,
have been transformed by their interaction with the movement. As men-
tioned in chapter 6, on the Indigenous Environmental Network, Greenpeace restructured not only its national policy but its personnel as a result of its involvement with IEN and the Environmental Justice Movement. Because Greenpeace, one of the largest environmental groups in
the world, became involved at formative stages of IEN, high-level
Greenpeace leadership attended early conferences and learned about environmental issues on Indian lands. Their raised consciousness, combined with pressure from Native Americans and Greenpeace staffers,
helped push Greenpeace executives to commit resources to IEN and to
Native American issues; dialectically, the more Greenpeace got involved,
the deeper its understanding of and commitment to these issues became.

The involvement of Greenpeace, which had a decidedly mixed reputation in Indian country because of its opposition, in the 1970s, to the
hunting of fur seals by Native peoples, was greeted with skepticism by
early IEN participants. To overcome that skepticism, Greenpeace leaders
devoted considerable resources to a new environmental protection effort, the Native Lands campaign. The group hired the respected Indian
leader Jackie Warledo as a full-time organizer on Indian issues. It also
hired the Indian activist Nilak Butler to work on nuclear issues—a main-
stay of Greenpeace's traditional advocacy—but to connect that work
with nuclear issues on Native lands. And, in perhaps the greatest show of
inclusion, the Native activist Winona LaDuke was elected to Greenpeace
USA's five-member Board of Directors.

All of these developments indicated a profound transformation in the
organization, which moved from being vilified by Native activists for its
ethnocentric anti-seal-hunting policies to being praised by Indian leaders for its strong support of Native struggles. More than any other traditional environmental group, Greenpeace grappled with the issue of environmental justice, owned up to its past mistakes, and brought Native
Americans into the fold, as staff and as decision makers. The institution

was transformed at the policy, staff, and board levels. The Environmental Justice Movement changed the course of Greenpeace USA's activism for almost a decade. Unfortunately, funding problems in the late 1990s forced Greenpeace to abandon its Native Lands campaign (as well as to lay off 50 percent of its staff and to close all of its U.S. offices except the one in Washington, D.C.).

"It did have a big impact," notes Warledo. "It's historic, actually. We didn't get as far as we wanted to, but Greenpeace moved farther than anyone else did." She pauses for a moment. "But, you know," she continues thoughtfully, noting the paucity of Native American staff at Greenpeace today, "I'm the one Native lands toxics campaigner, so, on the one hand, yes, we made great steps, but, on the other hand, it was never really fully accepted." Although Greenpeace's transformation proved impermanent, it was significant nonetheless; it resulted in the application of significant resources to community-identified issues and struggles, resources that would not have been available to those communities otherwise.

Turning the Ocean Liner: Transforming National Policy

One lasting success of the Environmental Justice Movement is that its goals and principles have been institutionalized as federal policy, representing a profound institutional transformation on the widest scale. This institutionalization has occurred within individual federal agencies and across the executive branch of the federal government.

The Environmental Justice Movement reached what may have been its apogee of transforming national policy on February 11, 1994, when President Bill Clinton signed the Executive Order on Environmental Justice,[25] making environmental justice the policy of the federal government. This Order, among other things, directs each federal agency to "identify and address" the "disproportionately high and adverse human health or environmental effects" of its programs, policies, and activities on people of color and on low-income communities. The Executive Order was a concrete realization of the Movement's goals of influencing decision makers; many Movement leaders were invited to the Oval Office to watch the signing ceremony.

The Executive Order was the result of dozens of local environmental justice struggles, and it is possible to trace the agency of individuals involved in those local fights to specific changes in federal policy through the Order. The struggle of Latino Kettleman City residents for translation of environmental documents into Spanish, noted in the Preface of this book, for example, led—through the national publicity their struggle received and the networking of environmental justice activists across the country—directly to the provision in the Executive Order, at Section 5-5(b), that "[e]ach Federal agency may, whenever practicable and appropriate, translate crucial public documents, notices, and hearing relating to human health or the environment for limited English-speaking populations."[26] Thus, an idea first discussed in the living rooms and kitchens of Latino farm-worker activists in a small California town was transformed, through the movement for environmental justice, into national policy.

The transformations throughout the federal government go far beyond the Executive Order, however; they affect law and policy across a broad spectrum of agencies and in Congress. Some of the impact of the transformation was sudden and unexpected: the Nuclear Regulatory Commission, for example, cited the Executive Order as the basis for its denial of a permit for a uranium-enrichment facility in rural Louisiana, the first permit ever denied in the NRC's history, because of significant questions raised over the racial fairness of the siting of the plant in an African American community.

Elsewhere, the transformation has been slower, and deeper. Nowhere is the movement's transformation of national policy more evident than at the Environmental Protection Agency, which has undergone a profound shift in perspective in the past eight years. Beginning with several tentative and uncomfortable meetings between environmental justice advocates and the then administrator of EPA, William Reilly, in 1991, movement pressure has transformed the EPA into an agency that pays significant attention to the idea of environmental justice. As noted in chapter 1, activists pressured Reilly to respond to their findings of disproportionate impact. Reilly set up the Office of Environmental Equity and directed agency staffers to study the allegations of disproportionate impact. The results of the agency's efforts, found in the Environmental Protection Agency's *Report from the Environmental Equity Workgroup*, have been roundly criticized as myopic and superficial.[27] These first missteps, however, paved the way for a more active role for environmental justice advocates and ideas within the EPA.

When Bill Clinton defeated George Bush in the 1992 presidential election, two national environmental justice leaders, the Rev. Benjamin Chavis and Dr. Robert Bullard, were named to Clinton's transition team. As part of the "natural resources" cluster, Chavis and Bullard had direct input into the policies the new administration would attempt to implement, and thus environmental justice became a cornerstone of the Clinton EPA's stated program. Clinton's choice to head EPA, Carol Browner, announced, in 1993, that environmental justice was one of four priorities for her administration at EPA. One of the first changes made was in the name of the Office of Environmental Equity, which was changed to the Office of Environmental Justice. Browner also created the National Environmental Justice Advisory Council (known by its acronym NEJAC, pronounced "knee-jack"), a group of twenty-five "stakeholders" from the movement, government, academia, and industry who advise the EPA on how to best achieve environmental justice.

NEJAC raised the stature of the Environmental Justice Movement to new heights and institutionalized the movement's transformative power over agency policy. Although some—including members of NEJAC— have openly doubted its power and influence, NEJAC has succeeded in its five years of existence in suffusing environmental justice thinking into many of the agency's offices. It has also provided a vehicle for community groups seeking increased attention to their local struggles; hundreds of community residents have testified before NEJAC on issues ranging from birth defects to garbage dumps to pesticides to federal military facilities. NEJAC has passed dozens of resolutions calling on EPA to investigate or resolve particular local problems. Although it serves in an advisory capacity only, NEJAC has had sufficient input into EPA decision making to effect specific changes in policy, both on a national and at a site-specific level.

In some cases, NEJAC was able to support the efforts of agency staffers who had tried, unsuccessfully, to bring environmental justice concerns to the fore in their work, by raising the issues with their supervisors or even the leadership of EPA itself. Some offices within EPA now operate with environmental justice as part of their approach; others are still actively hostile to it. However, the work that hundreds of EPA staffers have undertaken to push the idea of environmental justice has slowly borne fruit.

Larger Transformations: Movement Fusion

An institutional transformation at a different level is the important power building that is occurring between the Environmental Justice Movement and other social justice activism, what we call "movement fusion": the coming together of two (or more) different social movements in a way that expands the base of support for both movements by developing a common agenda. As we explained in chapter 1, environmental justice advocates, like their predecessors in the civil rights and the anti-toxics movements, understand that environmental problems are a manifestation of other, larger problems endemic to our social and economic structure. In addition to the fusion of civil rights and anti-toxics concepts and strategies that are evident in the Environmental Justice Movement, other examples of movement fusion offer a glimpse of the transformative possibilities of this fusion.

In the San Francisco Bay Area, the women's organization Breast Cancer Action has shifted from focusing on a *cure* for breast cancer to focusing on *prevention* of the disease. Its members are women who have had breast cancer, and they recognize that the cure can be as devastating as the disease for many women. In a fusion that has national implications, the group is linking up with environmental justice activists to challenge the use of endocrine-disrupting chemicals by industry. Breast Cancer Action has worked with Bay Area environmental justice groups like Greenaction and Communities for a Better Environment to sponsor an annual "Cancer Industry Tour" of downtown San Francisco, including stops at Chevron (accused of dumping dioxin, a carcinogen, into San Francisco Bay), Bechtel (accused of constructing polluting nuclear reactors), and the EPA (accused of not stopping pollution).

This movement fusion is bringing together other (perhaps unlikely) allies. Members of the Environmental Justice Movement and the immigrants' rights movement formed a coalition to beat back an attempt by right-wing environmentalists to have the Sierra Club oppose immigration on environmental grounds. The United Farm Workers has fused the two issues of labor rights and environmental toxicity for the past three decades, calling attention to the effects of pesticides on workers. The recently formed Just Transition movement, bringing together the Oil, Chemical and Atomic Workers Union and environmental justice networks like IEN and the Southwest Network for Environmental and Economic Justice, continues this fusion. Workers and environmental justice activists recognize that steps taken to protect workers also protect the communities that surround industrial facilities or fields. Workers want sustainable, clean, and safe jobs; residents want safe neighborhoods, and neighbors.

Movement fusion is a necessary ingredient for the long-term success of the Environmental Justice Movement because, put simply, environmental justice advocates do not have a large enough power base to win the larger struggle for justice on their own.[28] But this fusion is transformative, not only for its possibilities of generating the power necessary to win policy debates but because cross-fertilization brings new ideas, such as pollution prevention and more democratic decision-making processes, to the fore.

The Environmental Justice Movement remains one of the most active social movements in the United States today. The individual transformations—the "aha! moments"—that take place across America every day are the energy that drives countless local struggles, struggles that are transforming our communities and the nation. The movement fusion that occurs as a result of this activity not only changes the terrain and terms of the debate, but also offers a glimpse of the possibilities for broad-based, progressive coalitions of women, workers, immigrants, people of color, and environmentalists, working together to transform society, in a way that could both lead to, and transcend, environmental justice.

An Annotated Bibliography of Studies and Articles That Document and Describe the Disproportionate Impact of Environmental Hazards by Race and Income

African American Environmentalist Ass'n, et al., OUR UNFAIR SHARE: A SURVEY OF POLLUTION SOURCES IN OUR NATION'S CAPITAL (1994) (finding that the cleanest area in Washington, D.C., is Ward 3, 88 percent of whose residents are white, whereas 65 percent of the overall population of the city is black).

Agency for Toxic Substances Disease Registry, U.S. Department of Health and Human Services, THE NATURE AND EXTENT OF LEAD POISONING IN CHILDREN IN THE UNITED STATES: A REPORT TO CONGRESS, I-12 (1988) (childhood blood lead levels have disproportionate impact by race and income, with race independent of class).

Anderson, Andy B., et al., *Environmental Equity: Evaluating TSDF Siting over the Past Two Decades*, WASTE AGE, July 1994, at 83 (reporting that analysis based on 1990 Census data did not find significant evidence that people of color disproportionately live near hazardous waste facilities).

Anderton, Douglas L., et al., *Environmental Equity: The Demographics of Dumping*, 31 DEMOGRAPHY 229 (1994) (reporting that analysis using 1980 Census data did not find significant evidence that people of color disproportionately live near hazardous waste facilities; study funded by Waste Management, Inc.).

Anderton, Douglas L., and Andrew B. Anderson, *Environmental Equity: Hazardous Waste Facilities: "Environmental Equity" Issues in Metropolitan Areas*, 18 EVALUATION REVIEW 123 (1994) (finding that the percentage of people of color who live in neighborhoods that host commercial hazardous waste treatment facilities is not greater than the percentage in areas without such treatment facilities; study funded by Waste Management, Inc.).

Asch, Peter, and Joseph J. Seneca, *Some Evidence on the Distribution of Air Quality*, 54 LAND ECONOMICS 278 (1978) (reporting a study of Cleveland, Chicago, and Nashville that showed poorer census tracts to be exposed consistently to higher pollution levels than more affluent tracts; people of color have higher pollution levels than whites in Chicago and Nashville; a study of urban areas in twenty-three states that found particulate pollution was higher in cities with low-income characteristics and in communities of color).

Attah, E. B., *Demographics and Siting Issues in EPA Region IV*, in PROCEEDINGS OF THE CLARK ATLANTA UNIVERSITY AND ENVIRONMENTAL PROTECTION AGENCY REGION IV CONFERENCE ON ENVIRONMENTAL EQUITY (B. Holmes, ed., 1992) (study of CERCLIS sites in eight southeastern states revealed that the number of sites per census tract increases as the percentage of people of color population increases in the tract).

Baden, Brett, and Don Coursey, *The Locality of Waste Sites within the City of Chicago: A Demographic, Social, and Economic Analysis*, Harris School of Public Policy Studies, Working Paper 97:2 (February 5, 1997)(analyzing hazardous waste sites in Chicago and concluding there was no evidence of environmental racism against African Americans).

Been, Vicki, and Francis Gupta, *Coming to the Nuisance or Going to the Barrios? A Longitudinal Analysis of Environmental Justice Claims*, 24 ECOLOGY LAW QUARTERLY 1 (1997) ((examining 544 communities, using 1990 Census data, that hosted active commercial hazardous waste treatment storage and disposal facilities and finding no substantial evidence that commercial hazardous waste facilities that began operating between 1970 and 1990 were sited in areas that had disproportionate African American or low-income populations, but finding evidence that lower-income Latinos were disproportionately more likely to live near such facilities).

Been, Vicki, *Locally Undesirable Land Uses in Minority Neighborhoods: Disproportionate Siting or Market Dynamics*, 103 YALE LAW REVIEW 1383 (1994) (containing a listing and critique of disproportionate impact studies).

Berry, Brian J. L., et al., THE SOCIAL BURDENS OF ENVIRONMENTAL POLLUTION: A COMPARATIVE METROPOLITAN DATA SOURCE (1977) (reporting that solid waste sites in Chicago are distributed inequitably by income and race; air pollution in thirteen major areas is distributed inequitably by income and race; pesticide poisoning in Chicago is distributed inequitably by income and race; noise pollution in three major urban areas is distributed in-

Appendix

equitably by income and race; and risk of rat bites in Chicago is inequitably distributed by race).

Bingham, Taylor H., et al., *Distribution of the Generation of Air Pollution*, 14 JOURNAL OF ENVIRONMENTAL ECONOMY & MANAGEMENT 30 (1987) (the rich both generate more pollution and pay proportionally less for environmental protection than the poor).

Boer, J. Tom, et al., *Is There Environmental Racism? The Demographics of Hazardous Waste in Los Angeles County*, 78 SOCIAL SCIENCE QUARTERLY 793 (1997) (finding that working-class communities of color in industrial areas of Los Angeles are most affected by hazardous waste treatment storage and disposal facilities).

Boerner, Christopher, and Thomas Lambert, ENVIRONMENTAL JUSTICE IN THE CITY OF ST. LOUIS: THE ECONOMICS OF SITING INDUSTRIAL AND WASTE FACILITIES (Center for the Study of American Business Working Paper 156, 1995) (in St. Louis neighborhoods that host active waste facilities and inactive CERCLIS sites, the percentages of the poor and people of color increased at a faster rate than in nonhost neighborhoods, and both mean family income and median housing values in host areas fell relative to those for nonhost neighborhoods).

Bowen, William M., et al., *The Spatial Association Between Race, Income, and Industrial Toxic Emission in Cuyahoga County, Ohio 1* (1995) (unpublished paper prepared for the Annual Meetings of the Association of American Geographers, Atlanta, Georgia) (air emissions inequitably distributed).

Bowen, William, Mark Sailing, Kingsley Haynes, and Ellen Cyran, *Toward Environmental Justice: Spatial Equity in Ohio and Cleveland*, 85 ANNALS OF THE ASSOCIATION OF AMERICAN GEOGRAPHERS 641 (1995) (at county level there was a positive association between percentage of blacks in an area and the amount of toxins released, while at the Census tract level this same association did not exist).

Brodine, Virginia, *A Special Burden*, 13 ENVIRONMENT 22 (March 1971) (reporting on studies presented at a 1970 American Medical Association conference, including a study that showed that nonwhites and people from low socioeconomic groups suffered disproportionate exposure to potentially fatal pollution).

Brody, D., et al., *Blood Lead Levels in the U.S. Population*, 272 JOURNAL OF THE AMERICAN MEDICAL ASSOCIATION 277 (1994) (national blood lead levels dropping but children of color have disproportionately high levels).

Brueggemann, Martin R., *Environmental Racism in Our Backyard: Solid Waste Disposal in Holly Springs, North Carolina* (1993) (unpublished M.A. thesis, University of North Carolina) (solid waste disposal sites in Wake County, North Carolina, inequitably distributed by race and income).

Appendix

Bryant, Bunyan, and Elaine Hockman, *Hazardous Waste and Spatial Relations According to Race and Income in the State of Michigan* (1994) (unpublished paper) (in Michigan, largest proportions of people of color live in zip codes that house commercial hazardous waste facilities, zip codes that surround incinerator sites, and zip codes with incinerators; zip codes with incinerators and/or commercial hazardous waste facilities have the greatest exposure to environmental pollution from sites required to report emissions to the federal Toxic Release Inventory and from leaking underground storage tanks; race, not income, is the determining factor: "Locations containing and locations near incinerator/hazardous waste sites are more heavily populated with minorities than are locations at a distance from these sites. Income distribution is not significant.").

Bullard, Robert D., *Environmental Inequities Suffered by People of Color: A Case Study on Houston,* in ENVIRONMENTAL RACISM: ISSUES AND DILEMMAS (Bunyan Bryant and Paul Mohai, eds., 1991) (describing discriminatory siting of garbage dumps in Houston, Texas).

Bullard, Robert D., INVISIBLE HOUSTON: THE BLACK EXPERIENCE IN BOOM AND BUST 70–75 (1987) (distribution of municipal landfills and incinerators in Houston had disproportionate racial impact, independent of class).

Bullard, Robert D., *Solid Waste Sites and the Houston Black Community,* 53 SOCIAL INQUIRY 273 (1983) (finding that although African Americans made up only 28 percent of the Houston population in 1980, six of Houston's eight incinerators and mini-incinerators and fifteen of seventeen landfills were located in predominantly African American neighborhoods).

Bullard, Robert D., and Beverly Hendrix Wright, *The Politics of Pollution: Implications for the Black Community,* 47 PHYLON 71 (1986) (noting that black neighborhoods, which account for one-quarter of Houston's population, are home to six of the city's eight garbage incinerators and all five city-owned garbage landfills).

Burch, William R., *The Peregrine Falcon and the Urban Poor: Some Sociological Interrelations,* in HUMAN ECOLOGY: AN ENVIRONMENTAL APPROACH (Peter J. Richerson and James McEvoy, eds., 1976) (finding air pollution in New Haven, Connecticut, is distributed inequitably by income but not by race).

Burke, Lauretta, ENVIRONMENTAL EQUITY IN LOS ANGELES (National Center for Geographic Information and Analysis, 1993) (in Los Angeles, the poorer the area and the higher the population of people of color, the greater the number of Toxic Release Inventory facilities in the area; race slightly more important than class in predicting presence of TRI facilities).

Burke, Lauretta, *Race and Environmental Equity: A Geographic Analysis of Los Angeles,* 3 GEO INFO SYSTEMS 44 (October 1993) (the number of Toxic Release Inventory facilities increases with an increase in percentage of people of color in a Census tract and with a decrease in per capita income; Latinos and African Americans are disproportionately exposed to TRI facilities; race has "slightly stronger relationship" than class to occurrence of TRI facilities).

Burns, James E., *Organochlorine Pesticide and Polychlorinated Biphenyl Residues in Biopsied Human Adipose Tissue—Texas 1969–72*, 7 PESTICIDE MONITORING JOURNAL 122 (1974) (reporting that study in southern Texas found significantly higher residues of the pesticides DDT, DDE, and dieldrin in Mexican-Americans than in Anglo-Americans).

Butts, Cassandra Q., *The Color of Money: Barriers to Access to Private Health Care Facilities for African-Americans*, 26 CLEARINGHOUSE REVIEW 159 (1992) (stating that African Americans in both urban and rural areas are more likely than whites to face geographic barriers to health care and health care providers and that a disproportionate share of hospital closings affect African Americans with "the likelihood of closures . . . directly related to the percentage of African-Americans in the population of a city").

Carter-Pokras, Olivia, et al., *Blood Lead Levels of 4–11-Year-Old Mexican American, Puerto Rican, and Cuban Children*, 105 PUBLIC HEALTH REPORT (1990) (study of 1,390 children found that Mexican-American children living in poverty have higher blood lead levels than Mexican-American children not living in poverty and that Mexican-American and Puerto Rican children probably have a higher risk of lead poisoning than whites because a disproportionate number of them are poor).

Centers for Disease Control, PREVENTING LEAD POISONING IN YOUNG CHILDREN (1991) (lead poisoning levels much higher in African American communities than in white communities; rates vary also with income levels).

Citizens for a Better Environment, RICHMOND AT RISK: COMMUNITY DEMOGRAPHICS AND TOXIC HAZARDS FROM INDUSTRIAL POLLUTERS (1989) (reporting that the Contra Costa County neighborhoods closest to polluting industries in Richmond were also those with the lowest income and highest concentrations of people of color).

Clean Sites, HAZARDOUS WASTE SITES AND THE RURAL POOR: A PRELIMINARY ASSESSMENT 48–51 (1990) (concluding that potential Superfund sites in rural poor communities were placed on the NPL at just half the rate of other potential sites but that, once a site in such a community was placed on the NPL, its cleanup progressed as quickly or more quickly than the cleanup at the rest of the sites).

Cole, Luke, *Empowerment as the Means to Environmental Protection: The Need for Environmental Poverty Law*, 19 ECOLOGY LAW QUARTERLY 619 (1992) (extensive bibliography of studies demonstrating disproportionate impact by both income and race, with race predominating as a factor; also noting that all three of California's Class I toxic waste landfills are in low-income communities 63 to 95 percent of whose populations are people of color).

Cole, Luke, and Susan S. Bowyer, *Pesticides and the Poor in California*, 2 RACE, POVERTY & THE ENVIRONMENT 1 (Spring 1991) (noting that farm-workers, with average annual earnings of $8,800 for a family of four, are at greatest risk of pesticide poisoning).

Commission for Racial Justice, United Church of Christ, TOXIC WASTES AND RACE IN THE UNITED STATES: A NATIONAL REPORT ON THE RACIAL AND SOCIO-ECONOMIC CHARACTERISTICS OF COMMUNITIES WITH HAZARDOUS WASTE SITES (1987) (reporting that mean household income is lower nationally in areas with toxic waste sites than in areas without sites; that three of the five largest hazardous waste landfills in the United States are in black or Latino communities; that the mean percentage of people of color in areas with toxic waste sites is twice that of areas without toxic waste sites; and that race is a more reliable predictor of location of hazardous waste sites than income).

Committee on Environmental Hazards and Committee on Accident and Poison Prevention, American Academy of Pediatrics, *Statement on Childhood Lead Poisoning*, 79 PEDIATRICS 475 (1987) (finding lead poisoning to be particularly prevalent in areas of urban poverty).

Costner, Pat, and Joseph Thornton, PLAYING WITH FIRE: HAZARDOUS WASTE IN-CINERATION (1990) (compared average proportion of white residents and home owners and average income, home value, and rent for zip codes that host sixteen existing commercial hazardous waste incinerators and twenty-four proposed incinerators with the U.S. average values and found average percentage of people of color in zip code areas with facilities was 89 percent higher than the U.S. average; average income was 15 percent lower).

Council on Environmental Quality, THE SECOND ANNUAL REPORT OF THE COUN-CIL ON ENVIRONMENTAL QUALITY (1971) (finding air pollution in Chicago to be distributed inequitably by income).

Crawford, Colin, *Analyzing Evidence of Environmental Justice: A Suggestion for Professor Been*, 12 JOURNAL OF LAND USE & ENVIRONMENTAL LAW 103 (Fall 1996) (critiquing the methodology of recent disproportionate impact studies, particularly those of Vicki Been).

Davies, John E., et al., *The Role of Social Class in Human Pesticide Pollution* 96 AMERICAN JOURNAL OF EPIDEMIOLOGY 334 (1972) (discussing survey of 800 residents of Dade County, Florida, that showed blood levels of the pesticides DDT and DDE to be significantly higher in poor people than in the more affluent).

Davies, John E. et al., *Problems of Prevalence of Pesticide Residues in Humans*, 2 PESTICIDE MONITORING JOURNAL 80 (1968) (discussing survey in Dade County, Florida, that showed blacks to have higher blood and fat tissue levels of DDT than whites).

Davis, Morris E., *The Impact of Workplace Health and Safety on Black Workers: Assessment and Prognosis*, 31 LABOR LAW JOURNAL 1 723 (1980) ("Black workers have a 37% greater chance than whites of suffering occupational injury or illness. Black workers are one and one-half times more likely than whites to be severely disabled from job injuries and illnesses and face a 20% greater chance than whites of dying from job-related injuries and illnesses.").

Division of Labor Statistics and Research, California Department of Industry Relations, 1988: CALIFORNIA WORK INJURIES AND ILLNESSES 42–50 (1989) (in 1988, approximately 30 percent of all injured or ill workers in California—those who missed a day or more of work as a result of occupational injury or illness—made less than $250 per week; just under two-thirds made less than $400 per week).

Division of Labor Statistics and Research, California Department of Industry Relations, 1987: OCCUPATIONAL DISEASE IN CALIFORNIA 5 tbl. 3 (1989) (California craftsworkers, operatives, laborers, farm-workers, and service workers, all in traditionally low-paying, nonunion sectors of the economy, accounted for 72 percent of all reported occupational diseases in 1987).

Dorfman, Nancy S., and Arthur Snow, *Who Will Pay for Pollution Control? The Distribution by Income of the Burden of the National Environmental Protection Program, 1972–1980*, 28 NATIONAL TAX JOURNAL 101 (1975) (environmental controls have a regressive impact).

Dorfman, Robert, *Incidence of the Benefits and Costs of Environmental Programs*, 67 AMERICAN ECONOMIC ASSOCIATION OF PAPERS AND PROCEEDINGS 333, 334 (1977) (environmental controls have a regressive impact).

Ducsik, Dennis, SHORELINE FOR THE PEOPLE 46–47 (1974) (discussing "the problem of the inability of low income, less mobile groups to find suitable coastal recreational facilities anywhere but in the immediate vicinity of urban centers, where the pollution problems are most severe, and where fewer beaches are available and oftentimes inaccessible due to gross overcrowding.").

Florida Environmental Equity and Justice Commission, FINAL REPORT 9–36 (1996) (low-income communities and communities of color suffer disproportionate environmental impacts at the sites studied in Florida).

Freeman, Myrick, *The Distribution of Environmental Quality*, in ENVIRONMENTAL QUALITY ANALYSIS (Allen V. Kneese and Blair T. Bower, eds., 1972) (air pollution is distributed inequitably by income in Kansas City, St. Louis, and

Washington, D.C., and inequitably distributed by race in Kansas City; race independent of income, and a stronger determinant).

Freeman, A. Myrick, III, *The Incidence of the Cost of Controlling Automotive Air Pollution*, in THE DISTRIBUTION OF ECONOMIC WELL-BEING 163 (F. T. Juster, ed., 1977) (environmental controls have a regressive impact).

Friedman-Jiménez, George, *Occupational Disease in African-American and Latino Workers*, in MINORITIES AND THE ENVIRONMENT, PUBLIC HEARING BEFORE NEW YORK STATE ASSEMBLY ENVIRONMENTAL CONSERVATION COMMITTEE 7 (September 20, 1991) (finding that blacks and Latinos in New York City are clustered in high-risk occupations, while whites are overrepresented in low-risk occupations).

Friedman-Jiménez, George, *Occupational Disease among Minority Workers: A Common and Preventable Occupational Health Problem*, 37 AMERICAN ASSOCIATION OF OCCUPATIONAL HEALTH NURSES JOURNAL 64 (1989) (describing two case studies showing that workers of color are overrepresented in the most hazardous jobs and as a result are at a high risk of developing occupational disease).

Gelobter, Michel, *The Distribution of Air Pollution, by Income and Race* (1989) (unpublished M.A. thesis, University of California at Berkeley (Energy and Resources Group)) (finding that the poor face higher levels of air pollution than the rich).

Gelobter, Michel, *Toward a Model of Environmental Discrimination*, in RACE AND THE INCIDENCE OF ENVIRONMENTAL HAZARDS: A TIME FOR DISCOURSE (Bunyan Bryant and Paul Mohai, eds., 1992) (the damage caused by air pollution in urban areas is inequitably distributed by income).

Gianessi, Leonard P., Henry M. Peskin, and Edward Wolff, *The Distributional Effects of Uniform Air Pollution Policy in the United States*, 93 QUARTERLY JOURNAL OF ECONOMICS 281, 293–300 (1979) (concluding that U.S. air pollution policy implies a redistribution of benefits toward a minority composed largely of nonwhite inhabitants of polluted urban areas; also, the rich both generate more pollution and pay less for environmental protection than the poor).

Gianessi, Leonard P., and Henry M. Peskin, *The Distribution of the Costs of Federal Water Pollution Control Policy*, 56 LAND ECONOMICS 85, 95 (1980) (environmental controls have a regressive impact; the rich both generate more pollution and pay less for environmental protection than the poor).

Glickman, Ted, and Robert Hersh, EVALUATING ENVIRONMENTAL EQUITY: THE IMPACTS OF INDUSTRIAL HAZARDS ON SELECTED SOCIAL GROUPS IN ALLEGHENY COUNTY, PENNSYLVANIA (1995) (Resources for the Future Discussion Paper 95-13) (data at the census tract and block group level indicate that Toxic Release Inventory [TRI] communities contain a lower percentage of African Americans [10 percent] and people of color [11 percent] than non-TRI communities [11 and 13 percent, respectively]; conversely, data for half-mile circles indicate that TRI communities have a greater percentage of African Americans [14 percent] and people of color [15 percent] than non-TRI communities [11 and 12 percent, respectively]).

Godsil, Rachel D., *Remedying Environmental Racism*, 90 MICHIGAN LAW REVIEW 394 (1991) (pointing out that the common result of opposition to hazardous waste facilities by well-meaning, NIMBY environmentalists in affluent communities is that the sites are placed in predominantly poor, powerless communities of color).

Goldman, Benjamin A., and Laura Fitton, TOXIC WASTES AND RACE REVISITED: AN UPDATE OF THE 1987 REPORT ON THE RACIAL AND SOCIOECONOMIC CHARACTERISTICS OF COMMUNITIES WITH HAZARDOUS WASTE SITES (1994) (finding that, between 1980 and 1993, the concentration of people of color living in zip codes with commercial hazardous facilities increased from 25 percent to almost 31 percent of the average population around the facilities and that in 1993 people of color were 47 percent more likely than whites to live near a commercial hazardous waste facility).

Goldman, Benjamin A., NOT JUST PROSPERITY: ACHIEVING SUSTAINABILITY WITH ENVIRONMENTAL JUSTICE (National Wildlife Federation, 1994) (listing sixty-four studies that document disproportionate impact of environmental hazards by race, income, or both).

Gould J., QUALITY OF LIFE IN AMERICAN NEIGHBORHOODS: LEVELS OF AFFLUENCE, TOXIC WASTE, AND CANCER MORTALITY IN RESIDENTIAL ZIP CODE AREAS (Council on Economic Priorities, 1986) (finding that communities with the highest incomes have the lowest amounts of toxic waste).

Greenberg, Michael, and Richard Anderson, *Hazardous Waste Sites: The Credibility Gap* (1984) (summarizing a study of 567 communities in New Jersey that found communities with the greatest number of toxic waste sites to have more low-income and black residents than other communities).

Greenberg, Michael, *Proving Environmental Inequity in Siting Locally Undesirable Land Uses*, 4 RISK-ISSUES HEALTH & SAFETY 235 (1993) (survey of 192 waste-to-energy facilities [WTEFs] found that the "larger facility-populous town" combination had statistically significant inequities for per capita income and people of color, while the "smaller facility-less populated town" combination had slightly higher per capita income than their service areas and much less inequity for people of color; WTEF towns had lower per capita incomes than the United States as a whole and lower incomes than their service areas and averaged 45 percent more people of color than their service areas).

Haan, Mary, et al., *Poverty and Health: Prospective Analysis from Alameda County Study*, 125 AMERICAN JOURNAL OF EPIDEMIOLOGY 989, 994 (1987) (study analyzing the differences in overall morbidity and mortality between low-income groups and people of color groups and their more affluent white counterparts, controlling for certain risk factors, including blood pressure, heart disease, employment status, access to medical care, health insurance coverage, smoking, alcohol consumption, physical activity, body fat, and marital and social status, finds an average age adjusted difference in mortality of more than 50 percent).

Hamilton, James, *Testing for Environmental Racism: Prejudice, Profits, Political Power?* 14 JOURNAL OF POLICY ANALYSIS AND MANAGEMENT 107 (1995) (levels of political activism, not race, were negatively associated with the probability of expansion, controlling for socioeconomic and other factors, demonstrating that companies, when calculating where to expand hazardous waste processing capacity, are more likely to target areas with lower levels of potential political activity).

Hamilton, James, *Politics and Social Costs: Estimating the Impact of Collective Action on Hazardous Waste Facilities*, 24 RAND JOURNAL OF ECONOMICS 101 (1993) (using 1970 and 1980 Census data, finding that (1) both race and median household income were statistically significant in predicting sitings of hazardous waste processing facilities; (2) race and income were not statistically significant in predicting expansion of existing facilities; (3) facilities were less likely to plan to reduce their capacity as their counties' population of people of color increased; and (4) percentage of registered voters [a measure of political efficacy] was statistically significant in predicting expansion and reduction plans).

Handy, Femida, *Income and Air Quality in Hamilton, Ontario*, ALTERNATIVES (Spring 1977) (finding that air pollution in Hamilton, Ontario, is distributed inequitably by income).

Harrison, David, WHO PAYS FOR CLEAN AIR: THE COST AND BENEFIT DISTRIBUTION OF AUTOMOBILE EMISSIONS STANDARDS (1975) (air pollution inequitably distributed by income in urban areas, but not nationally; emission controls impose regressive costs).

Hird, John, SUPERFUND: THE POLITICAL ECONOMY OF ENVIRONMENTAL RISK (1994) (Superfund sites are more likely to be found in counties that are more affluent than in economically disadvantaged ones; Superfund sites are more likely to be located in counties with a higher percentage of nonwhites).

Hoffman, William S., et al., *Relation of Pesticide Concentration in Fat to Pathological Changes in Tissues*, 15 ARCHIVES ENVIRONMENTAL HEALTH 758 (1967) (discussing study of fat tissue of 700 patients from Chicago that found a higher concentration of DDT in blacks than in whites).

Inform, Toxics Watch 1995, 374 (listing studies that show environmental regulations' disproportionate impact on people of color and on low-income communities).

Joint Legislative Audit and Review Commission of the Virginia General Assembly, Solid Waste Facility Management in Virginia: Impact on Minority Communities (1995) (in Virginia, facilities in communities in which more than half the population was African American were inspected less frequently than other facilities, and, when violations of applicable environmental protection laws were found, the median length of time to bring the facility into compliance was longer in these communities).

Kay, Jane, *Minorities Bear Brunt of Pollution: Latinos and Blacks Living in State's "Dirtiest Neighborhood,"* San Francisco Examiner (April 7, 1991), at A1, A12 (finding that based on Toxics Release Inventory data, 59 percent of the population of the California zip code bearing the greatest total pounds of toxic release was black, and 38 percent was Latino).

Kay, Jane, *State's Toxic Threat: Work Place Poison*, San Francisco Examiner (April 10, 1987), at A1 (finding that workers stay in hazardous work places because they cannot afford not to work).

Ketkar, Kusum, *Hazardous Waste Sites and Property Values in the State of New Jersey*, 24 Applied Economics 647 (1992) (an analysis of seven urban counties in New Jersey found that municipalities with the highest percentage of people of color also had a large number of toxic waste sites).

Kruvant, W. J., *People, Energy and Pollution*, in The American Energy Consumer (K. K. Newman and D. Day, eds., 1975) (distribution of air pollutants in Washington, D.C., inequitable by race and income, with income more important determinant).

Kutz, F. W., et al., *Racial Stratification of Organochlorine Insecticide Residues in Human Adipose Tissue*, 19 Journal of Occupational Medicine 619 (1977) (national study detected almost twice as much of the pesticide DDT in the fat tissue of African Americans as in the fat tissue of whites; the pesticide lindane was detected more than twice as often in African Americans as in whites).

Lambert, Thomas, and Christopher Boerner, *Environmental Inequity: Economic Causes, Economic Solutions*, 14 Yale Journal on Regulation 195 (Winter 1997) (using data from 1970, 1980, and 1990 Censuses and finding no statistical relationship between active hazardous and solid waste storage facilities and incinerators and presence of minority residents in St. Louis, but finding a weak relationship between presence of minority and poor residents and facilities if inactive sites are added to the data set).

Appendix

Landrigan, Philip J., and John W. Graef, *Pediatric Lead Poisoning in 1987: The Silent Epidemic Continues,* 79 Pediatrics 582 (1987) (study conducted from 1976–1980 found 9.1 percent of all preschool children in the United States had blood lead levels over 25 milligrams per deciliter, while 24.5 percent of black children had blood levels this high).

Lavelle, Marianne, and Marcia Coyle, *Unequal Protection: The Racial Divide in Environmental Law, A Special Investigation,* National Law Journal, September 21, 1992, at S1 ("[t]here is a racial divide in the way the U.S. government cleans up toxic waste sites and punishes polluters. White communities see faster action, better results and stiffer penalties than communities where blacks, Hispanics and other minorities live. This unequal protection often occurs whether the community is wealthy or poor." Finds that penalties under hazardous waste laws at sites located near the greatest white population were about 500 percent higher than penalties at sites near the greatest population of people of color; for all the federal environmental laws aimed at protecting citizens from air, water, and waste pollution, penalties in white communities were 46 percent higher than those in communities of color; under the Superfund cleanup program, abandoned hazardous waste sites in communities of color take 20 percent longer to be placed on the national priority action list than those in white areas).

Lloyd, J. William, et al., *Long-Term Mortality Study of Steelworkers,* 12 Journal of Occupational Medicine 151 (1970) (finding that African Americans working in coke oven operations showed double the expected mortality rate from malignant neoplasms).

Lucas, Robert E. B., *The Distribution of Job Characteristics,* 56 Review of Economy & Statistics 530 (1974) (African American men have a 27 percent greater chance than whites of facing safety hazards and a 60 percent greater chance of facing health hazards in the workplace; African American women face a 106 percent greater chance than white women of facing safety hazards and a 91 percent greater chance of facing health hazards).

Mahaffey, Kathryn R., et al., *National Estimates of Blood Lead Levels: United States, 1976–1980,* 307 New England Journal of Medicine 573 (1982) (discussing a national health survey that found "significantly higher prevalence" of elevated levels of lead in children whose families have incomes of less than $6,000 compared to those whose families have incomes of more than $6,000; poor black children have six times the lead poisoning rate of poor white children.).

Mann, Eric, L.A.'s Lethal Air: New Strategies for Policy, Organizing, and Action (1991) (finding that in Los Angeles, 71 percent of African Americans and 50 percent of Latinos live in areas with the worst air pollution, compared to 34 percent of whites).

McCaull, Julian, *Discriminatory Air Pollution: If Poor Don't Breathe* 19 ENVI-RONMENT 26 (March 1976) (air pollution inequitably distributed).

McMichael, A. J., et al., *Mortality among Rubber Workers: Relationship to Specific Jobs*, 18 JOURNAL OF OCCUPATIONAL MEDICINE 178 (1976) (reporting that a study of 6,678 rubber workers found 27 percent of black workers but only 3 percent of white workers worked in the most dangerous areas).

Mohai, Paul, and Bunyan Bryant, *Environmental Racism: Reviewing the Evidence*, in RACE AND THE INCIDENCE OF ENVIRONMENTAL HAZARDS: A TIME FOR DISCOURSE (Bunyan Bryant and Paul Mohai, eds., 1992) (finding that poor people are more likely than the more affluent to live near commercial hazardous waste sites in Detroit and that, in Michigan, commercial hazardous waste facilities are located disproportionately where people of color live; that out of the fifteen systematic studies done since 1971 that examine disproportionate impact of environmental hazards by race or class, nearly every study has found an inequitable distribution of pollution by income; all but one have found distribution inequitable by race; and five of the eight studies that compared race and income found race to be a stronger predictor).

Mohai, Paul, and Bunyan Bryant, *Race, Class and Environmental Quality in the Detroit Area*, in ENVIRONMENTAL RACISM: ISSUES AND DILEMMAS (Bunyan Bryant and Paul Mohai, eds., 1991) (finding that African Americans in Detroit are four and a half times more likely than whites to live within a mile of a commercial hazardous waste facility and that race is a stronger predictor of such proximity than income).

Mohai, Paul, and Bunyan Bryant, *Environmental Injustice: Weighing Race and Class as Factors in the Distribution of Environmental Hazards*, 63 UNIVERSITY OF COLORADO LAW REVIEW 921 (1992) (summarizing the results of sixteen studies on disproportionate impacts and concluding that race and income biases exist in the distribution of environmental hazards).

Mohai, Paul, *The Demographics of Dumping Revisited: Examining the Impact of Alternate Methodologies in Environmental Justice Research*, 14 VIRGINIA ENVIRONMENTAL LAW JOURNAL 615 (1995) (comparing the methodological approaches of the national United Church of Christ and the University of Massachusetts studies, which reached conflicting results as to the disproportionate impact of the siting of TSDFs).

Moore, Marjorie W., *Environmental Health and Community Action*, NEW YORK STATE BAR ASSOCIATION ENVIRONMENTAL LAW JOURNAL (February–May 1991) (five out of Manhattan's seven municipal bus depots are in predominantly African American and Latino West Harlem).

Moses, Marion, A FIELD SURVEY OF PESTICIDE-RELATED WORKING CONDITIONS IN THE U.S. AND CANADA: MONITORING THE INTERNATIONAL CODE OF CONDUCT ON THE DISTRIBUTION AND USE OF PESTICIDES IN NORTH AMERICA (1988) (noting that 70 percent of farm-workers in a 1984 survey reported being exposed to pesticides, and 90 percent reported making less than $5,000 annually).

Moses, Marion, Eric S. Johnson, and W. Kent Angler, *Environmental Equity and Pesticide Exposure*, 9 TOXICOLOGY & INDUSTRIAL HEALTH 913, 916 (1993) ("People of color and low-income groups bear a disproportionate share of the potential health risks from exposure to pesticides.").

Needleman, H., and D. Bellinger, *The Developmental Consequences of Childhood Exposure to Lead*, in 7 ADVANCES IN CLINICAL PSYCHOLOGY 195 (Benjamin B. Lahey and Alan E. Kazdin, eds., 1984) (discussing a 1972 study by the National Center for Health Statistics that found that 4 percent of all children in United States have elevated blood lead levels, while the rate was 18.6 percent for black children living below the poverty level).

Oakes, John Michael, et al., *A Longitudinal Analysis of Environmental Equity in Communities with Hazardous Waste Facilities*, 25 SOCIAL SCIENCE RESEARCH 125 (1996) (nationwide study comparing changes in the demographics of areas that are hosting TSDFs to those of nonhost areas with varying levels of industrial employment and finding no significant differences in the changes).

Perfecto, Ivette, and Baldemar Velásquez, *Farm Workers: Among the Least Protected*, EPA JOURNAL (March–April 1992) (noting that as many as 313,000 of approximately 2 million farm-workers in the United States may suffer from pesticide-related illnesses annually).

Perfecto, Ivette, *Hazardous Waste and Pesticides: An International Tragedy*, in ENVIRONMENTAL RACISM: ISSUES AND DILEMMAS (Bunyan Bryant and Paul Mohai, eds., 1991) (noting that 90 percent of farm-workers in the United States are people of color).

Peskin, Henry, *Environmental Policy and the Distribution of Benefits and Costs*, in CURRENT ISSUES IN U.S. ENVIRONMENTAL POLICY 144, 159 (Paul R. Portney, ed., 1978) (environmental controls have a regressive impact).

Pfaff, Dennis, *Pollution and the Poor*, DETROIT NEWS (November 26, 1989), at A1 (reporting on the high concentration of pollution sources in low-income communities; forty-one of Detroit's top air polluters, twenty-five of the thirty-three most toxic chemical contaminated sites, and four of the five licensed hazardous waste storage treatment facilities are located in neighborhoods with average per capita incomes of less than $10,000 per year).

Poirier, Marc R., *Essays on Environmental Justice: Environmental Justice/*

Appendix

Racism/Equity; Can We Talk? 96 WEST VIRGINIA LAW REVIEW 1083, n.4 (1994) (providing examples of early studies relating to the disproportionate impact of environmental hazards on people of color).

Pollock, Philip H., III and M. Elliot Vittes, *Who Bears the Burdens of Environmental Pollution? Race, Ethnicity, and Environmental Equity in Florida,* 76 SOCIAL SCIENCE QUARTERLY 294 (June 1995) (race, ethnicity, and income are critical in explaining proximity to Toxic Release Inventory [TRI] facilities in Florida; households of people of color and low-income households were found to be overrepresented close to the facilities and underrepresented at greater distances, even controlling for urban versus overall population, manufacturing versus all workers, median house age, and median house value; black households were overrepresented near to each source, as were low-income black households compared to low-income white households).

Ringquist, Evan J., *Equity and the Distribution of Environmental Risk: The Case of TRI Facilities,* 78 SOCIAL SCIENCE QUARTERLY 811 (1997) (finding that Toxic Release Inventory facilities and pollutants are concentrated in residential zip codes with large populations of people of color).

Robinson, James C., *Exposure to Occupational Hazards Among Hispanics, Blacks, and Non-Hispanic Whites in California,* 79 AMERICAN JOURNAL OF PUBLIC HEALTH 629 (1989) (discussing study that found Latino men to have more than double the risk of work-related illness or injury of white men; black men had a 41 percent greater risk than white men).

Robinson, James C., *Racial Inequality and the Probability of Occupation-Related Injury or Illness,* 62 MILBANK QUARTERLY 567 (1984) (finding that the average African American worker is in an occupation that is 37 percent to 52 percent more likely to produce serious accident or illness than the occupation of the average white worker and that African American workers with the same level of education and job training as whites, on average, find themselves in substantially more dangerous occupations).

Robinson, James C., *Trends in Racial Inequality and Exposure to Work-Related Hazards 1968–1986,* 65 MILBANK QUARTERLY 404 (1987) (reporting that a survey of disabling injuries in 1968, 1977, and 1986 found that blacks faced risks of on-the-job injury one and one-half times those faced by whites and that, in 1986, black women faced risks almost double those of white women).

Robinson, James C., TOIL AND TOXICS: WORKPLACE STRUGGLES AND POLITICAL STRATEGIES FOR OCCUPATIONAL HEALTH (1991) (blacks have significantly higher exposure to occupational hazards than whites, and blacks and Latinos have much higher occupational injury and illness rates than whites).

Stretesky, Paul, and Michael J. Hogan, *Environmental Justice: An Analysis of Superfund Sites in Florida,* 45 SOCIAL PROBLEMS 268, 277–84 (1998) (in

Appendix

Florida, a higher percentage of blacks, Latinos, the poor, and lower-income households are located in Census tracts containing Superfund sites than are located in tracts without such sites; race independent of class as a determinant; in Census tracts containing Superfund sites the percentage of blacks and Hispanics has increased between 1970 and 1990).

Szasz, Andrew, Michael Meuser, Hal Aronson, and Hiroshi Fukurai, *The Demographics of Proximity to Toxic Releases: The Case of Los Angeles County* (1993) (paper presented at the 1993 Meetings of the American Sociological Association, Miami, Florida; available at <http://www.mapcruzin.com/scruztri/docs/seek55.htm>) (average county air emissions exceeded where Latinos or Latinos and African Americans together exceed 30 percent of Census tract population; income a factor, too, although race is statistically more important when both are considered together).

Szasz, A., and M. Meuser, *Environmental Inequality: Silicon Valley Toxics and Demographics* (1997) (published on the web at <http://www.mapcruzin.com/EI/index.html>) (neighborhoods closest to toxic emitters in Santa Clara County tend, generally, to be poorer and more Latino than the rest of the county).

Unger, Donald, et al., *Living Near a Hazardous Waste Facility: Coping with Individual and Family Distress*, 62 AMERICAN JOURNAL OF ORTHOPSYCHIATRY 55 (1992) (finding that residents who lived closest to a hazardous waste facility in Pinewood, South Carolina, were poor and African American, while more affluent whites lived further away).

U.S. Commission on Civil Rights, GOVERNMENT, INDUSTRY, AND PEOPLE: THE BATTLE FOR ENVIRONMENTAL JUSTICE IN LOUISIANA (1993) (finding disproportionate siting of hazardous waste facilities among low-income areas with high percentages of African Americans in the industrial corridor from Baton Rouge to New Orleans).

U.S. Council on Environmental Quality, THE SECOND ANNUAL REPORT OF THE COUNCIL ON ENVIRONMENTAL QUALITY (1971) (finding air pollution to be distributed inequitably by income).

U.S. Department of Health and Human Services, STRATEGIC PLAN FOR THE ELIMINATION OF CHILDHOOD LEAD POISONING (1991) (concluding that "poor, minority children in the inner cities" are particularly vulnerable to lead poisoning).

U.S. General Accounting Office, GAO/PEMD-92-6, HISPANIC ACCESS TO HEALTH CARE: SIGNIFICANT GAPS EXIST (1992) (reporting that 33 percent of Latinos had neither private nor public medical insurance in 1989, compared with 19 percent of African Americans and 12 percent of whites).

U.S. General Accounting Office, SITING OF HAZARDOUS WASTE LANDFILLS AND

THEIR CORRELATION WITH RACIAL AND ECONOMIC STATUS OF SURROUNDING COMMUNITIES (1983) (finding that three out of the four commercial hazardous waste sites in eight southern states are located in communities with a majority of people of color, while the fourth is in a community where 38 percent of the residents are black; at least 26 percent of the population in all four communities have incomes below the poverty line).

Villones, Rebecca, *Women in the Silicon Valley,* in MAKING WAVES: AN ANTHOLOGY OF WRITINGS BY AND ABOUT ASIAN AMERICAN WOMEN (Asian Women United of California, ed., 1989) (people of color, and especially immigrant workers, are concentrated in the most dangerous and lowest-paying jobs in the electronics industry).

Wernette, Dee R., and L.A. Nieves, *Breathing Polluted Air: Minorities Are Disproportionately Exposed,* EPA JOURNAL 16, 16–17 (March–April 1992) (people of color bear disproportionate burden of air pollution in urban areas).

West, Patrick G., *Invitation to Poison? Detroit Minorities and Toxic Fish Consumption from the Detroit River,* in RACE & ENVIRONMENTAL HAZARDS, IN RACE AND THE INCIDENCE OF ENVIRONMENTAL HAZARDS: A TIME FOR DISCOURSE 96 (Bunyan Bryant and Paul Mohai, eds., 1992) (disproportionate impact from consumption of fish laden with toxics).

West, Patrick G., et al., *Minority Anglers and Toxic Fish Consumption: Evidence from a Statewide Survey of Michigan,* in RACE AND THE INCIDENCE OF ENVIRONMENTAL HAZARDS: A TIME FOR DISCOURSE 100 (Bunyan Bryant and Paul Mohai, eds., 1992) (finding, in a Michigan study, that African American and Native American anglers eat more fish than white anglers irrespective of income and more than is assumed by state health authorities who set discharge limits).

White, Harvey, *Hazardous Waste Incineration and Minority Communities,* in RACE AND THE INCIDENCE OF ENVIRONMENTAL HAZARDS: A TIME FOR DISCOURSE (Bunyan Bryant and Paul Mohai, eds., 1992) (in the Baton Rouge area, communities of color had an average of one hazardous waste incineration facility per 7,349 residents, while white communities had only one site per 31,100 residents).

Zimmerman, Rae, *Social Equity and Environmental Risk,* 13 RISK ANALYSIS 649, 660–63 (1993) (finding that the higher the percentage of African American residents in communities hosting Superfund National Priority List (NPL) sites, the less likely it was that these sites would progress to the final pre-cleanup stage, but noting that progress appeared to be correlated primarily with time on the NPL, which was itself correlated with race).

Zupan, Jeffrey M., THE DISTRIBUTION OF AIR QUALITY IN THE NEW YORK REGION (1973) (finding that air pollution is distributed inequitably by income in New York).

NOTES

Notes to the Preface

1. This story is drawn from one of the authors' work, over a period of many years, with the community group El Pueblo para el Aire y Agua Limpio. The author, Luke Cole, began work as the group's attorney in October 1989 and continues to represent the group today.

2. CALIFORNIA CODE REGS, Title 14, §15072(a).

3. Cerrell Associates, POLITICAL DIFFICULTIES FACING WASTE-TO-ENERGY CONVERSION PLANT SITING 17–30 (1984) (commissioned by the California Waste Management Board).

4. Bureau of the Census, U.S. Department of Commerce, 1990 CENSUS OF POPULATION AND HOUSING, SUMMARY POPULATION AND HOUSING CHARACTERISTICS: CALIFORNIA 62, 66, 73 (table 4, Sex, Race and Hispanic Origin: 1990) (1991).

5. Robert D. Bullard, DUMPING IN DIXIE: RACE, CLASS AND ENVIRONMENTAL QUALITY (1994).

6. Bureau of the Census, U.S. Department of Commerce, *Community Area 51, Population and Housing Characteristics*, in 1980 CENSUS OF POPULATION AND HOUSING, at 205.

7. According to 1980 Census data, 77 percent of the Census Tract that includes the Port Arthur facility is African American and 2 percent is Latino, compared to Jefferson County as a whole, 55 percent of whose population is white. U.S. Department of Commerce, Selected Demographic and Housing Data, 1980 CENSUS OF POPULATION AND HOUSING (1980).

8. "[T]he census tracts surrounding Sauget and Trade Waste Incineration [are] more than 96% black. The average racial composition of the first five Census tracts to the north of Sauget . . . is 97.6 black with 40% of the population under the poverty level. The average racial composition of the four Census Tracts to the east of Sauget . . . is 95% black with 43% of the population under the poverty level. These results are significant considering that the average proportion of black people in the St. Louis SMSA is only 17 percent." Martin G. Rosen, *A Case Study of Environmental Racism in Sauget Illinois*, (unpublished manuscript prepared for RACE AND ENVIRONMENT 269, University of California at Los Angeles) (on file with author). We thank Robert Bullard for his extensive

help in compiling the demographic figures on Chem Waste facilities nationwide.

9. The Tijuana incinerator was denied a permit by the Mexican government after long community opposition, including a meeting between Kettleman City activists and Mexican environmentalists. Joel Simon, *U.S. and Mexican Activists Stop Incinerator Project*, CALIFORNIA LAWYER 89 (February 1993); see also Mark Grossi, *Tijuana Activists to Visit Waste Site in Kettleman City*, FRESNO BEE (March 7, 1992).

10. California Assembly Office of Research, TODAY'S TOXIC DUMP SITES: TO-MORROW'S TOXIC CLEANUP SITES 19, 24 (1986) ("In 1985, the EPA fined CWM Kettleman $7 million for improper groundwater monitoring, dumping incompatible wastes into ponds, keeping inadequate records, and more than 1,500 incidents of over-filling ponds. CWM settled by agreeing to pay EPA $2.1 million and DHS $1.1 million."). See also County of Ventura, Department of Sheriff, WASTE MANAGEMENT, INC. (1991), Attachment 6; Edwin L. Miller, Jr., District Attorney, FINAL REPORT: WASTE MANAGEMENT, INC. (San Diego District Attorney's Office, March 1992).

11. See Casey Bukro, *A $587,900 Lesson on Whistle-blowing: Incinerator Staffer's Retaliatory-Firing Suit Zaps Chemical Waste*, CHICAGO TRIBUNE (October 24, 1994); David Young, *Waste Firm Agrees to Pay $4.3 Million More*, CHICAGO TRIBUNE (December 24, 1991).

12. Cyndee Fontana, *Kettleman Incinerator Draws Fire: Firm's Poor Record in Illinois Cited*, FRESNO BEE (January 17, 1990). Balanoff told the people of Kettleman City that Chem Waste is "not a company that can be trusted at all." Id. See also Ron Nielsen, *Illinois Politician Denigrates Burner*, HANFORD SENTINEL (January 17, 1990), at 1.

13. Jeff Bailey, *Tough Target: Waste Disposal Giant, Often under Attack, Seems to Gain from It; Waste Management's Jousts with Environmentalists Deter Rivals from Field; How It Sanitizes Its Image*, WALL STREET JOURNAL (May 1, 1991), at A1.

14. Memorandum from John D. Dingell, Chair, Subcommittee on Oversight and Investigations of the Committee on Energy and Commerce, to members of the subcommittee (dated September 9, 1992), at 4–5, 24–30 (detailing storage of dioxin contaminated material at David's Mini-U-Storage in a residential neighborhood of Baton Rouge) (reproduced in Subcommittee on Oversight and Investigations of the Committee on Energy and Commerce, U.S. House of Representatives, EPA's CRIMINAL ENFORCEMENT PROGRAM, Serial No. 102-163 [September 1992], at 13–14, 32–39). According to Rep. Dingell,

Rather than immediately alerting the EPA, ChemWaste initiated a cover-up effort, designed to protect the reputation and interests of

Chem Waste at the expense of the public. . . . The dioxin-contaminated drums were falsely manifested as an "unknown" and delivered by night to ChemWaste's facility at Emelle, Alabama. Emelle had no permit to received dioxin-contaminated waste.

Id. at 14. A criminal prosecution ensued and a trial in Louisiana resulted in felony convictions of several individuals in 1991. Id.

15. San Diego District Attorney's Report, supra note 10, at 57. According to the District Attorney,

Waste Management, Inc.'s methods of doing business and history of civil and criminal violations has established a predictable pattern which has been fairly consistent over a significant number of years. The history of the company presents a combination of environmental and anti-trust violations and public corruption cases which must be viewed with considerable concern. Waste Management has been capable of absorbing enormous fines and other sanctions levied against it while still maintaining a high earnings ratio. We do not know whether these sanctions have had any punitive effect on the company or have merely been considered as additional operating expenses. . . .

Our examination of the activities of Waste Management in San Diego County causes us additional concern. When viewed in the context of their established history of business practices, it is clear that Waste Management engages in practices designed to gain undue influence over government officials.

Id. at 57–58.

16. Jeff Bailey, *Waste Management Unit Pleads Guilty to Violations, Will Pay $11.6 Million*, WALL STREET JOURNAL (October 12, 1992), at 1.

17. Remarks of Chair Mike Wheatley, Kings County Planning Commission, in Reporter's Transcript, Kings County Planning Commission Special Meeting, Public Hearing for Conditional Use Permit No. 1480, November 14–15, 1990, at 172.

18. Testimony of Mary Lou Mares, in Reporter's Transcript, Kings County Planning Commission Special Meeting, Public Hearing for Conditional Use Permit No. 1480, November 14–15, 1990, p. 257; testimony of Ephraim Camacho, id. at 180; testimony of Allen Brent, id. at 149.

19. CALIFORNIA HEALTH AND SAFETY CODE §25149.5.

20. See Tracy Correa, *County to Share Chem Waste Tax*, HANFORD SENTINEL (November 16, 1991) (County revenues from 10 percent tax on Chem Waste were $6.1 million in 1990–1991, $7.4 million in 1989–1990).

21. *El Pueblo para el Aire y Agua Limpio v. County of Kings*, Sacramento

Superior Court No. 366045, Ruling on Submitted Matter, Gunther, J. (December 30, 1991), 22 Environmental Law Reporter 20, 357.

22. *El Pueblo para el Aire y Agua Limpio v. County of Kings*, California Court of Appeals, Third District, No. 3 Civil 014017.

23. This knowledge was transmitted through a number of stories mentioning the Kettleman City struggle that appeared in local, regional, and national media, including Julia Flynn Siler, *"Environmental Racism": It Could Be a Messy Fight*, Business Week (May 20, 1991), at 116; Jeff Bailey, *Tough Target: Waste Disposal Giant, Often under Attack, Seems to Gain from It*, supra; Roberto Suro, *Pollution-Weary Minorities Try Civil Rights Tack*, New York Times (January 11, 1993), at A1; Marcia Coyle, *Lawyers Try to Devise New Strategy*, National Law Journal (September 21, 1992), at S8; Katherine L. Ratcliffe, *Fusing Civil, Environmental Rights Hispanic Residents Claim Racism in Protest over Plan to Build Incinerator in Their Fertile Valley*, Christian Science Monitor (May 24, 1991), at 12; as well as segments on National Public Radio and on the McNeil-Lehrer News Hour.

24. Chemical Waste Management, Inc., *Chem Waste Withdraws Incinerator Proposal for Kettleman Hills*, News Release (September 7, 1993).

25. Id.; Jeff Bailey, *WMX Pulls Its Application for Incinerator*, Wall Street Journal (September 8, 1993), at A4.

26. Dennis Pfaff, *Enemies of Toxics Incinerator Are Cheered by End of Project; California Rural Legal Assistance Had Opposed the Construction, Once Slated for a Hispanic Community*, Daily Journal (San Francisco) (September 8, 1993), at 3.

27. Mark Grossi, *Chemwaste Won't Build Kettleman Incinerator*, Fresno Bee (September 8, 1993)

Notes to the Introduction

1. See Appendix A for a bibliography of studies, and chapter 3 for discussion of studies.

2. Exec. Order No. 12898, 59 Fed. Reg. 7,629 (1994). The Order directs each federal agency to make achieving environmental justice part of its mission by addressing disproportionately high and adverse health and environmental effects of its programs on minority and low-income populations. To comply, agencies must issue detailed reports outlining their plan to eliminate racially disparate environmental effects.

3. Iris M. Young, *Communication and the Other: Beyond Deliberative Democracy*, in Democracy and Difference: Contesting the Boundaries of the Political 131 (Seyla Benhabib, ed., 1996).

4. As we have written elsewhere,

Engaging in what some critical race theorists and critical legal scholars have called "unmasking," grassroots activists have uncovered, through their own experiences, the hidden power dynamics of pollution and environmental laws. They have acquired an "institutional" understanding of the political economy of pollution.

Luke W. Cole, *Empowerment as the Key to Environmental Protection: The Need for Environmental Poverty Law*, 19 Ecology Law Quarterly 619, 642–43 (1992) (footnotes omitted).

5. See generally Sheila Foster, *Race(ial) Matters: The Quest for Environmental Justice*, 20 Ecology Law Quarterly 721, 731–35 (1994); Cole, *Empowerment as the Key to Environmental Protection: The Need for Environmental Poverty Law*, supra. See also Alan D. Freeman, *Legitimizing Racial Discrimination through Anti-Discrimination Law: A Critical Review of Supreme Court Doctrine*, 62 Minnesota Law Review 1049, 1052–57 (1978).

6. Giovanna Di Chiro, *Nature as Community: The Convergence of Environment and Social Justice*, in Uncommon Ground: Rethinking the Human Place in Nature 298–320 (William Cronon, ed., 1995).

7. See Laura Pulido, *A Critical Review of the Methodology of Environmental Racism Research*, 28 Antipode 142, 149 (1996) (noting that the real challenge in environmental racism research is to "understand how racism operates in conjunction with a particular political economic system").

8. See also Environmental Equity Workgroup, U.S. Environmental Protection Agency, Environmental Equity: Reducing Risk for All Communities, Workgroup Report to the Administrator, EPA230-R-92-008, page 10 (1992) (hereafter "Environmental Equity")

9. This view is shared by an increasing number of commentators. See, e.g., Eileen Guana, *The Environmental Justice Misfit: Public Participation and the Paradigm Paradox*, 17 Stanford Environmental Law Journal 3 (1998); Ellison Folk, *Public Participation in the Superfund Cleanup Process*, 18 Ecology Law Quarterly 173 (1991); Jonathan Poisner, *A Civic Republican Perspective on the National Environmental Policy Act's Process for Citizen Participation*, 26 Environmental Law 53 (1996); Eileen Gay Jones, *Risky Assessments: Uncertainties in Science and the Human Dimensions of Environmental Decision Making*, 22 William & Mary Environmental Law & Policy Review 1 (1997); Lawrence Susskind, *Overview of Developments in Public Participation*, in Public Participation in Environmental Decision Making 2–4 (ABA Standing Committee on Environmental Law, 1994); Luke W. Cole, *Macho Law Brains, Public Citizens, and Grassroots Activists: Three Models of Environmental Advocacy*, 14 Virginia Environmental Law Journal 687, 698 (1995).

10. For example, Anne Simon has called for decision-making processes to be both transparent and permeable. Anne Simon, *Valuing Public Participation*, 25 ECOLOGY LAW QUARTERLY 757 (1999).

11. Susskind, *Overview of Developments in Public Participation*, in ABA Standing Committee on Environmental Law, supra.

12. Charles Lee, *Environment: Where We Live, Work, Play and Learn*, 6 RACE, POVERTY & THE ENVIRONMENT (Winter–Spring 1996), at 6.

13. As Regina Austin and Michael Schill explain, "[I]n the view of many people of color, environmentalism is associated with the preservation of wildlife and wilderness, which simply is not more important than the survival of people and the communities in which they live; thus, the mainstream [environmental] movement has its priorities skewed." Regina Austin and Michael Schill, *Black, Brown, Red, and Poisoned*, in UNUSUAL PROTECTION: ENVIRONMENTAL JUSTICE AND COMMUNITIES OF COLOR 58 (Robert Bullard, ed., 1994).

14. Cynthia Hamilton, *Women, Home & Community: The Struggle in an Urban Environment*, RACE, POVERTY & THE ENVIRONMENT (April 1990), at 3.

15. See Peter L. Reich, *Greening the Ghetto: A Theory of Environmental Race Discrimination*, 41 KANSAS LAW REVIEW 271 (1992).

16. See, e.g., *Principles of Environmental Justice* ratified at the First National People of Color Environmental Leadership Summit in Washington, D.C., in October 1991, printed in 2 RACE, POVERTY & THE ENVIRONMENT 32 (Fall 1991/Winter 1992).

Notes to Chapter 1

1. Robert D. Bullard, *Environmental Justice for All: It's the Right Thing to Do*, 9 JOURNAL OF ENVIRONMENTAL LAW & LITIGATION 281, 285 (1994).

2. Bullard, supra, at 285; Robert D. Bullard, *Environmental Justice for All*, in UNEQUAL PROTECTION: ENVIRONMENTAL JUSTICE AND COMMUNITIES OF COLOR (Robert D. Bullard, ed., 1994), at 3–4.

3. We thank Charles Lee for this metaphor.

4. See, e.g., Charles M. Payne, I'VE GOT THE LIGHT OF FREEDOM: THE ORGANIZING TRADITION AND THE MISSISSIPPI FREEDOM STRUGGLE (1995); Aldon Morris, THE ORIGINS OF THE CIVIL RIGHTS MOVEMENT: BLACK COMMUNITIES ORGANIZING FOR CHANGE (1984); Clayborne Carson, IN STRUGGLE: SNCC AND THE BLACK AWAKENING OF THE 1960s (1981); THE EYES ON THE PRIZE CIVIL RIGHTS READER: DOCUMENTS, SPEECHES, AND FIRSTHAND ACCOUNTS FROM THE BLACK FREEDOM STRUGGLE, 1954–1990 (Clayborne Carson et al., eds. 1991); Taylor Branch, PARTING THE WATERS: AMERICA IN THE KINGS YEARS, 1954–63 (1988).

5. Chavis helped bring national attention to the Warren County struggle

through his national, church-based network. He was a key leader in the Environmental Justice Movement from the early 1980s through the early 1990s. He later went on to head the National Association for the Advancement of Colored People (NAACP). Also prominent in the Warren County struggle was District of Columbia congressional delegate Walter Fauntroy, who was a product of the civil rights movement as well.

6. 500 YEARS OF CHICANO HISTORY IN PICTURES 129–37 (Elizabeth Martinez, ed., 1991).

7. Bullard, *Environmental Justice for All*, in UNEQUAL PROTECTION: ENVIRONMENTAL JUSTICE AND COMMUNITIES OF COLOR (Robert D. Bullard, ed., 1994), at 3, 5; Ken Geiser and Gerry Waneck, *PCBs and Warren County*, in UNEQUAL PROTECTION: ENVIRONMENTAL JUSTICE AND COMMUNITIES OF COLOR (Robert D. Bullard, ed., 1994), at 43, 44.

8. See Congressman John Lewis, *Foreword*, in UNEQUAL PROTECTION: ENVIRONMENTAL JUSTICE AND COMMUNITIES OF COLOR, (Robert D. Bullard, ed. 1994), at vii–x. This act would have targeted the 100 most polluted locations in the United States for federal attention. These areas would have been designated environmental high-impact areas and require assessment of health conditions in communities that have high concentrations of polluting facilities. Id. at viii–ix.

9. Id. at viii.

10. See, e.g., Andrew Szasz, ECOPOPULISM: TOXIC WASTE AND THE MOVEMENT FOR ENVIRONMENTAL JUSTICE 38–102 (1994).

11. Nicholas Freudenberg and Carol Steinsapir, *Not in Our Backyards: The Grassroots Environmental Movement*, 4 SOCIETY & NATURAL RESOURCES 237; see also LOIS M. GIBBS, LOVE CANAL: MY STORY (1982).

12. Andrew Szasz, ECOPOPULISM: TOXIC WASTE AND THE MOVEMENT FOR ENVIRONMENTAL JUSTICE, supra, at 40.

13. Id. at 41.

14. Id. at 69–102.

15. CCHW is now known as the Center for Health, Environment, and Justice.

16. See, e.g., Freudenberg and Steinsapir, *Not in Our Backyards: The Grassroots Environmental Movement*, supra, 235, 242; Barry Commoner, MAKING PEACE WITH THE PLANET 103–40, 178–90 (1990); Luke W. Cole, *Empowerment as the Means to Environmental Protection: The Need for Environmental Poverty Law*, 19 ECOLOGY LAW QUARTERLY 619, 645 (1992).

17. See Richard Moore and Louis Head, *Building a Net That Works: SWOP*, in UNEQUAL PROTECTION: ENVIRONMENTAL JUSTICE AND COMMUNITIES OF COLOR 191 (Robert D. Bullard, ed., 1994).

18. See generally Paul Mohai and Bunyan Bryant, *Environmental Racism:*

Reviewing the Evidence, in RACE AND THE INCIDENCE OF ENVIRONMENTAL HAZ-ARDS: A TIME FOR DISCOURSE 163 (Bunyan Bryant and Paul Mohai, eds., 1992) (reviewing early studies finding distributional inequities by income and race).

19. At the end of the meeting, the seven asked for an informal meeting of only the African American staffers present, without Reilly or any other white EPA staffers; at that post-meeting, EPA staffers informed the Michigan Group about the reality of working as a person of color in the EPA.

20. Robert D. Bullard, *Introduction,* in UNEQUAL PROTECTION: ENVIRONMEN-TAL JUSTICE AND COMMUNITIES OF COLOR (Robert D. Bullard, ed., 1994), at vii, xvii–xviii.

21. Interview with Mary Lou Mares, Kettleman City, June 15, 1998.

22. *Bean v. Southwestern Waste Management Corp.,* 482 F.Supp. 673 (S.D. Tex. 1979). See generally *A Pioneer in Environmental Justice Lawyering: A Conversation with Linda McKeever Bullard,* 5 RACE, POVERTY & THE ENVIRONMENT 17 (Fall 1994/Winter 1995). Linda Bullard convinced her husband, Bob, to conduct a study of the demographics of those living around garbage dumps in the Houston area as part of the *Bean* case.

23. *In the Matter of Louisiana Energy Services, L.P.,* Decision of the Nuclear Regulatory Commission Atomic Safety and Licensing Board, May 1, 1997 (using the testimony of Dr. Robert Bullard to establish that the siting process at issue was biased and that racial considerations were a factor in the site selection process).

24. President William J. Clinton, MEMORANDUM ON ENVIRONMENTAL JUSTICE, February 11, 1994.

25. Vine Deloria, Jr., BEHIND THE TRAIL OF BROKEN TREATIES: AN INDIAN DEC-LARATION OF INDEPENDENCE 8–21 (1985).

26. Peter Matthiessen, IN THE SPIRIT OF CRAZY HORSE (1983); Edward Lazarus, BLACK HILLS, WHITE JUSTICE: THE SIOUX NATION VERSUS THE UNITED STATES, 1775 TO THE PRESENT (1991).

27. Cole, *Empowerment as the Means to Environmental Protection,* supra, 636 n. 51.

28. For a nice history of the environmental movement and its underlying ideology, see Anna Bramwell, ECOLOGY IN THE 20TH CENTURY: A HISTORY (1989).

29. For a provocative indictment of the second-wave environmentalists, see Peter Montague, *What We Must Do: A Grassroots Offensive against Toxics in the '90s,* 14 THE WORKBOOK 90, 92 (1989).

30. By the term "traditional environmental group," we mean primarily the "Group of Ten" environmental organizations, which are national in scope, advocacy, and membership. The "Group of Ten" label was first used by these

groups—the nation's ten largest traditional environmental groups—in 1985. Robert Gottlieb, *Earth Day Revisited*, Tikkun (March–April 1990), at 55.

31. Robert Bullard and Beverly Hendrix Wright, *Blacks and the Environment*, 14 Humboldt Journal of Social Relations 165, 167 (Fall/Winter and Winter/Spring 1986–87).

32. Charles Jordan and Donald Snow, *Diversification, Minorities, and the Mainstream Environmental Movement, in* Voices from the Environmental Movement: Perspectives for a New Era 71, 78 (Donald Snow, ed., 1991). Many Earth Day speeches in 1970 made the direct connection between environmental issues and social and racial justice. There was, to be sure, tension between the often affluent environmentalists and activists in the civil rights movement, such as that surrounding the burial of a car at an Earth Day event in San Jose, California. While the white environmentalists saw the interment of a brand new car as a statement of antimaterialism, local inner-city residents criticized them for squandering resources that could be put to better use.

33. Id. at 93.

34. For example, by 1983, the heads of the Sierra Club, the Sierra Club Legal Defense Fund, the Natural Resources Defense Council, the Audubon Society, the Environmental Defense Fund, and the Wilderness Society were all attorneys. Christopher Manes, Green Rage: Radical Environmentalism and the Unmaking of Civilization 255 n. 8 (1990). For analysis of the second wave and its focus on litigation, see generally Tom Turner, *The Legal Eagles*, Amicus Journal (Winter 1988), at 25; Melia Franklin, *What's Four-Legged and Green All Over? . . . Sorting out the Environmental Movement*, California Tomorrow (Fall 1988), at 14. In a Sierra Club national membership survey in 1972, "lawsuits and lobbying were strongly endorsed as appropriate methods. . . . More than two-thirds of the members, in each case, *strongly* agreed that they were appropriate. Only five percent disapproved." Don Coombs, *The Club Looks at Itself,* Sierra Club Bulletin (July–August 1972), at 38 (emphasis in original).

35. "[T]he legal victories won in the late sixties and early seventies formed the foundation on which the modern environmental movement is built," according to John Adams, the executive director of NRDC. Tom Turner, *The Legal Eagles*, Amicus Journal (Winter 1988), at 27–28. Another pioneer of the environmental law field states, "In no other political and social movement has litigation played such an important and dominant role. Not even close." Id. at 27 (quoting David Sive).

36. Id. at 27 (quoting Frederick Sutherland).

37. There are notable exceptions to this overgeneralization. For example, the Sierra Club worked with the Urban Environment Conference and the National Urban League to put on the City Care conference on the urban environment in

1979. See National Urban League et al., *City Care*, in National Conference on the Urban Environment Proceedings (1979); Urban Environment Conference, Resource Book—"Taking Back Our Health": An Institute on Surviving the Toxics Threat to Minority Communities (January 1985) (conference handbook).

38. Coombs, *The Club Looks at Itself*, supra, at 35, 37.

39. See Jordan and Snow, *Diversification, Minorities, and the Mainstream Environmental Movement*, supra, 75–78 (detailing racist exclusion of people of color from early conservation clubs and hunting preserves). Several southern California chapters of the Sierra Club, for example, formerly deliberately excluded blacks and Jews from membership; when the San Francisco chapter tried in 1959 to introduce a policy of inclusion of the "four recognized colors" into the Sierra Club, the resolution failed. Id. at 76; Stephen Fox, John Muir and His Legacy: The American Conservation Movement 349 (1981).

40. Grassroots leaders have seen traditional environmentalists as enemies when those groups accept contributions from industry and have appointed executives of corporations such as Waste Management to their boards at the same time activists were fighting the companies. As Dana Alston writes about the National Wildlife Federation, those "who are engaged in life and death struggles with Waste Management were hard-pressed to understand why such a corporation is represented on the board of directors of one of the largest and most influential environmental organizations." Dana Alston, *Transforming a Movement*, Race, Poverty & the Environment (Fall 1991–Winter 1992), at 1, 29. As one environmental justice advocate asserted,

> We are not always well served by the Environmentalist establishment in Washington. Perhaps with the best of intentions they have legitimated a system of destruction. Their batteries of lawyers and lobbyists battle over insignificant or irrelevant measures while implicitly recognizing the right of polluters to carry on business as usual. They are caught up in a deadly game, thrilled at the prospect of being "players."

Paul deLeon, *The STP Schools: Education for Environmental Action*, New Solutions (Summer 1990), at 22, 23.

41. See Luke W. Cole, *Foreword: A Jeremiad on Environmental Justice and the Law*, 14 Stanford Environmental Law Journal ix, xiii–xv.

42. See, e.g., Peter Montague, *What We Must Do: A Grassroots Offensive against Toxics in the '90s*, supra. Even one of the authors of this book has referred to the Environmental Justice Movement as the "third wave."

43. Letter from SouthWest Organizing Project to "Group of 10" National Environmental Organizations (February 21, 1990) (letter on behalf of more than 100 community leaders of color).

Notes to Chapter 2

44. Philip Shabecoff, *Environmental Groups Told They Are Racist in Hiring*, NEW YORK TIMES, (February 1, 1990), at A16.

45. Donald Unger et al., *Living Near a Hazardous Waste Facility: Coping with Individual and Family Distress*, 62 AMERICAN JOURNAL OF ORTHOPSYCHIATRY 55, 57 (1992). Anecdotal evidence shows that even among children living near toxic waste sites, there was a "loss of faith in governmental institutions." Id; see also Freudenberg and Steinsapir, *Not in Our Backyards: The Grassroots Environmental Movement*, supra, at 235, 237, 239 (noting that in one survey of grassroots groups, 45 percent of those responding claimed that government agencies had blocked their access to needed information).

Notes to Chapter 2

1. See Craig Offman, *Trouble Comes to Toxic Town USA*, GEORGE (March 1998), at 94; Brent Staples, *Life in the Toxic Zone*, NEW YORK TIMES (September 15, 1996), at A14. See also *Chester Residents Concerned for Quality Living v. Seif*, 132 F.3d 925, 928 n. 1 (3rd Cir. 1997), *cert. granted*, 118 S.Ct. 2296 (U.S. June 8, 1998), *vacated and remanded*, 1998 WESTLAW 477242 (U.S. August 17, 1998) (noting that 91 percent of the population of Delaware County is white and 32 percent of that of Chester is white).

2. See Mark Jaffe, *Waste-Site Ruling Aids Chester Activists*, PHILADELPHIA INQUIRER (January 1, 1998), at A1; Staples, *Life in the Toxic Zone*, supra (noting that the five permits issued in Chester were for waste facilities that had the capacity to handle more than two million tons of waste per year; the permits issued in the rest of the county were for waste plants with the capacity to process less than 1 percent as much waste).

3. Michael Janofsky, *Suit Says Racial Bias Led to Clustering of Solid Waste Sites*, NEW YORK TIMES (May 29, 1996), at A15.

4. LAID TO WASTE: A CHESTER NEIGHBORHOOD FIGHTS FOR ITS FUTURE (DUTV television broadcast, April 1996) (on file with author). "DUTV" stands for Drexel University Television. The station is an educational access channel operated by Drexel University under agreement with the City of Philadelphia, Department of Public Property.

5. See id. (quoting one resident describing her feeling of being "in jail").

6. See *A Review of Waste to Energy Trash Incinerators in the U.S.A.*, WORK ON WASTE (January 1992), at 1. The facility has also not been the best neighbors. It was fined thousands of dollars for exceeding its permitted levels of sulfur dioxide, hydrochloric acid, carbon monoxide, and other pollutants between 1992 and 1995. See Martin Indars, *Westinghouse Settles over Chester Facility; Agreement Involves State, Federal Agencies*, LEGAL INTELLIGENCER (May 27, 1997), at

| 195 |

6 (reporting the agreement among Westinghouse, the EPA, and the DEP involving a $400,000 settlement for the clean-air emissions violations, which includes a $100,000 fine and company sponsorship of a $100,000 lead abatement program).

7. Meta Mendel-Reyes, RECLAIMING DEMOCRACY (1995), at 155.

8. See United States Environmental Protection Agency Region III, *Environmental Risk Study for City of Chester, Pennsylvania* (June 1995), <http://.epa.gov/reg3hwmd/chester.html> (noting that two facilities are believed to account for half the long-term cancer risk).

9. See LAID TO WASTE, supra.

10. Russell, *The Perpetrators . . . Russell, Rea, and Zappala* (November 9, 1997) <http://www.envirolink.org/orgs/pen/crcql/rrz.html> (CRCQL Web page).

11. See Michael de Courcy Hinds, *Pennsylvania City Hopes It's Bouncing Back from the Bottom*, NEW YORK TIMES (January 5, 1992), at A14.

12. Morgan Kelly, *History of Chester* (November 9, 1997) <http://www.envirolink.org/orgs/pen/crcql/history.html> (CRCQL Web page).

13. See id. (noting that Chester was also "well know [*sic*] for its jazz scene and it's [*sic*] good educational system"); see also Hinds, *Pennsylvania City Hopes It's Bouncing Back from the Bottom*, supra (noting that the city "thrived for 175 years, building the first iron-clad ships and becoming one of the world's busiest shipyards").

14. See Kelly, *History of Chester*, supra; see also Hinds, *Pennsylvania City Hopes It's Bouncing Back from the Bottom*, supra (reporting that at an increasing pace over the past forty years, because of high labor costs and increased competition, all but two major companies closed or moved to the South; at the same time, more southern blacks moved into Chester and many white residents moved to the suburbs); Staples, *Life in the Toxic Zone*, supra (describing Chester as a "declining factory town" but "[o]nce a muscular city of 66,000" before "Chester lost a third of its population—and more than 40,000 jobs—between the end of World War II and the coming of Ronald Reagan").

15. See Hinds, *Pennsylvania City Hopes It's Bouncing Back from the Bottom*, supra (reporting that "about one of every six residents lives in public housing, one family in three receives public assistance and about one adult in three is unemployed").

16. See, e.g., Frank Reeves, *City Schools Reform Plan Includes Vouchers; State Panel's Report Seeks Changes in 24 Ailing Urban Districts*, PITTSBURGH POST-GAZETTE (December 16, 1997), at C1 (noting that Chester-Upland School District meets state commission's criteria for "educationally distressed," which include high dropout rates, failure of a quarter or more of district students to meet

statewide standards, high teacher absenteeism, and student attendance rates 10 percent or more below national norms); Associated Press, *Master: Chaos Is the Norm in Chester Schools; Students Fail Because No One Cares, Feds Say*, HARRIS-BURG PATRIOT (May 14, 1996), at A4 (reporting that Chester-Upland School District is on the verge of collapse, according to a federal master, because of poor student performance, high truancy, and bankruptcy).

17. See Casey Combs, *Statistics Show Crime Is Worse in Smaller Cities*, PITTS-BURGH POST-GAZETTE (April 28, 1996), at F1 (supporting analysis with 1996 FBI figures based on incidents reported by the police).

18. LAID TO WASTE, supra (quoting resident and noting that the Mayor of Chester and other politicians pleaded with the City of Philadelphia to transport and process its waste in Chester).

19. A summary of Chester's political history appears on a CRCQL Web site. In part, the author explains the history as follows:

Chester's political history is closely linked to its economic history. Since the turn of the century, with one exception, Chester has been ruled by a corrupt and extremely powerful political machine. The machine began in 1910 with a Swarthmore dropout named John McClure. McClure consolidated power over Chester through a campaign founded in racketeering and bootlegging.

. . . McClure and the Republican party kept tight control over the city's votes by controlling [*sic*] public funds in such a way that every government function was delivered as a personal favor. . . . They were largely responsible for controlling who got jobs. . . . A paper in 1967 noted that, when asked why they voted for machine candidates, most African-Americans responded that it was so they would be able to get a job. Whether or not this was true, the rumor, the fear of losing a job, was all that was necessary. The machine held the people in the palm of its hand. By delivering favors on an individual basis it kept the poor from organizing and bargaining collectively. Effectively, it removed any power people had in the political process.

After McClure died in 1965, Jack Nacrelli, a local mobster, took control of the party. He served as mayor until 1979 when he was convicted on tax evasion, bribery and racketeering. His control was still felt from jail however, and in 1985, his secretary Willie Mae Leake became the first black mayor of Chester.

Kelly, *History of Chester*, supra; see also Hinds, *Pennsylvania City Hopes It's Bouncing Back from the Bottom*, supra; see also Mark Fazlollah, *Chester Softball Fund Probed*, PHILADELPHIA INQUIRER (January 4, 1992), at B3 (reporting that recent investigations have found evidence of corruption in the Chester City

Council, the Redevelopment Authority, and the Resources Recovery Authority, as well as possible malfeasance involving the City's softball fund). The *New York Times* reported:

Chester's Republican Party machine, one of the nation's oldest, has also been called one of the most corrupt in recent decades by state officials. The Pennsylvania Crime Commission, an investigative agency of the State Legislature, said in a recent report last year that Chester's government had been dominated by a triad of criminals, corrupt politicians and rogue law-enforcement officers since the 1960s.

Hinds, *Pennsylvania City Hopes It's Bouncing Back from the Bottom*, supra.

Of course, political corruption is not unique to a city like Chester. Poor, disenfranchised cities are known to have a history of corruption in city government. See David L. Kirp et al., Our Town: Race, Housing and the Soul of Suburbia 19, 30 (1995) (describing the political corruption that has haunted Camden, New Jersey, one of the state's poorest cities).

20. Laid to Waste, supra. Kostmayer is now director of Zero Population Growth (ZPG). See *ZPG Online* (April 9, 1998) <http://www.zpg.org/>.

21. See Rick Teaff, *Westinghouse, RR&Z Team Up on Waste-to-Energy Plant*, Pittsburgh Business Times & Journal (February 8, 1987), at 1; see also Don Hopey, *Protestors Target Firm Helping Build Waste Disposal Sites*, Pittsburgh Post-Gazette (April 13, 1996), at B5.

22. Russell, *Perpetrators*, supra; see also Teaff, *Westinghouse, RR&Z Team Up on Waste-to-Energy Plant*, supra (noting that U.S. Senator John Heinz, R-PA, inserted a provision into the 1986 tax bill that specifically retained tax benefits for the incinerator).

23. See *Corporate Structure of Russell, Rea & Zappala* (November 10, 1997) <http://www.envirolink.org/orgs/pen/crcql/rrz-structure.html> (CRCQL Web page).

24. See Laid to Waste, supra.

25. Hopey, *Protestors Target Firm Helping Build Waste Disposal Sites*, supra (reporting that the representative also noted that "all of the businesses were approved by the City of Chester" and that "all of the incinerators have proper permits from the State").

26. Id. (emphasis added).

27. Environmental assessment criteria can include factors such as avoiding a certain degree of proximity to wells, surface waters, residences, recreational areas, wetlands, and endangered species habitat. See Solid Waste Management Act (SWMA), 1980 Pa. Laws 380 (codified as amended at 35 Pennsylvania Consolidated Statutes Annotated 6018.101-6018.1003 (West 1993)); Pennsylvania Department of Environmental Protection Regulations, 25 Pennsylva-

NIA CODE § 271.127 (West Supp. 1997) (listing environmental assessment requirements for municipal waste permits).

28. See LAID TO WASTE, supra; see also *Township of Chartiers v. William H. Martin, Inc.*, 542 A.2d 985 (Pa. 1988) (holding that "natural expansion doctrine" requires municipalities to allow landfills and similar facilities to expand); 25 PENNSYLVANIA CODE § 271.126(b)(3) (West Supp. 1997) (exempting permit modification applications that are not considered "major" from environmental assessment process); Michael B. Gerrard, WHOSE BACKYARD, WHOSE RISK: FEAR AND FAIRNESS IN TOXIC AND NUCLEAR WASTE SITING 55 (1994).

29. LAID TO WASTE, supra.

30. Interview with Zulene Mayfield, chairperson of CRCQL, in Chester, Pennsylvania (April 14, 1996) [hereinafter "Mayfield Interview"]. Unless otherwise noted, all factual background and quotes in this section are from the Mayfield Interview

31. Arguably there is not much of a substantive difference between the two, other than semantics. The storage and processing of such waste is regulated under the Resource Conservation and Recovery Act of 1976, Pub. L. No. 94-580, 90 Stat. 2795 (now codified at 42 U.S.C. § 6901-87) (West 1995) (RCRA). RCRA defines a "resource recovery facility" as one "at which solid waste is processed for the purpose of extracting, converting to energy, or otherwise separating and preparing solid waste for reuse." 42 U.S.C. § 6903 (24) (West 1995). Incineration is one way of treating and/or processing solid wastes. The Westinghouse facility is a trash-to-energy incinerator.

32. LAID TO WASTE, supra (quoting unnamed Chester resident).

33. Autoclaving sterilizes objects in an apparatus using superheated steam. *Chester Residents Concerned for Quality Living v. Commonwealth of Pennsylvania, Department of Environmental Resources*, 668 A.2d 110, 111 n. 1 (Pa. 1995).

34. See 25 PENNSYLVANIA CODE § 271.141 (West Supp. 1997) (listing public notice and comment as general requirements for permits and permit applications). This section requires that the permit applicant publish notice of its application once a week for three consecutive weeks in a "newspaper of general circulation in the area where the proposed facility is located." Id. Permit applicants must also give separate notice via certified mail to "owners and occupants of land contiguous to the site or the proposed permit area." Id. This notice is intended to give the community a formal opportunity to review applications and comment on them within a specific period of time.

35. *Waste Management Permits* (November 8, 1997) <http://www.dep.state .pa.us/dep/DEPUTATE/enved/_go_with_inspector/resource/Waste_Manage_Permit.htm.> (Penn. Dep't of Envtl. Protection Home Page). Once the applicant submits its application to the DEP, it must send a copy to the city. See 25

PENNSYLVANIA CODE § 271.141(d) (West 1997). City officials are then free to raise objections, or give their support, directly to the DEP. If, as in this case, local officials are in favor of a facility for economic reasons, the community's health and quality of life concerns are not likely to be raised or addressed in the decision-making process.

36. Russell, *Perpetrators*, supra. The resident's belief is based upon a Pennsylvania law that advises the state to hold a public hearing when, among other things, there is significant public interest in the permit application. The relevant section, however, is more permissive than mandatory. See 25 PENNSYLVANIA CODE § 271.143 (a) (West Supp. 1997) ("The Department may conduct public hearings for the purpose of receiving information on an application for a new permit . . . wherever there is significant public interest or the Department deems a hearing appropriate").

37. "Infectious wastes are those contaminated by disease producing microorganisms which may harm or threaten human health." *Chester Residents Concerned for Quality Living v. Department of Environmental Resources*, 655 A.2d 609, 610 (Pa. Commw. Ct.), *rev'd* 668 A.2d 110 (Pa. 1995).

38. Id. at 610. Of the 13,335 tons generated, approximately 5,800 tons per year are "incinerated or otherwise disposed [of]" at the sites where the waste is generated. Id. Thus, 7,755 tons per year are generated within the eastern zone and must be transported to a covered facility for disposal. Id.

39. See id. This figure assumes that "all of the infectious waste generated in the eastern zone were shipped to this single facility for incineration." Id.

40. The DEP found that the total quantity of infectious and chemotherapeutic wastes generated throughout all of Pennsylvania is 26,500 tons per year. See id. at 609.

41. See *Commonwealth v. Onda*, 103 A.2d 90, 91 (Pa. 1954) (citing Act of May 22, 1722, 1 Sm. L. 131, 17 P.S. § 41, and Act of June 16, 1836, P.L. 784 § 1, 17 P.S. § 41).

42. 42 PENNSYLVANIA CONSOLIDATED STATUTES ANNOTATED § 726 (West 1981).

[N]otwithstanding any other provision of law, the Supreme Court may, on its own motion or upon petition of any party, in any matter pending before any court or district justice of this Commonwealth involving an issue of immediate public importance, assume plenary jurisdiction of such matter at any stage thereof and enter a final order or otherwise cause right and justice to be done.

Id. See also *In re Petition of Blake*, 593 A.2d 1267 (Pa. 1991) (construing section 726 as an elaboration of the King's Bench powers); *Commonwealth v. Lang*, 537 A.2d 1361, 1363 n.1 (Pa. 1988) (same).

43. Bernard F. Scherer, *The Supreme Court of Pennsylvania and the Origins of King's Bench Power*, 32 DUQUESNE LAW REVIEW 525, 525–26 (1994).

44. See, e.g., Frank Reeves, *Special Power of State Court Challenged*, PITTS-BURGH POST-GAZETTE (July 23, 1995), at A1 (reporting on the House Judiciary Committee's plans to hold hearings on King's Bench power and Thermal Pure decision and noting that state representatives have questioned the power in the past).

45. Interview with Jerome Balter, attorney for CRCQL, in Philadelphia (December 3, 1996).

46. See *Chester Residents Concerned for Quality Living v. Department of Environmental Resources*, 668 A.2d 110 (Pa. 1995).

47. See Brian O'Neill, *Zappala Slips His Family Ties*, PITTSBURGH POST-GAZETTE (August 24, 1994), at C1 (noting Justice Zappala's admission that he bought securities in Russell, Rea & Zappala).

48. Russell, *Perpetrators*, supra.

49. See, e.g., Reeves, *Special Power of State Court Challenged*, supra ("It is another example of the exercise of the 'King's Bench' authority by the court for no apparent reason and where a member of the court, although he has recused himself, has an apparent familial interest in the case") (quoting Rep. Jeffrey Piccola of Dauphin County).

50. Many environmental justice advocates view struggles to stop the proliferation of hazardous waste sites as inherently political, not legal, problems. As Luke Cole points out, "because someone in the government has decided to allow a company to dump in their neighborhood," what is required to change that decision is a "political tool." Luke W. Cole, *Empowerment as the Key to Environmental Protection: The Need for Environmental Poverty Law*, ECOLOGY LAW QUARTERLY, 619, 648 (1992). As such, litigation and most legal strategies are viewed as vehicles for broader political organizing and community empowerment. See Luke W. Cole, *Remedies for Environmental Racism: A View From the Field*, 90 MICHIGAN LAW REVIEW 1991, 1995–97 (1992); see also Derrick A. Bell, Jr., *Serving Two Masters: Integration Ideals and Client Interests in School Desegregation Litigation* 85 YALE LAW JOURNAL 470, 513 (1976) ("Litigation can and should serve lawyer and client as a community-organizing tool, an educational forum, a means of obtaining data, a method of exercising political leverage, and a rallying point for public support").

51. See generally Luke W. Cole, *Environmental Justice Litigation: Another Stone in David's Sling*, 21 FORDHAM URBAN LAW JOURNAL 523 (1994).

52. See Robert Bullard, *Environmental Blackmail in Minority Communities*, in RACE AND THE INCIDENCE OF ENVIRONMENTAL HAZARDS: A TIME FOR DISCOURSE (Bunyan Bryant and Paul Mohai, eds., 1992), at 85–86, 90–91.

53. Kelley, *History of Chester*, supra; see also Hinds, *Pennsylvania City Hopes It's Bouncing Back from the Bottom*, supra (noting that "Republicans, who outnumber Democrats 2 to 1 in this predominantly black city, have controlled the government since 1866," and characterizing the recent Democratic victory as a "stunning upset," largely attributable to "a grass roots voter-registration drive").

54. Russell, *Perpetrators*, supra.

55. Russell, *Perpetrators*, supra.

56. The threat of lawsuits against active community members or groups, widely known as SLAPPS—Strategic Lawsuits Against Public Participation—has been reported as a growing phenomenon. See George W. Pring and Penelope Canan, SLAPPs: GETTING SUED FOR SPEAKING OUT (1996). This may or may not have been the motivation behind the Westinghouse threat. Nevertheless, the effect of the threat was to motivate the group into broadening its base.

57. See Monica Yant, *From One Man's Strength, a Choir Camp That Chops: Disciplining Voices and Character*, PHILADELPHIA INQUIRER (July 3, 1997), at A1 (describing a summer camp for the Chester Boys Choir that offers tai chi, karate, math and reading, and baseball and swimming classes).

58. In its denial letter, the DEP listed various reasons for denying of the waste permit. The DEP also denied Cherokee's application for an air permit. See *Cherokee Biotechnology Plant Defeated!* (February 1, 1998) <http://www.envirolink.org/orgs/pen/crcql/cherokee_goes_down.html> (CRCQL Web site) (summarizing the letter).

59. See Victoria Rivkin, *Chester Residents Achieve Environmental Victory: Unique Settlement for $320,000 Calls for Environmental Justice*, LEGAL INTELLIGENCER (December 24, 1997), at 5; see also Ramona Smith, *320G Fine Helps Fight Lead Paint*, PHILADELPHIA DAILY NEWS (December 19, 1997), at 28. DELCORA has denied any wrongdoing in the consent decree. Id.

60. 40 CFR § 735(b) (1997). There are obvious benefits to suing under the regulations, as opposed to the statute itself. The United States Supreme Court has ruled that a violation of the statute requires proof of discriminatory intent, whereas proof of discriminatory effect suffices to establish liability when the suit is brought to enforce regulations issued pursuant to the statute, rather than the statute itself. See *Guardians Association v. Civil Service Common of New York*, 463 U.S. 582, 591–93 (1983).

61. See *Chester Residents Concerned for Quality Living v. Seif*, 132 F.3d 925, 928 n.1 (3rd Cir. 1997), *cert. granted*, 118 S.Ct. 2296 (U.S. June 8, 1998), *vacated and remanded*, 1998 WESTLAW 477242 (U.S. August 17, 1998)

62. See, e.g., Dan Hardy, *Chester Mayor Says Council Is Usurping Power*, PHILADELPHIA INQUIRER (July 8, 1992), at B1 (reporting that the Democractic mayor, Barbara Bohannan-Sheppard, sued four City Council colleagues and the

city solicitor, contending they usurped her powers to manage her own administration). Dan Hardy, *Council Coalition Keeps Chester Mayor on Outside*,
PHILADELPHIA INQUIRER (April 30, 1992), at B4 (reporting that the City Council intensified its assault on the Democratic Mayor, stripping her of much of her
staff and filling council vacancies with Republicans; this move was the latest in
the escalating conflict between the Mayor and the City Council—struggle that
virtually paralyzed city government).

63. Demonstrators described the protest as "unorthodox." According to its
participants, the number of protesters never exceeded twenty individuals, and
the demonstration was staged in an industrial park far from regular traffic.
CRCQL and C4 members marched on the street in front of the Authority's offices, demanded a meeting with SWA to discuss waste shipments to Chester, and
probably were noticed only by the Waste Authority personnel. Barely an hour
passed before SWA officials met with the protesters. They agreed to meet later in
the month to discuss the Chester residents' concerns. At this meeting, CRCQL
presented SWA with a record of Westinghouse's emission violations. SWA expressed genuine surprise at the long list of transgressions, which included the
emission of some pollutants at levels exceeding what is deemed safe for the surrounding community. See Andy Murray, *Chester Residents and Supporters Protest
In Delaware* (November 9, 1997) <http://www.envirolink.org/orgs/seac13/
c4/dswa.html> (C4 Web page) (on file with author); Green Delware, *Urgent
Action! Delaware Solid Waste Authority Votes to Continue Burning Delaware
Garbage In Chester, PA*, News Release (May 1, 1997), at 1–2.

64. Mendel-Reyes, RECLAIMING DEMOCRACY, supra, at 158 (citation omitted).

Notes to Chapter 3

1. Commission for Racial Justice (United Church of Christ), TOXIC WASTES
AND RACE IN THE UNITED STATES xii (1987). The UCC study defines "hazardous
wastes" as the term is used by the EPA: as "by-products of industrial production
which present particularly troublesome health and environmental problems." Id.
The study goes on to explain that

> [n]ewly generated hazardous wastes must be managed in an approved "fa-
> cility," which is defined by the EPA as any land structures thereon which
> are used for treating, storing or disposing of hazardous wastes (TSD facil-
> ity). Such facilities may include landfills, surface impoundments or incin-
> erators. A "commercial" facility is defined as any facility (public or private)
> which accepts hazardous wastes from a third party for a fee or other re-
> muneration.

Id. The term "uncontrolled toxic waste sites" refers to closed and abandoned sites on the EPA's list of sites that pose a present and potential threat to human health and the environment. As of 1985, the EPA inventoried approximately 200 uncontrolled toxic wastes sites across the nation. See id.

2. These areas included Memphis, Tenn. (173 sites), St. Louis, Mo. (160 sites), Houston, Tex. (152 sites), Cleveland, Ohio (106 sites), Chicago, Ill. (103 sites), and Atlanta, Ga. (91 sites). Id.

3. See, e.g., Vicki Been, *Coming to the Nuisance or Going to the Barrios? A Longitudinal Analysis of Environmental Justice Claims*, 24 ECOLOGY LAW QUARTERLY 1 (1997) (finding in a nationwide study that commercial hazardous waste treatment facilities sited between 1970 and 1990 were sited in areas disproportionately populated by lower-income Hispanics, but finding no evidence that these facilities were sited in disproportionately African American areas or in areas with high concentrations of the poor). Some regional studies also report results that vary by ethnic group. See, e.g., Brett Baden and Don Coursey, THE LOCALITY OF WASTE SITES WITHIN THE CITY OF CHICAGO: A DEMOGRAPHIC, SOCIAL AND ECONOMIC ANALYSIS (Irving B. Harris Graduate School of Public Policy Studies Working Paper Series 97-2, 1997) (finding that, in 1990, waste sites tended to be located in low population density areas near commercial waterways and commercial highways, that more African Americans do appear to live in proximity to historical solid waste disposal sites, that there is no evidence that African Americans live in areas with higher concentrations of hazardous waste than whites or Hispanics, and that the percentage of Hispanics in an area is significant in describing the location of waste sites); Douglas L. Anderton et al., *Hazardous Waste Facilities: "Environmental Equity" Issues in Metropolitan Areas*, 18 EVALUATION REVIEW, 123–40 (April 1994) (finding no racial disparity in the location of commercial hazardous waste facilities, using the 1990 census). The Anderton study was funded by the world's largest waste management firm, WMX Technologies, Inc.

4. See, e.g., Benjamin A. Goldman and Laura Fitton, TOXIC WASTE AND RACE REVISITED: AN UPDATE OF THE 1987 REPORT ON THE RACIAL AND SOCIOECONOMIC CHARACTERISTICS OF COMMUNITIES WITH HAZARDOUS WASTE SITES I (Center for Policy Alternatives, NAACP, United Church of Christ Commission for Racial Justice, 1994). Id. at 2 (finding statistical significance at the 0.001 level, which means that the probability that the observed change is merely a random fluctuation is less than one in a thousand). No similar pronounced disparities by socioeconomic status were discovered, though the researchers indicated that the data were not examined with the same detail as in the original 1987 study. Id. at 5 (also noting that sixty-three out of sixty-four of most recent studies continue to document racial disparities in the location of noxious facilities, toxic releases and exposures, ambient levels of air pollution, and environmental health effects).

"People of color" includes the total population less non-Hispanic whites. The demographics of the zip code areas, including socioeconomic status, are taken from the 1990 census. Id.

5. Id. at 17 (but also noting that "no matter what the causes, the distribution of these facilities shows how some of the most hazardous inefficiencies of our economy can also pose significant social inequities").

6. Anderton et al., *Hazardous Waste Facilities,* supra; Douglas L. Anderton et al., *Environmental Equity: The Demographics of Dumping,* 31 DEMOGRAPHY 229 (1994) (results using 1980 census data); Andy B. Anderson et al., *Environmental Equity: Evaluating TSDF Siting over the Past Two Decades,* WASTE AGE 83–100 (July 1994).

7. SADRI researchers reasoned that only tracts in the same metropolitan or rural county as a facility could serve as possible alternative sites for the same market. See Andy B. Anderson et al., *Evaluating TSDF Siting,* supra, at 92, 96, 100. For an effective rebuttal of this argument, see Vicki Been, *Analyzing Evidence of Environmental Justice,* 11 JOURNAL OF LAND USE & ENVIRONMENTAL LAW 1, 12–13 (1995) (demonstrating that limiting analysis of census data to metropolitan areas or rural counties that have at least one facility reduces the differences in the ethnic and racial composition of host and nonhost tracts) and Been, *Coming to the Nuisance or Going to the Barrios?* supra, at 15–17 (arguing that the effect of SADRI's limitation reduced the differences between the racial and ethnic composition of host and nonhost tracts).

8. Been, *Coming to the Nuisance or Going to the Barrios?* supra. Been attributes her results, which differ compared to those of the SADRI study, to the fact that the SADRI study "did not control for density." Id. at 34.

9. See, e.g., Marianne Lavelle and Marcia Coyle, *Unequal Protection: The Racial Divide in Environmental Law,* NATIONAL LAW JOURNAL (September 21, 1992), at S1, S2 (concluding that there is a racial disparity in the way the U.S. government cleans up toxic waste sites and punishes polluters). The *National Law Journal* study is not without its critics. See Mary Bryant, *Unequal Justice? Lies, Damn Lies, and Statistics Revisited,* SONREEL (American Bar Association Section of Natural Resources, Energy, and Environmental Law) NEWS (September–October 1993), at 3 (critiquing the NLJ study for not defining key terms, not disclosing sample sizes, not disclosing the size of studied communities, and not adjusting the data for time).

10. The concept of "baselines" belongs to Cass Sunstein. See Cass Sunstein, THE PARTIAL CONSTITUTION 3–4 (1993) (when the state chooses "status quo neutrality," in taking existing social practices and distributions as its baseline for being neutral toward public and private actors, it produces injustice).

11. See Environmental Equity Workgroup, U.S. Environmental Protection

Agency, EPA 230-R-92-008, ENVIRONMENTAL EQUITY: REDUCING RISK FOR ALL
COMMUNITIES, WORKGROUP REPORT TO THE ADMINISTRATOR 1 (1992).

12. When it is available to them, people of color have a more difficult time
getting adequate medical care than do whites. U.S. General Accounting Office,
GAO/PEMD-92-6, Hispanic Access to Health Care: Significant Gaps Exist 10
(1992) (reporting that 33 percent of Latinos had neither private nor public medical insurance in 1989, compared with 19 percent of blacks and 12 percent of
whites); Cassandra Q. Butts, *The Color of Money: Barriers to Access to Private
Health Care Facilities for African-Americans*, 26 CLEARINGHOUSE REVIEW 159,
160 n. 5, 161–62 (1992); Marilyn Yaquinto, *Latinos Cited as Having Least Medical Coverage*, LOS ANGELES TIMES (February 19, 1992), at A5; Stephanie Pol-
lack and JoAnn Grozuczak, REAGAN, TOXICS & MINORITIES 2 (1984) (Policy Report for the Urban Environment Conference, Inc.) (noting that one in six and
one-half black families had trouble getting medical care in 1982, as compared to
one in eleven white families). As Cassandra Butts notes, African Americans in
both urban and rural areas are more likely than whites to face geographic barriers to health care and health care providers, and a disproportionate share of hospital closings affect African Americans, with "the likelihood of closures . . . directly related to the percentage of African-Americans in the population of a city."
Butts, *The Color of Money*, supra. The problem is particularly acute for undocumented Latino farm-workers, who are concentrated in low-paying, high-risk
jobs and who are prohibited by law from receiving most government health benefits. See Peter L. Reich, *Jurisprudential Tradition and Undocumented Alien
Entitlements*, 6 GEORGETOWN IMMIGRATION LAW JOURNAL 1 (1992); Peter L.
Reich, *Public Benefits for Undocumented Aliens: State Law into the Breach Once
More*, 21 NEW MEXICO LAW REVIEW 219, 220–23 (1991); Susan B. Drake, *Immigrants' Right to Health Care*, 20 CLEARINGHOUSE REVIEW 498, 503–4 (1986);
U.S. General Accounting Office, GAO/HRD-92-46, HIRED FARMWORKERS:
HEALTH AND WELL-BEING AT RISK 3, 24–25 (1992). Additionally, doctors who
treat poor people, people of color, and rural residents also often have fewer re-
sources at their disposal and therefore less to offer those patients. Diana B. Dut-
ton, *Children's Health Care: The Myth of Equal Access*, in IV BETTER HEALTH FOR
OUR CHILDREN: A NATIONAL STRATEGY 375 (U.S. Department of Health &
Human Services, ed., 1981).

13. See Beverly H. Wright, *Effects of Occupational Injury, Illness, and Disease
on the Health Status of Black Americans: A Review*, in RACE AND THE INCIDENCE
OF ENVIRONMENTAL HAZARDS: A TIME FOR DISCOURSE (Bunyan Bryant and Paul
Mohai, eds., 1992), at 118 (explaining "victim blaming").

14. Vicki Been, *What's Fairness Got to Do with It? Environmental Justice and
the Siting of Locally Undesirable Land Uses*, 78 CORNELL LAW REVIEW 1001,

1016 (1993); see also Vicki Been, *Locally Undesirable Land Uses in Minority Neighborhoods: Disproportionate Siting or Market Dynamics*, 103 YALE LAW JOURNAL 1383, 1389 (1994). See also Thomas Lambert and Christopher Boerner, *Environmental Inequity: Economic Causes, Economic Solutions*, 14 YALE JOURNAL ON REGULATION 195, 202 (1997); Lynn Blais, *Environmental Racism Reconsidered*, 74 NORTH CAROLINA LAW REVIEW 75, 93 (1996).

15. Been, *Locally Undesirable Land Uses*, supra, at 1388–89.

16. See also Lambert and Boerner, *Environmental Inequity*, supra, at 206, 212 (finding that their analysis supports the theory that "minority and poor [individuals] voluntarily move into areas surrounding industrial and waste sites" in St. Louis).

17. In fact, a chief proponent of such theories has proved the opposite proposition through her empirical research: that market dynamics do *not* lead people of color to "come to the nuisance." See, e.g., Been, *Coming to the Nuisance or Going to the Barrios?* supra (finding that the areas surrounding commercial hazardous waste treatment facilities currently are disproportionately populated by lower-income Hispanics, and finding no evidence that these communities became poorer or increased in minority population after the waste facilities were sited); Been, *Locally Undesirable Land Uses in Minority Neighborhoods*, supra, at 1398–1400 (finding that the southeastern waste sites studied by the U.S. General Accounting Office in 1983 were all in communities that originally had both high levels of poverty and predominantly African American populations; finding that these communities did not become poorer or increase in African American percentage of population after the waste facilities were sited). But see Been, *Locally Undesirable Land Uses in Minority Neighborhoods*, supra, at 1400–1406 (finding that Houston waste sites studied in 1983 by Professor Robert Bullard were originally sited in disproportionately in African American communities, but that the communities did not originally have disproportionately low incomes; however, the percentage of African Americans rose and incomes fell after the solid waste facilities were sited); Lambert and Boerner, *Environmental Inequity*, supra, at 206–7 (finding a disproportionate increase of poor and minority individuals around waste sites in St. Louis between 1970 and 1990); Anderton, et al., *Hazardous Waste Facilities*, supra, at 135 (finding evidence of economic decline in communities with commercial hazardous waste facilities but no evidence of "white flight").

18. Been, *Locally Undesirable Land Uses*, supra, at 1389 (emphasis added); see also Lambert and Boerner, *Environmental Inequity*, supra, at 200–202.

19. See, e.g., Cass Sunstein, FREE MARKETS AND SOCIAL JUSTICE 13–31 (1997).

20. Been, *Locally Undesirable Land Uses*, supra, at 1389; Lambert and

Boerner, *Environmental Inequity*, supra, at 212 (finding that their analysis supports the theory that "minority and poor [individuals] voluntarily move into areas surrounding industrial and waste sites" in the St. Louis area but cautioning that "the conclusions drawn from this study may provide an incomplete picture of environmental justice" and that "other forms of racial discrimination may have been a factor influencing the subsequent migration of these residents to communities hosting polluting facilities"); Blais, *Environmental Racism*, supra, at 141. See also Douglas S. Massey and Nancy A. Denton, AMERICAN APARTHEID: SEGREGATION AND THE MAKING OF THE UNDERCLASS 114 (1993) (finding that "race is the dominant organizing principle" for "housing and residential patterns").

21. Been, *Locally Undesirable Land Uses*, supra, at 1389. See also Massey and Denton, AMERICAN APARTHEID, supra, at 114 (describing the various types of "exclusionary tactics" used by realtors to limit the likelihood of black entry into white neighborhoods and to channel black demand for housing into areas that are within or near existing ghettos; detailing the "white prejudice" that accompanies the movement of blacks into certain neighborhoods, making the area unattractive to further white settlement, and leading to "white flight"; and the pervasive discrimination in the allocation of mortgages and home improvement loans).

22. Regina Austin and Michael Schill, *Black, Brown, Poor and Poisoned: Minority Grassroots Environmentalism and the Quest for Eco-Justice*, 1 KANSAS JOURNAL OF LAW AND PUBLIC POLICY 69, 69–70 (1991).

23. Gerald Torres, *Understanding Environmental Racism*, 63 UNIVERSITY OF COLORADO LAW REVIEW 839 (1992).

24. *Washington v. Davis*, 426 U.S. 229 (1976) (adopting intent/purpose requirement as a prerequisite to proving race discrimination in equal protection jurisprudence).

25. See Alan D. Freeman, *Legitimizing Racial Discrimination through Antidiscrimination Law: A Critical Review of Supreme Court Doctrine*, 63 MINNESOTA LAW REVIEW 1049, 1052–57 (1978); Charles R. Lawrence III, *The Id, the Ego, and Equal Protection: Reckoning with Unconscious Racism*, 39 STANFORD LAW REVIEW 317, 318–19 (1987); Luke W. Cole, *Empowerment as the Key to Environmental Protection: The Need for Environmental Poverty Law*, 19 ECOLOGY LAW REVIEW 619, 642 (1992).

26. 768 F.Supp. 1144, 1149 (E.D. Va. 1991), *aff'd*, 977 F.2d 573 (4th Cir. 1992).

27. Id. at 1150. See also *Bean v. Southwestern Waste Management Corp.*, 482 F.Supp. 673 (S.D. Tex. 1979), *aff'd without op.*, 782 F.2d 1038 (5th Cir. 1986); (denying environmental racism claim for lack of discriminatory intent); *East Bibb*

Twiggs Neighborhood Assn. v. Macon-Bibb County Planning and Zoning Comm'n 706 F.Supp. 880 (M.D. Ga.), *aff'd* 896 F.2d 1264 (11th Cir.), *opinion replaced by* 846 F.2d 1264 (11th Cir. 1989) (same).

28. Lawrence, *The Id, the Ego, and Equal Protection,* supra at 322.

29. See Sheila Foster, *Intent and Incoherence,* 72 TULANE LAW REVIEW 1065 (1998).

30. Cole, *Empowerment as the Key to Environmental Protection,* supra at 648; Luke W. Cole, *Environmental Justice Litigation: Another Stone in David's Sling,* 21 FORDHAM URBAN LAW JOURNAL 523, 524 (1994); Luke W. Cole, *Remedies for Environmental Racism: A View from the Field,* 90 MICHIGAN LAW REVIEW 1991, 1997 (1992).

31. See, e.g., Michael Gelobter, *Toward a Model of "Environmental Discrimination,"* in RACE AND THE INCIDENCE OF ENVIRONMENTAL HAZARDS: A TIME FOR DISCOURSE (Bunyan Bryant and Paul Mohai, eds., 1992), at 76–80.

32. Presumably, market dynamics adherents would agree with this normative analysis. See Been, *Locally Undesirable Land Uses in Minority Neighborhoods,* supra, at 1391 n. 30 (noting that "[i]f market forces at issue are based on discrimination, i.e., if host neighborhoods became predominantly minority after the [facility] was sited because racial discrimination in the housing market relegated people of color to those neighborhoods, siting practices might have to change to account for persistent discrimination in the housing market").

33. Massey and Denton, AMERICAN APARTHEID, supra, at 1–16, 17–60.

34. Richard Ford, *The Boundaries of Race: Political Geography in Legal Analysis,* 107 HARVARD LAW REVIEW 1841, 1847–54 (1994).

35. Massey and Denton, AMERICAN APARTHEID, supra, at 83–114.

36. According to one study, among neighborhoods located within five miles of an established black neighborhood, white population loss is extremely likely, and this loss becomes virtually certain as the percentage of blacks increase. This pattern holds true for suburbs as well as for central cities. The probability that a central city tract located within five miles of a black neighborhood would lose white residents was .85 when its black percentage was 0%–5%; it rose to .92 when the black percentage reached 30%–40%. Massey and Denton, AMERICAN APARTHEID, supra, at 80. See also id. at 74, 113–14 (comparing the segregation of Caribbean Latinos with that of blacks and concluding that the average level of segregation increases steadily as one moves from being identified as white Hispanics, to mixed-race Hispanic to black Hispanic, the last having an "index" of segregation comparable to that for African Americans).

37. Ford, *Boundaries of Race,* supra, at 1857.

38. Id. at 1854.

39. Massey and Denton, AMERICAN APARTHEID, supra, at 114, 96–109.

40. Yale Rabin, *Expulsive Zoning: The Inequitable Legacy of* Euclid, in ZONING AND THE AMERICAN DREAM 101 (Charles M. Haar and Jerold S. Kayden, eds., 1990).

41. Massey and Denton, AMERICAN APARTHEID, supra, 118–30, Ford; *Boundaries of Race*, supra, at 1851–52.

42. John Calmore, *Racialized Space and the Culture of Segregation: "Hewing a Stone of Hope from a Mountain of Despair,"* 143 UNIVERSITY OF PENNSYLVANIA LAW REVIEW 1233, 1235 (1995).

43. Susan J. Smith, *Residential Segregation and the Politics of Racialization*, in RACISM, THE CITY, AND THE STATE 128, 133 (Malcolm Cross and Michael Keith, eds., 1993).

44. William Julius Wilson, WHEN WORK DISAPPEARS: THE WORLD OF THE NEW URBAN POOR 51–86 (1996). Wilson writes that social isolation deprives inner-city residents not only of conventional role models but also of the social resources provided by mainstream social networks that facilitate social and economic advancement in a modern industrial society; social isolation also contributes to the formation and crystallization of ghetto-related cultural traits and behaviors.

45. Margaret Weir, *From Equal Opportunity to the New Social Contract*, in RACISM, THE CITY, AND THE STATE (Malcolm Cross and Michael Keith, eds., 1993), 104; see also Wilson, WHEN WORK DISAPPEARS, supra, at 184–85 ("[t]he growing suburbanization of the population influences the extent to which national politicians will support increased federal aid to large cities and the poor . . . we can associate the sharp drop in federal support for basic urban programs since 1980 with the declining political influence of cities and the rising influence of electoral coalitions in the suburbs").

46. Sunstein, THE PARTIAL CONSTITUTION, supra, at 3–4 (when the state chooses "status quo neutrality," in taking existing social practices and distributions as its baseline for being neutral toward public and private actors, it produces injustice); see also Ford, *Boundaries of Race*, supra, at 1852 (making similar point in the context of housing segregation).

47. Public opposition, and often direct protest, is considered by industry to be the "greatest single obstacle to the successful siting of" hazardous facilities, with middle and upper socioeconomic groups possessing greater resources to effectuate their opposition. Cerrell Associates, POLITICAL DIFFICULTIES FACING WASTE-TO-ENERGY CONVERSION PLANT SITING 43 (1984) (prepared for the California Waste Management Board) (counseling that "middle and higher socioeconomic strata neighborhoods should not fall within the one-mile and five-mile radius of the proposed site"); Richard Lazarus, *Pursuing "Environmental Justice": The Distributional Effects of Environmental Protection*, 87 NORTHWESTERN

UNIVERSITY LAW REVIEW 787, 806 (1993) (noting that few proposals survive the public review that often accompanies the announcement of the recommended siting of a hazardous waste facility).

48. Joan Bernstein, *The Siting of Commercial Waste Facilities: An Evolution of Community Land Use Decisions*, 1 KANSAS JOURNAL OF LAW & PUBLIC POLICY 83 (1991)(waste companies look for cheap land); Michael B. Gerrard, WHOSE BACKYARD, WHOSE RISK: FEAR AND FAIRNESS IN TOXIC NUCLEAR WASTE SITING 47 (1994); Paul Mohai and Bunyan Bryant, *Race, Poverty, and the Distribution of Environmental Hazards: Reviewing the Evidence*, in RACE, POVERTY, AND THE ENVIRONMENT (Fall 1991–Winter 1992), at 24.

49. Cerrell Associates, POLITICAL DIFFICULTIES, supra, at 65 (noting that "older, conservative, and lower socioeconomic neighborhoods" are least likely to resist sitings).

50. Bernstein, *The Siting of Commercial Waste Facilities*, supra.

51. Cerrell Associates, POLITICAL DIFFICULTIES, supra, at 29.

52. See Rabin, *Expulsive Zoning*, supra, at 101–2. "Such patterns, once established, are difficult to alter. Locally Unwanted Land Uses (LULUs) result in depressed residential property values which, in turn, reduce the municipal tax base and discourage other upscale development which would help boost property values." Jason Wilson, *Environmental Inequity: Which Came First, Poverty or Pollution*, NEW JERSEY REPORTER 40 (March/April 1997).

53. Conner Bailey and Charles E. Faupel, *Environmentalism and Civil Rights in Sumter County, Alabama*, in RACE AND THE INCIDENCE OF ENVIRONMENTAL HAZARDS: A TIME FOR DISCOURSE 140 (Bunyan Bryant and Paul Mohai, eds., 1992) (noting that "among Alabama's 67 counties, the ten with the lowest population densities also have average per capita incomes well below the state average" and noting that blacks are a majority in six of ten Alabama counties with the lowest population densities and lower than average per capita income); Gerrard, WHOSE BACKYARD, WHOSE RISK, supra (noting that "most of the anecdotes and much of the data concerning discriminatory siting come from the southeastern United States . . . [and that] is a region where, for obvious historical reasons, rural areas have large black populations; in the northeast, where the rural areas are mostly white, most proposed sites have been in white areas").

54. *African Americans for Environmental Justice v. Mississippi Department of Environmental Quality*, No. 1R-93-R4 (filed Sept. 24, 1993) (study of Mississippi's siting process revealed that population density in Mississippi was directly inversely correlated with race so that the less dense, the more African American an area was, leading to siting in only black areas). See also Luke W. Cole, *Civil Rights, Environmental Justice, and the EPA: The Brief History of Administrative*

Complaints under Title VI of the Civil Rights Act of 1964, 9 JOURNAL OF ENVI-RONMENTAL LAW AND LITIGATION 309, 345 (1994).

55. See, e.g., *North Carolina Department of Transportation v. Crest Street Community Council, Inc.,* 479 U.S. 6 (1986) (freeway through African American neighborhood fought on civil rights grounds); *Coalition of Concerned Citizens against I-670 v. Damian,* 608 F.Supp. 110 (S.D. Ohio 1984) (same); *Clean Air Alternatives Coalition v. United States Department of Transportation,* No. C-93-0721-VRW (N.D. Cal. filed March 2, 1993) (same).

56. *In the Matter of Louisiana Energy Services, L.P.,* Decision of the Nuclear Regulatory Commission Atomic Safety and Licensing Board, LBP-97-8, 45 NRC 367, 390–92 (May 1, 1997). On appeal, NRC Commissioners reversed the Board's requirement of an inquiry into racial discrimination in the siting process. It based its reversal on the Board's failure to find that intentional racism had tainted the decisional process and the Board's failure to make clear the legal basis for its decision to order an investigation of possible racism in the section of the site. *In the Matter of Louisiana Energy Services,* Decision of the Nuclear Regulatory Commission, CLI-98-3 (April 3, 1998).

57. RCRA allows states to establish solid and hazardous waste programs that are more restrictive than the federal minimum. 42 U.S.C. 6902 (b), 6929. RCRA explicitly acknowledges that "the collection of solid wastes should continue to be primarily the function of State, regional and local agencies." Id. at 1002(a)(4). See also Celeste P. Duffy, *State Hazardous Waste Facility Siting: Easing the Process through Local Cooperation and Preemption,* 11 BOSTON COLLEGE ENVIRONMENTAL AFFAIRS LAW REVIEW 755, 757–58, 766–67 (1984); Rodolfo Mata, *Hazardous Waste Facilities and Environmental Equity: A Proposed Siting Model,* 13 VIRGINIA ENVIRONMENTAL LAW REVIEW 375, 395–400 (1994).

58. U.S. Environmental Protection Agency, SW-865, HAZARDOUS WASTE FACILITY SITING: A CRITICAL PROBLEM 7 (1980).

59. See, e.g., Andrew Szasz, ECOPOPULISM: TOXIC WASTE AND THE MOVEMENT FOR ENVIRONMENTAL JUSTICE 183 n. 26 (1994) (describing as "passive" approach); Duffy, *State Hazardous Waste Facility Siting,* supra, 755, 766–769 (describing as "ad hoc" approach); see also Rachel D. Godsil, *Remedying Environmental Racism,* 90 MICHIGAN LAW REVIEW 394, 403–4 (1991) (describing approach as "super review"). See generally Sheila Foster, *Impact Assessment,* in THE LAW OF ENVIRONMENTAL JUSTICE: THEORIES AND PROCEDURES TO ADDRESS DISPROPORTIONATE RISKS 256, 285–89 (Michael B. Gerrard, ed., 1999) (reviewing state siting processes).

60. See generally A. Dan Tarlock, *State versus Local Control of Hazardous Waste Facility Siting: Who Decides in Whose Backyard?* in RESOLVING LOCATIONAL CONFLICT 137, 148–50 (Robert W. Lake, ed., 1987).

61. See, e.g., ALABAMA CODE § 22-30-5.1(d) (1990) (requiring selection committee to consider and include in its written report the "social and economic impacts of the proposed facility on the affected community, including changes in property values, community perception and other costs"); KENTUCKY REVISED STATUTE ANNOTATED § 244.855(1)(c) (Michie 1995) (requiring agency to consider "social and economic impacts of the proposed facility" on the "affected community," including "changes in property values, community perceptions and other psychic costs"); MARYLAND ENVIRONMENTAL CODE ANNOTATED 7-402 (1997) (providing that hazardous waste facilities be subject to "due consideration" of the "equitable geographic distribution of sites" and that consideration be given to those "subdivisions that presently have sites" and avoiding "to the extent feasible" siting additional facilities "disproportionately in any one subdivision"); MISSISSIPPI CODE ANNOTATED 17-18-15 (1997) (requiring consideration of "socioeconomic factors," which include but are not limited to "impact on local land uses, property values and governmental services"); NORTH CAROLINA GENERAL STATUTE § 160A-325 (a) (1996) (requiring considerations of "socioeconomic and demographic data" in selecting or approving a site for a new sanitary landfill that is located within one mile of an existing sanitary landfill). Some proposed legislation contains similar soft criteria. See also H.B. 518, 90th Leg., 1st Sess. § 15 (Ill. 1997) (requiring a community impact statement "written in plain language and limiting the use of technical terms" to provide information about, among other things, "the presence of any other existing toxic chemical facilities and hazardous waste sites in the affected community"); H.B. 2103, 1st Sess. § 7 (1997 Tex.) (requiring consideration of "cumulative risks," including the combined level of noise, odor, and other impacts, in an administrative proceeding involving the siting or expansion of operation of a facility in an area where other facilities are located).

62. See, e.g., CALIFORNIA PUBLIC RESOURCE CODE § 21151.1 (1997) (specifically subjecting hazardous waste facility permits to environmental impact statement requirement) and CALIFORNIA CODE OF REGULATIONS § 15131 (1997) (requiring consideration of social and economic impacts); LOUISIANA REVISED STATUTES § 30:2018 (1998) (requiring environmental assessment statement for new permits; requiring consideration of social and economic benefits of the facility); CODE MASSACHUSETTS § 11.25 (1997) (requiring environmental impact report for certain facilities); MINNESOTA STATUTE ANNOTATED §§ 115A.194 (1997) (requiring environmental impact statement before issuing permit for hazardous waste facility) and 116D.04 (requiring analysis of economic, employment, and sociological impacts in environmental impact statement); NEW YORK CODE OF RULES AND REGULATIONS § 361.3 (requiring application for permit to contain a draft environmental impact statement).

63. See, e.g., ALABAMA CODE ANNOTATED 22-30-5.1 (providing that no more than one commercial hazardous waste facility or disposal site shall be situated within any one county of the state); ARKANSAS CODE ANNOTATED § 8-6-1501 (Michie 1993) (creating a rebuttable presumption against permitting a "high impact solid waste management facility" within twelve miles of any other existing "high impact solid waste management facility"); GEORGIA CODE ANNOTATED § 12-8-25.4 (Harrison 1996) (prohibiting the permitting of any solid waste handling facility within an area that already includes all or a portion of three or more landfills in a two-mile radius); WISCONSIN STATUTE ANNOTATED 289.29 (1997) (prohibiting siting of a solid waste facility in a "3rd class city" if two or more approved solid waste facilities are in operation in that city).

When choosing potential sites under the far less common active approach to siting, state regulations suffer from a similar myopia. Some states mandate consideration of equitable geographic distribution. See MARYLAND ENVIRONMENTAL CODE ANNOTATED § 7-402 (1997) (providing for "due consideration" of the "equitable geographic distribution of sites" and that consideration be given to those "subdivisions that presently have sites" and avoiding "to the extent feasible" siting additional facilities "disproportionately in any one subdivision"). Other states proclaim a preference for locating hazardous waste sites in industrial areas, ensuring that high impact land uses are clustered in certain neighborhoods. UTAH CODE ANNOTATED § 19-6-205 (1997).

64. While ostensibly designed to identify significant environmental impacts, the environmental review process is only as good as the government agency conducting it. Across the country, agencies have failed to consider certain impacts or communities as a result of incompetence or design. Luke W. Cole, *Macho Law Brains, Public Citizens, and Grassroots Activists: Three Models of Environmental Advocacy*, 14 VIRGINIA ENVIRONMENTAL LAW JOURNAL 687, 701 (1995).

Sharon Carr Harrington notes the inaccuracy of the Environmental Impact Statement for a Louisiana Energy Services uranium enrichment facility located between two historical African American communities near Homer, Louisiana:

The draft EIS failed to consider any impact of the facility on Forest Grove and Center Springs—the communities closest to the proposed site. In fact, neither of the communities appear on any of the numerous maps included in the 400-page document although more distant, predominantly white communities of similar size are noted.

Sharon Carr Harrington, *Fighting Toxics on the Bayou*, RACE, POVERTY & THE ENVIRONMENT (Fall 1994–Winter 1995), at 48, 49. The plaintiffs made the same observation in *Residents of Sanborn Court, et al. v. California Department of Toxic Substances Control*, No. 95CS01074 (Sacramento Sup. Ct., May 5, 1995).

In this case, the State of California prepared environmental review documents for a toxic waste treatment facility just one block from a complex that housed Latino farm-workers and more than seventy children:

> Remarkably, the Initial Study failed to mention that there was a substantial concentration of people living very close to the proposed toxic facility. The site map included in the Initial Study showed the neighborhood surrounding the toxic plant, and conveniently stopped across the street from the Sanborn Court residential complex.

Plaintiffs' Memorandum of Points and Authorities in Support of Petition for Writ of Mandate.

65. For instance, Mississippi grants a volunteer host community $1 million after a commercial hazardous waste facility is permitted and construction has commenced. The community may also negotiate with the state environmental agency for a percentage of annual gross receipts from the facility, as well as a host of other incentives (e.g., education and outreach programs). MISSISSIPPI CODE ANNOTATED 17-18-37 (1997). But see Robert Bullard, *Environmental Blackmail in Minority Communities*, in RACE AND THE INCIDENCE OF ENVIRONMENTAL HAZARDS: A TIME FOR DISCOURSE 83–84 (Bunyan Bryant and Paul Mohai, eds., 1992) (explaining that minority communities are often vulnerable to economic inducements and may minimize their opposition to sitings whose risks might outweigh their benefits because these communities are beset by rising unemployment, extreme poverty, a shrinking tax base, and decaying business infrastructure).

66. The following material was drawn from many sources. For general information about Cancer Alley and the Shintech dispute, see M. Kirz, *Environment: The Color of Poison*, NATIONAL LAW JOURNAL (July 11, 1998); OCR, EPA, TITLE VI ADMINISTRATIVE COMPLAINT RE: LOUISIANA DEP'T OF ENV'T QUALITY/PERMIT FOR PROPOSED SHINTECH FACILITY 20–21 (EPA File No. 4R-97-R6).

67. *NAACP v. Engler*, Case No. 95-38228-CV, Genesee County Circuit Court, May 29, 1997, at 45.

68. See Robert A. Dahl, DEMOCRACY AND ITS CRITICS 163–75 (1989) (arguing that certain rights, goods, and interests are integral to a legitimate democratic process).

Notes to Chapter 4

1. California Health & Safety Code §25199(a)(3).

2. See also Luke W. Cole, *Environmental Justice and the Three Great Myths of White Americana*, 3 HASTINGS WEST-NORTHWEST JOURNAL OF ENVIRONMENTAL LAW AND POLICY 449, 450–54 (1996). The myth described by Solorio-Garcia,

that the "government is on our side," is widely held in white communities, but sometimes surfaces in communities of color as well. Id. at 452–54.

3. The community group El Pueblo para el Aire y Agua Limpio filed suit in February 1991, charging that the EIR and the process used to develop it were inadequate under California law. In December 1991, Judge Jeffrey Gunther of the Sacramento Superior Court found the EIR did not adequately examine cumulative and agricultural impacts of the project and that the people of Kettleman City had not been "meaningfully included" in the environmental review process, as required by California law. *El Pueblo para el Aire y Agua Limpio v. County of Kings*, Sacramento Superior Court, Civ. No. 366045, Ruling on Submitted Matter, December 30, 1991.

4. This reconception of power relations is well described in Steven Winter, *The "Power" Thing*, 82 VIRGINIA LAW REVIEW 721, 835 (1996):

> To understand power as a property of a social system of relations is to see power as a shared resource that can be activated from many different positions within that system. Once power is understood as relational, it becomes apparent that at least some of what the dominant "have" must already be available to the subordinated. Indeed, there is an important sense in which this second point is the same as the first. The deconstruction of power is also the deconstruction of the agency and autonomy of the traditional liberal subject. This means that responsibility for subordination and inequality cannot be localized in certain identifiable agents; it is widely distributed throughout the social network. To the exact degree that this understanding of power diminishes the agency of the dominant, it amplifies the agency of the subordinated. What it subtracts from one part of the network, it necessarily redistributes to the other.

5. Transcript of Kern County Board of Supervisors meeting, December 12, 1994, at 193.

6. *El Pueblo para el Aire y Agua Limpio v. County of Kings*, 22 ENVIRONMENTAL LAW REPORTER (Environmental Law Institute) 20,357.

7. See Luke W. Cole, *Empowerment as the Key to Environmental Protection: The Need for Environmental Poverty Law*, 19 ECOLOGY LAW QUARTERLY 619, 674–79 (1993); Luke W. Cole, *The Struggle of Kettleman City: Lessons for the Movement*, 5 MARYLAND JOURNAL OF CONTEMPORARY LEGAL ISSUES 67, 74–78 (1994).

8. See Ralph Santiago Abascal, *Tools for Combating Environmental Injustice in the 'Hood: Title VIII of the Civil Rights Act of 1968*, 29 CLEARINGHOUSE REVIEW 345 (1995). Abascal's theory is that

> Title VIII's definition of "fair housing" can be read to prohibit discriminatory siting of environmental LULUs [Locally Unwanted Land Uses].

Discriminatory siting of environmental LULUs denies people of color access to environmentally safe housing and worsens the quality of neighborhoods suffering from the impact of racial discrimination. Those with the capacity for "exit," who tend to be white, leave. The people of color who are left behind are joined by more of the same because of the lower housing values, thereby perpetuating segregated residential housing patterns. This market dynamic is key to a Title VIII environmental justice claim.

Id. at 348.

9. See Cole, *Empowerment as the Key to Environmental Protection,* supra, at 619, 641–54; Cole, *The Struggle of Kettleman City,* supra, at 67, 77–79.

10. See Luke W. Cole, *Civil Rights, Environmental Justice and the EPA: The Brief History of Administrative Complaints under Title VI,* 9 JOURNAL OF ENVIRONMENTAL LAW AND LITIGATION 309 (1994); Luke W. Cole, *Community-based Administrative Advocacy under Civil Rights Law: A Potential Environmental Justice Tool for Legal Services Advocates,* 29 CLEARINGHOUSE REVIEW 360 (1995).

Notes to Chapter 5

1. Iris Marion Young, JUSTICE AND THE POLITICS OF DIFFERENCE 31 (1990).

2. See, e.g., NATIONAL ENVIRONMENTAL POLICY ACT, 42 U.S.C.A. §§ 4332(C), 4368; COMPREHENSIVE ENVIRONMENTAL RESPONSE, COMPENSATION AND LIABILITY ACT, 42 U.S.C.A. §§ 9617, 9659; EMERGENCY PLANNING AND COMMUNITY RIGHT-TO-KNOW ACT, 42 U.S.C.A. §§ 11044, 11046; CLEAN WATER ACT, 33 U.S.C.A. §§ 1365, 1344(o), 1342(j); TOXIC SUBSTANCES CONTROL ACT, 15 U.S.C.A. §§ 2619–2620; COASTAL ZONE MANAGEMENT ACT, 16 U.S.C.A. §§ 1457, 1458(b); SURFACE MINING CONTROL AND RECLAMATION ACT, 30 U.S.C.A. § 1270.

3. See, e.g., the *Principles of Environmental Justice,* 2 RACE, POVERTY & THE ENVIRONMENT 32 (Fall 1991/Winter 1992); Carl Anthony, *Community-based Approach to Redevelopment: The Case of West Berkeley,* 3 HASTINGS WEST-NORTHWEST JOURNAL OF ENVIRONMENTAL LAW & POLICY 371, 372, 377 (1996); Charles Lee, *From Los Angeles, East St. Louis, and Matamoros: Developing Working Definitions of Urban Environmental Justice* 3/4 RACE, POVERTY & THE ENVIRONMENT 3, 3, 5 (Winter/Spring 1993); Clifford Rechtschaffen, *Fighting Back against a Power Plant: Some Lessons from the Legal and Organizing Efforts of the Bayview-Hunters Point Community,* 3 HASTINGS WEST-NORTHWEST JOURNAL OF ENVIRONMENTAL LAW & POLICY 407, 418 (1996) (quoting the testimony of Carl Anthony that "the desired community decisionmaking process when considering the siting of a new facility would be one in which the local community is 'recognized as an equal partner and sitting at the decision-making table'").

4. For very good explanations of pluralism, see Cass R. Sunstein, *Interest Groups in American Public Law*, 38 STANFORD LAW REVIEW 29 (1985); Cass R. Sunstein, *Beyond the Republican Revival*, 97 YALE LAW JOURNAL 1539 (1988); Robert A. Dahl, DILEMMAS OF PLURALIST DEMOCRACY (1982); Michael J. Walzer, SPHERES OF JUSTICE: A DEFENSE OF PLURALISM AND EQUALITY (1983).

5. Procedures for issuance of most environmental permits are contained in 40 Code of Federal Regulations, Part 124. This Part covers permit issuance, modification, revocation, and termination under numerous statutes. Included under the purview of this regulation are permits issued pursuant to the Resource Conservation and Recovery Act (RCRA), Safe Drinking Water Act (SDWA), Clean Water Act (CWA), and Clean Air Act (CAA). Specifically, it covers all RCRA, Underground Injection Control (UIC), Prevention of Significant Deterioration (PSD), and National Pollutant Discharge Elimination System (NPDES) permits. Part 124 also includes expanded public participation provisions that are unique to RCRA permits. For a general discussion of federal and state permitting regulations and, particularly, their public participation provisions, see Sheila Foster, *Public Participation*, in THE LAW OF ENVIRONMENTAL JUSTICE: THEORIES AND PROCEDURES TO ADDRESS DISPROPORTIONATE RISKS (Michael B. Gerrard, ed., 1999), at 185–229.

6. 42 U.S.C. §§ 4321–4370 (1994); See also 40 C.F.R. PARTS 1501–1508 (1993). The following discussion is influenced and informed by Peter Reich, *Greening the Ghetto: A Theory of Environmental Race Discrimination*, 41 UNIVERSITY OF KANSAS LAW REVIEW 271, 305–13 (1992). For more on state mini-NEPA laws, see generally Nicholas A. Robinson, *SEQRA's Siblings: Precedents from Little NEPAs in the Sister States*, 46 ALABAMA LAW REVIEW 1155 (1982), and Jeffrey T. Renz, *The Coming of Age of State Environmental Policy Acts*, 5 PUBLIC LAND LAW REVIEW 31 (1984); Stephen M. Johnson, *NEPA and SEPAs in the Quest for Environmental Justice*, 30 LOYOLA OF LOS ANGELES LAW REVIEW 565 (1997).

7. See generally Sheila Foster, *Impact Assessment*, in THE LAW OF ENVIRONMENTAL JUSTICE: THEORIES AND PROCEDURES TO ADDRESS DISPROPORTIONATE RISKS (Michael B. Gerrard, ed., 1999), at 285–87.

8. Eileen Gauna, *The Environmental Justice Misfit: Public Participation and the Paradigm Paradox*, 17 STANFORD ENVIRONMENTAL LAW JOURNAL 3, 25 (1998).

9. See Daniel J. Fiorino, *Environmental Risk and Democratic Process: A Critical Review*, 14 COLUMBIA JOURNAL OF ENVIRONMENTAL LAW 501, 525–29 (1989); see also Young, JUSTICE AND THE POLITICS OF DIFFERENCE, supra, at 184–85 ("Where some groups are materially privileged and exercise cultural imperialism, formally democratic processes often elevate the particular experiences

and perspectives of the privileged groups, silencing or denigrating those of oppressed groups."); Gauna, *The Environmental Justice Misfit: Public Participation and the Paradigm Paradox*, supra, at 37 (noting that undue reliance on a pluralistic model of participation is problematic because "preferences are defined by the relative power of self-interested subjects" and such preferences "may be distorted by existing inequalities, poorly construed as a result of exclusion and unequal political clout"); Eileen Gay Jones, *Risky Assessments: Uncertainties in Science and the Human Dimensions of Environmental Decision Making*, 22 WILLIAM & MARY ENVIRONMENTAL LAW AND POLICY REVIEW 1, 41–42 (1997) (arguing that "education provides the skills to debate with experts, a basis for criticizing personal habits relevant to the quality of the environment, and facilitates dialogue necessary to reach agreement among decision makers").

10. See, e.g., Bruce A. Williams and Albert R. Matheny, DEMOCRACY, DIALOGUE, AND ENVIRONMENTAL DISPUTES: THE CONTESTED LANGUAGE OF SOCIAL REGULATION 24, 57 (1995) (discussing Jurgen Habermas).

11. Christopher H. Foreman Jr., THE PROMISE AND PERIL OF ENVIRONMENTAL JUSTICE 41 (1998).

12. Omar Saleem, *Overcoming Environmental Discrimination: The Need for a Disparate Impact Test and Improved Notice Requirements in Facility Siting Decisions*, 19 CALUMET JOURNAL OF ENVIRONMENTAL LAW 211, 240–41 (1994).

13. Government agencies in some areas are beginning to address these obstacles by requiring, for instance, that public notices be of a size large enough to attract public attention, requiring that key government documents be translated into the community's language, and requiring that supporting permit documents be written in plain language and limit their use of technical terms. See, e.g., TEXAS HEALTH & SAFETY CODE § 361.0791 (1998) (requiring published notice be no smaller than 96.8 square centimeters or fifteen square inches, with the shortest dimension at least 7.6 centimeters or three inches); Council on Environmental Quality, ENVIRONMENTAL JUSTICE: GUIDANCE UNDER THE NATIONAL ENVIRONMENTAL POLICY ACT (December 10, 1997) <http://ceq.eh.doe.gov/nepa/nepanet.htm> (requiring that key government documents be translated into the community's language); EXEC. ORDER No. 12,898, 3 C.F.R. § 859 (1995) (same; these federal policies were based on the success of Kettleman City residents in *El Pueblo para el Aire y Agua Limpio v. County of Kings*, No. 366045 (Cal. Sup. Ct. Sacramento County April 13, 1992), where the Court ruled that Spanish-speaking residents had not been properly included in an environmental review process under California law because the Environmental Impact Report was in English only); H.B. 518, 90th Leg., 1st Sess. § 15 (Ill. 1997) (supporting the principle that permit documents must be written in plain language and limit use of technical terms).

14. Council on Environmental Quality, Executive Office of the President, THE NATIONAL ENVIRONMENTAL POLICY ACT: A STUDY OF ITS EFFECTIVENESS AFTER TWENTY-FIVE YEARS (1997), at 11.

15. Gauna, *The Environmental Justice Misfit: Public Participation and the Paradigm Paradox,* supra, at 65.

16. John S. Applegate, *Beyond the Usual Suspects: The Use of Citizens Advisory Boards in Environmental Decision Making,* 73 INDIANA LAW JOURNAL 903, 910 (1998).

17. See generally, Foster, *Public Participation,* supra, at 205–6.

18. There is not general agreement on all that a deliberative democratic process entails. Nevertheless, at the risk of simplifying the deliberative democratic theories, we offer some useful guiding principles. For excellent descriptions of deliberative democratic principles, upon which we rely, see Sunstein, *Beyond the Republican Revival,* supra, at 1539; Frank Michelman, *Law's Republic,* 97 YALE LAW JOURNAL 1493 (1988); Cynthia Ward, *The Limits of "Liberal Republicanism": Why Group-based Remedies and Republican Citizenship Don't Mix,* 91 CALUMET LAW REVIEW 581 (1991); Jonathan Poisner, *A Civic Republican Perspective on the National Environmental Policy Act's Process for Citizen Participation,* 26 ENVIRONMENTAL LAW 53 (1996); Amy Gutmann and Dennis Thompson, DEMOCRACY AND DISAGREEMENT (1996).

19. See generally Jim Rossi, *Participation Run Amok: The Costs of Mass Participation for Deliberative Agency Decisionmaking,* 92 NORTHWESTERN UNIVERSITY LAW REVIEW 173 (1997).

20. See Sunstein, *Beyond the Republican Revival,* supra, at 1539.

21. Applegate, *Beyond the Usual Suspects: The Use of Citizen Advisory Boards in Environmental Decision Making,* supra, at 921.

22. Other states, however, require the board to develop permit conditions and operational requirements, on the assumption that the facility will be permitted. Many boards are also directed to negotiate with the developer for compensation and incentives, to make siting the facility more palatable to the community. Hence, there is no room for the committee to decide that permitting the facility is not in the best interests of the community, or does not constitute the "common good." See, e.g., CALIFORNIA HEALTH & SAFETY CODE § 25199.7 (advisory committee has as its "primary function" giving advice to the appointing legislative body of the "terms and conditions under which the proposed hazardous waste facility project may be acceptable to the community"; also directing committee to negotiate with the facility proponent on behalf of local residents).

23. Applegate, *Beyond the Usual Suspects: The Use of Citizen Advisory Boards in Environmental Decision Making,* supra, at 921.

24. Michelle Leighton Schwartz and Mark R. Wolfe, *Reevaluating the California Tanner Act: Public Empowerment vs. Efficient Waste Disposal*, 13 CALIFORNIA REAL PROPERTY JOURNAL 44, 45 (1995).

25. Lynn M. Sanders, *Against Deliberation*, 25 POLITICAL THEORY 347, 353, 367, 368, 369 (June 1997).

26. Applegate, *Beyond the Usual Suspects: The Use of Citizen Advisory Boards in Environmental Decision Making*, supra, at 921.

27. The following account is based on interviews with community residents, including LAC members. The account, and its supporting materials, can be found in Luke W. Cole, *The Theory and Reality of Community-based Environmental Decision Making: The Failure of California's Tanner Act and Its Implications for Environmental Justice*, 25 ECOLOGY LAW QUARTERLY 733 (1999).

28. Bruce A. Williams and Albert R. Matheny, DEMOCRACY, DIALOGUE, AND ENVIRONMENTAL DISPUTES: THE CONTESTED LANGUAGE OF SOCIAL REGULATION 190 (1995).

29. Patricia J. Williams, THE ALCHEMY OF RACE AND RIGHTS: DIARY OF A LAW PROFESSOR 146–48 (1991); Richard Delgado, *Rodrigo's Twelfth Chronicle: The Problem of the Shanty*, 85 GEORGETOWN LAW REVIEW 667, 680–81 (1997).

30. Delgado, *Rodrigo's Twelfth Chronicle: The Problem of the Shanty*, supra, at 681. "Americans subscribe to two sets of values: the noble ones we apply during occasions of state, on the Fourth of July, when everyone is watching. During these times, the same person who might at other times—say, in a bar or private club—tell an ethnic joke or do something hurtful to a woman or minority, will behave in truly egalitarian fashion. Formality triggers the former values and tends to assure a better result, all other things being equal." Id.

31. Luke Cole, *Macho Law Brains, Public Citizens, and Grassroots Activists: Three Models of Environmental Advocacy*, 14 VIRGINIA ENVIRONMENTAL LAW JOURNAL 687, 697 (1995) (relating the view of many community activists).

32. In fact, a case brought by California Rural Legal Assistance on behalf of six farm-workers, later joined by the fledgling Environmental Defense Fund, succeeded in banning DDT. See *Environmental Defense Fund v. HEW*, 428 F.2d 1083 (D.C. Cir. 1970); *Environmental Defense Fund v. Hardin*, 428 F.2d 1093 (D.C. Cir. 1970); *Environmental Defense Fund v. Environmental Protection Agency*, 510 F.2d 1292 (D.C. Cir. 1975).

33. Nine of the terms used in the EIR could not be located in a Webster's unabridged dictionary. See generally Peter L. Reich, *Greening the Ghetto: A Theory of Environmental Race Discrimination*, 41 KANSAS LAW REVIEW 271, 308–10 (1992) (citing litigation documents). For more on this lawsuit, and the surrounding controversy, see Luke W. Cole, *The Struggle of Kettleman City: Lessons*

for the Movement, 5 MARYLAND JOURNAL OF CONTEMPORARY LEGAL ISSUES 67 (1993–94); Luke W. Cole, *Empowerment as the Means to Environmental Protection: The Need for Environmental Poverty Law*, 19 ECOLOGY LAW QUARTERLY 619, 674–79 (1992).

34. Council on Environmental Quality, *Environmental Justice: Guidance Under The National Environmental Policy Act* 12–13 (December 10, 1997) <http://ceq.eh.doe.gov/nepa/nepanet.htm>. EPA's NEPA guidance similarly suggests ways to encourage and facilitate more active participation by low-income communities and minority communities, particularly when the screening analysis indicates that there may be a disproportionately high and adverse effect on the host community. Where appropriate, EPA recommends that accessible information repositories be established and that technical documents contain a summary written to the lay public and translated into the "dominant language of the affected community." Environmental Protection Agency, *Interim Final Guidance For Incorporating Environmental Justice Concerns in EPA's NEPA Compliance Analysis*, Section 4.2 (September 30, 1997) <http://es.epa.gov/oeca/ofa/ejepa.html>.

35. The following account is taken from two opinions in the case of the Genesee Power Plant in Flint, Michigan, one from the U.S. Environmental Protection Agency Appeals Board, *In re Genesee Power Station Ltd. Partnership*, 1993 WL 484880 (E.P.A.) (October 22, 1993), and another from a state court suit, *NAACP v. Engler*, Genesee County Circuit Court, unpublished opinion, Case 95-38228-CV (May 29, 1997).

36. See generally Mary Greczyn, *Michigan Court Allows Permit*, WASTE NEWS (December 7, 1998), 1998 WL 8229771; See also *Alabama ex rel. Siegelman v. United States Environmental Protection Agency*, 911 F.2d 499 (11th Cir. 1990), in which a federal appeals court rejected the argument that the EPA failed to provide a meaningful opportunity for public participation. In rejecting the complaint that citizens did not have a meaningful opportunity for public comment, the *Siegelman* court relied on fact that EPA made available copies of relevant documents at the local pubic library, at the county probate judges' office, and at the state agency's trailer located near the facility. EPA also made available to anyone who requested it a seventeen-page fact sheet, which provided a detailed description of the draft permit and of the procedures that govern public comments. Though EPA held a public question-and-answer session on the same day as the public hearing, the court opined that there was adequate time afterward for written comments to be filed. The court found significant the fact that, though EPA was required to leave the comment period open for only forty-five days, it allowed sixty-eight days. EPA received 145 comments and seventy-eight oral statements.

37. *Bean v. Southwestern Waste Management Corp.*, 482 F. Supp. 673 (S.D. Texas 1979).

38. See Luke W. Cole, *Environmental Justice Litigation: Another Stone in David's Sling*, 21 FORDHAM URBAN LAW JOURNAL 523, 530 (1994). This strategy has its roots in a case from the early 1970s that sought to block the construction of the Century Freeway in Los Angeles. Brought on both civil rights and environmental grounds, the suit prevailed on environmental grounds, and the civil rights claims were not reached. *Keith v. Volpe*, 352 F. Supp. 1324 (C.D. Cal. 1972), *aff'd en banc sub nom Keith v. California Highway Commission*, 506 F.2d 696 (9th Cir. 1974), *cert. denied*, 420 U.S. 908 (1975). In a later action to enforce the consent decree arising out of the case, Title VIII claims were used to force local government agencies to provide replacement housing for those people displaced by the freeway project. *Keith v. Volpe*, 858 F.2d 467, 482–86 (9th Cir. 1988), *cert. denied* 493 U.S. 813 (1989).

39. All of the equal protection lawsuits that have been decided by the courts have encountered the same problem of proving intentional discrimination: after *Washington v. Davis*, 426 U.S. 229 (1976), the equal protection clause is no longer a viable cause of action in most cases. In three reported cases, *Bean v. Southwestern Waste Management*, *East Bibb Twiggs Neighborhood Association v. Macon-Bibb County Planning & Zoning Commission*, and *R.I.S.E., Inc. v. Kay*, community groups were tripped up by the intent requirement. In these cases, neighborhood groups challenged the siting of a garbage dump in a predominantly African American neighborhood on equal protection grounds, and in all cases the neighborhood groups lost because, the courts held, the groups had not shown an intent to discriminate on the part of local decision makers. The *R.I.S.E.* facts in particular, discussed more thoroughly in chapter 3, demonstrate the difficulty of proving intent in environmental justice cases. *Bean v. Southwestern Waste Management Corp.*, 482 F. Supp. 673 (S.D. Texas 1979); *East Bibb Twiggs Neighborhood Ass'n v. Macon-Bibb County Planning & Zoning Commission*, 706 F.Supp. 880 (M.D. Ga. 1989), *aff'd*, 896 F.2d 1264 (11th Cir. 1989); *R.I.S.E., Inc. v. Kay*, 768 F. Supp. 1144 (E.D. Va. 1991), *aff'd* 977 F.2d 573 (4th Cir. 1992). All three cases have been extensively discussed in the literature. See, e.g., Robert D. Bullard, DUMPING IN DIXIE: RACE, CLASS, AND ENVIRONMENTAL QUALITY 50–54 (1990) (*Bean*); Gerald Torres, *Environmental Burdens and Democratic Justice*, FORDHAM URBAN LAW JOURNAL 431, 441–42 (1994) (*R.I.S.E.*); Robert W. Collin, *Environmental Equity: A Law and Planning Approach to Environmental Racism*, 11 VIRGINIA ENVIRONMENTAL LAW JOURNAL 495, 524–27 (*Bean* and *East Bibb*), 527–33 (*R.I.S.E.*); Richard J. Lazarus, *Pursuing "Environmental Justice": The Distributional Effects of Environmental Protection*, 87 NORTHWESTERN UNIVERSITY LAW REVIEW 101, 144–45 (*Bean* and *East*

Bibb), 146 (*R.I.S.E.*) (1993); Anthony Chase, *Assessing and Addressing Problems Posed by Environmental Racism*, 45 RUTGERS LAW REVIEW 335–56 (*Bean* and *East Bibb*), 356–58 (*R.I.S.E.*).

40. *Guardians Association v. Civil Service Commission of City of New York*, 463 U.S. 582 (1983).

41. See, respectively, 40 C.F.R. § 7.35, 7 C.F.R. § 15.3(b)(2), 32 C.F.R. § 300.4(b)(2), 10 C.F.R. §1040.13(c)–(d), 43 C.F.R. § 17.3(b)(2)–(3). For a complete list of all federal cabinet Departments with Title VI regulations that codify the discriminatory effect standard, see Paul K. Sonn, *Fighting Minority Underrepresentation in Publicly Funded Construction Projects after* Croson: *A Title VI Litigation Strategy*, 101 YALE LAW JOURNAL 1577, 1581 n. 25 (1992).

42. 42 U.S.C. § 2000d–4a. For a compendium of the various federal grants to state and local governments, consult sources such as Office of Management and Budget and U.S. General Services Administration, 1991 CATALOG OF FEDERAL DOMESTIC ASSISTANCE (1991), or Advisory Committee on Intergovernmental Relations, A CATALOG OF FEDERAL GRANTS-IN-AID PROGRAMS TO STATE AND LOCAL GOVERNMENTS: GRANTS FUNDED FY 1989 (1989). As Paul Sonn points out, however, "in order for Title VI limits to attach, federal funds must go to the particular program or activity funded. Receipt of funds by one agency within a state government is not sufficient to extend Title VI coverage to activities of other agencies, even when all are subdivisions of the same chartered governmental unit." Paul K. Sonn, *Fighting Minority Underrepresentation in Publicly Funded Construction Projects after* Croson, supra, at 1577, 1580 n. 18. This is particularly true in the hazardous waste area, where most states receive federal monies under the Resource Conservation Recovery Act and the Comprehensive Environmental Response, Compensation and Liability Act ("Superfund"). See Lazarus, *Pursuing Environmental Justice*, supra, at 148 n. 211.

43. Steven A. Light and Kathryn R. L. Rand, *Is Title VI a Magic Bullet? Environmental Racism in the Context of Political-Economic Processes and Imperatives*, 2 MICHIGAN JOURNAL ON RACE AND THE LAW 1 (1996); James Colopy, *The Road Less Traveled: Pursuing Environmental Justice through Title VI of the Civil Rights Act of 1964*, 13 STANFORD ENVIRONMENTAL LAW JOURNAL 125 (1994); Lazarus, *Pursuing Environmental Justice*, supra, at 147–52. See also Paul K. Sonn, *Fighting Minority Underrepresentation in Publicly Funded Construction Projects after* Croson, supra, at 1577; Luke W. Cole, *Civil Rights, Environmental Justice, and the EPA: The Brief History of Administrative Complaints under Title VI of the Civil Rights Act of 1964*, 9 JOURNAL OF ENVIRONMENTAL LAW AND LITIGATION 309 (1994).

44. *North Carolina Department of Transportation v. Crest Street Community Council, Inc.*, 479 U.S. 6, 9–10 (1986). Another freeway case, arising out

of Cleveland, did not fare as well. In the Cleveland case, although the community group Concerned Citizens Against I-670 demonstrated that the routing of the proposed I-670 freeway would be through neighborhoods that ranged from 50 to 90 percent African American—according to the Court a *"prima facie* showing of disparate effect upon racial minorities"—the defendant was able to overcome that hurdle by showing that alternative routes would have had a greater negative impact on African American neighborhoods. *Coalition of Concerned Citizens Against I-670 v. Damian,* 608 F. Supp. 110, 127 (S.D. Ohio 1984). The Court explained that "it is plain from the record that construction of I-670 would have substantially less impact upon racial minorities than would the construction of a freeway along 17th Avenue, the major alternative location for a freeway." *Coalition of Concerned Citizens against I-670 v. Damian,* supra, at 127.

45. See *Chester Residents Concerned for Quality Living v. Seif,* 132 F.3d 925, 928 n. 1 (3rd Cir. 1997), *cert. granted,* 118 S.Ct. 2296 (U.S. June 8, 1998), *vacated and remanded,* 1998 WL 477242 (U.S. August 17, 1998)

46. See also Bradford Mank, *Is There a Private Right of Action under EPA's Title VI Regulations?* 24 COLUMBIA ENVIRONMENTAL LAW JOURNAL 1, 25–36 (1999).

47. 42 U.S.C. §§3601–3619, 3631.

48. *U.S. v. City of Black Jack, Missouri,* 508 F.2d 1179 (C.A. Mo. 1974), *cert. denied* 422 U.S. 1042, *rehearing denied* 423 U.S. 884 ("effect, not motivation, is the touchstone"); *U.S. v. City of Parma, Ohio,* 494 F. Supp. 1049 (D.C. Ohio 1980), *affirmed* 661 F.2d 562, *rehearing denied* 669 F.2d 1100, *cert. denied* 456 U.S. 926, *rehearing denied* 456 U.S. 1012; *Burney v. Housing Authority of Beaver County,* 551 F. Supp. 746 (D.C. Pa. 1982); *Williamsburg Fair Housing Committee v. New York City Housing Authority,* 493 F. Supp. 1225 (D.C.N.Y. 1980); *NAACP v. Town of Huntington,* 844 F.2d 926 (C.A.2 NY), *review declined in part, affirmed* 109 S.Ct. 276, *rehearing denied* 109 S.Ct. 824; *Familystyle of St. Paul, Inc. v. City of St. Paul, Minn.,* 728 F. Supp. 1396 (D. Minn. 1990), *affirmed* 923 F.2d 91. Some of the limitations on Title VIII approaches are discussed in Ralph Santiago Abascal, *Tools for Combating Environmental Injustice in the "Hood": Title VII of the Civil Rights Act of 1968,* 29 CLEARINGHOUSE REVIEW 345 (1995); and Lazarus, Pursuing Environmental Justice, supra, at 153–55.

49. Yale Rabin, *Expulsive Zoning: The Inequitable Legacy of* Euclid, in ZONING AND THE AMERICAN DREAM 101 (Charles Haar and Jerrold Kayden, eds., 1990). An example might be changing zoning laws to allow a chemical plant or garbage incinerator in a residential community. See id. at 109–13; Bob Anderson, *Industries Crowding out Communities: Lack of Siting Law Leaves Tiny Towns*

Enclosed, Enraged, Baton Rouge Sunday Advocate (May 10, 1992), at 1A (local decision makers quick to change zoning laws to allow industry into residential neighborhoods).

50. For clues to surmounting the first hurdle, one recent case involving the siting of a facility is instructive. In the case, which challenged the siting of a baseball stadium to house the Chicago White Sox, members of the South Armour Square Neighborhood Association argued that the site was selected, and the neighborhood accordingly destroyed, for discriminatory reasons. *Laramore v. Illinois Sports Facilities,* 722 F.Supp. 443 (N.D. Ill. 1989). The second hurdle, proving segregative effect, may be less difficult to overcome. Anecdotally, and on the basis of common sense, one can easily argue that once a locally unwanted land use is allowed into a neighborhood, whites tend to move out—thus, the facility has had the effect of increasing segregation. This has been true in several situations in California. Eighty-four percent of the population of Kettleman City, for example, was Latino in 1980, just one year after the Chemical Waste Management toxic dump was sited nearby; ten years later, 95 percent were Latino. New looks at old studies on the disproportionate impact have also documented this dynamic. See Vicki Been, *Locally Undesirable Land Uses in Minority Neighborhoods: Disproportionate Siting or Market Dynamics,* 103 Yale Law Journal 1383 (1994).

Such proof in a case involving the siting of a new facility might involve longitudinal studies that look at a series of similarly situated communities, charting the demographic makeup of a community when a facility is first built and over the years following; if indeed, as one might suspect, the siting of the facilities had segregative effect in similar communities, it could be plausibly argued that the proposed facility would have similar effect and thus violate Title VIII. When a company is seeking to renew a permit for an existing facility, or to expand such a facility, studies of the demographics of the surrounding neighborhood before the facility was sited, when it was sited, and at various intervals since it was sited would be useful; if permit renewals or expansions have been approved in the past, the resulting effect (if any) of those on the racial composition of the neighborhood could similarly be charted.

51. See William L. F. Felstiner et al., *The Emergence and Transformation of Disputes: Naming, Blaming and Claiming,* 15 Law & Society Review 631 (1981).

52. Julia Siler Flynn, *Environmental Racism: It Could Get Messy,* Business Week (May 20, 1991), at 116.

53. David H. Harris Jr., *Farm Land, Hog Operations and Environmental Justice,* 5 Race, Poverty & the Environment (Fall 1994–Winter 1995), at 31, 33.

Notes to Chapter 6

1. Monica Pieper, *Navajos Say No to Waste*, SUN (Phoenix, Ariz.) (March 8, 1989), at 2.
2. Betty Reid, *Dilcon nixes dump*, INDEPENDENT (Gallup, NM) (March 8, 1989), at 1, 2.
3. Id., at 1, 2.
4. *Keep It in Your Own Yard: Navajo Community of Dilcon Says No to Toxic Wastes*, INTERNATIONAL INDIAN TREATY COUNCIL NEWSLETTER (Fall 1989), at 6.
5. "We're talking in terms of .001 percent of residue left in the form of sterile ash," one company spokesperson was quoted as saying. Pieper, *Navajos Say No to Waste*, supra, at 2.
6. Reid, *Dilcon nixes dump*, supra, at 1, 2.
7. *Keep It in Your Own Yard*, supra, at 6.
8. *Resolution of the Dilkon Chapter, Rescinding the Resolution of August 1, 1988, Which Approved the Locating of High-Tech Recycling in Dilkon; Recognizing the C.A.R.E. Committee*, March 6, 1989.
9. Id. The resolution was passed by a 26-0 vote.
10. *Keep It in Your Own Yard*, supra, at 6.
11. Id., at 6.
12. All quotes from Jackie Warledo are from an interview with her at Fort Belknap, Montana, on August 6, 1997, by Luke Cole.
13. All quotes from Tom Goldtooth are from an interview with him in Bemidji, Minnesota, on July 14, 1997, by Luke Cole.
14. Peiper, *Navajos Say No to Waste*, supra, at 2.
15. *Keep It in Your Own Yard*, supra, at 6.
16. This transformation is explored in more detail in chapter 7.

Notes to Chapter 7

1. Sara M. Evans and Harry C. Boyte, FREE SPACES: THE SOURCES OF DEMOCRATIC CHANGE IN AMERICA xix (1986).
2. Robert D. Bullard, DUMPING IN DIXIE: RACE, CLASS, AND ENVIRONMENTAL QUALITY 2 (2d ed., 1990).
3. Bullard, DUMPING IN DIXIE, supra, at 2.
4. Our use of the term "agency" in the context of this chapter mirrors its use in recent feminist legal literature. Like Kathryn Abrams, we use the term "in a way that acknowledges an internal, as well as an external or outwardly-oriented, aspect to agency, and that highlights the oppressed circumstances of many who seek to exercise it." Kathryn Abrams, *Sex Wars Redux: Agency and Coercion in*

Feminist Legal Theory, 95 Columbia Law Review 304, 307 n. 11 (1995). Agency thus denotes the "ability to develop and act on conceptions of oneself that are not determined by dominant, oppressive conceptions." Id.

5. Steven L. Winter, *The "Power" Thing*, 82 Virginia Law Review 721, 835 (1996) (interpreting Michel Foucault's conception of power as not a "thing" nor quality, capacity, or possession of particular people but rather as an emergent quality than can take shape only through the joint agency of all those who participate in a given set of social relations).

6. Abrams, *Sex Wars Redux*, supra, at 347–48; see also Tracy E. Higgins, *Democracy and Feminism*, 110 Harvard Law Review 1657, 1696 (1997).

7. Higgins, *Democracy and Feminism*, supra, at 1691.

8. See Abrams, *Sex Wars Redux*, supra, at 348 n.4 ("As contrasted with transcendent agency, internal agency is hard-won and almost always partial or incomplete. So long as coercion and devaluation of women continue in society, women must struggle with the tension between the 'outside' and 'inside' visions of themselves, or among the multiple voices that make up their identities.").

9. John Gaventa, Power and Powerlessness: Quiescence and Rebellion in an Appalachian Valley 211 (1980).

10. See Luke W. Cole, *Empowerment as the Means to Environmental Protection: The Need for Environmental Poverty Law*, 19 Ecology Law Quarterly 619, 676–77 n. 251 (1992). This transformed understanding is similar to that experienced by participants in feminist "consciousness-raising" groups, which were (and are) a "process of developing an awareness of group political oppression through the sharing of individual experiences." Angela Harris, *On Doing the Right Thing: Education Work in the Academy*, 15 Vermont Law Review 125, 125 n. 3; see also Catherine MacKinnon, Toward a Feminist Theory of the State 83–105 (1989) (arguing that consciousness-raising groups lead women, through their participation, to become conscious of their oppression as common rather than individual).

11. In environmental justice struggles, collective action is crucial to success. As Denis Brion notes, "The atomistic individual could accomplish little in isolation, but could accomplish great things when organized into a group." Denis J. Brion, *An Essay On LULU, NIMBY, and the Problem of Distributive Justice*, 15 Boston College Environmental Affairs Law Review 437, 452 (1988).

12. Luke W. Cole, *Environmental Justice and the Three Great Myths of White Americana*, 3 Hastings West-Northwest Journal of Environmental Law and Policy 449, 452–54 (1996).

13. Cole, *Empowerment as the Means to Environmental Protection*, supra, at 643.

14. Gaventa, Power and Powerlessness, supra, at 205.

15. Id. at 212.

16. R. Gregory Roberts, *Comment: Environmental Justice and Community Empowerment: Learning from the Civil Rights Movement*, 48 AMERICAN UNIVERSITY LAW REVIEW 229, 256 n. 150 (1998). Roberts continues, "This is precisely what happened in the Civil Rights Movement. Civil rights activists educated individuals about their rights and the law, which led to the education of entire communities, which in turn empowered individuals and communities to unite in a national movement that successfully exerted significant pressure on politicians nationwide."

17. Gaventa, POWER AND POWERLESSNESS, supra.

18. Id. at 140.

19. The information on Ironbound contained in this chapter is based upon one of the author's interviews with Arnold Cohen, former cochair of the Ironbound Committee against Toxic Waste; June Kruszewski, community resident; Joseph Della Fave, executive director of Ironbound Community Corporation; and Tiwana M. Steward-Griffin, former staff member.

20. In 1991, six companies in Ironbound released more than half a million pounds of hazardous materials each. Ironbound is now the home of the Essex County Resource Recovery Facility, New Jersey's largest garbage incinerator, which alone burns more than one million tons of garbage per year. Ironbound is also host to the primary sewage treatment plant for the thirty-three municipalities and 1.5 million people served by the Passaic Valley Sewage Commission. And the old Diamond Alkali plant, where the herbicide Agent Orange was once produced, is now part of the Federal Superfund program to clean up contaminated sites, and it remains a constant source of concern among Ironbound residents. Adding to the pollution released from these sources, Ironbound is also bounded by at least five major roads, including the New Jersey Turnpike, as well as by Newark Airport. Fernando Linhares, *Environmental Equity: Focus on Ironbound* 4–5 (1995) (paper on file with the authors) (citing J. Mark Zdpeski, *Industrial Development, Urban Land-Use Practices and Resulting Groundwater Contamination*, JMZ GEOLOGY, at 1–2, Pre-print NGWA Focus Eastern Conference, October 12–15, 1992).

21. Jesus Rangel, *The Talk of Ironbound: In a Thriving Community, Ties That Bind Also Chafe*, NEW YORK TIMES (June 27, 1988), at B1 (quoting Arnold Cohen, a spokesperson for the Ironbound Committee against Toxic Waste).

22. This coalition ultimately included the Ironbound Health Project, Greenpeace, the Coalition for a United Elizabeth, Rutgers Law School Environmental Law Clinic, the Environmental Law Council, the New Jersey Public Interest Research Group, and the Essex County Sea Alliance.

23. IRONBOUND VOICES, vol. 8, no. 8 (1986).

24. Id.

25. President William Jefferson Clinton, *Executive Order* 12,898, *Federal Actions to Address Environmental Justice in Minority Populations and Low-Income Populations* (February 11, 1994), published in 59 Federal Register 7629 (February 16, 1994).

26. Id. at §5–5(b).

27. See Environmental Equity Workgroup, U.S. Environmental Protection Agency, EPA 230-R-92-008, Environmental Equity: Reducing Risk For All Communities, Workgroup Report to the Administrator 1 (1992). See also the discussion in chapter 3.

28. See Cole, *Empowerment as the Means to Environmental Protection*, supra, at 634. Cf. Richard Delgado, *Zero-based Racial Politics: An Evaluation of Three Best-Case Arguments on Behalf of the Nonwhite Underclass*, 78 Georgetown Law Journal 1929, 1930 (1990), noting the importance of building coalitions because the "black and brown middle class is too small to carry out a rescue operation of the magnitude needed" to achieve social justice.

INDEX

Abascal, Ralph: and Buttonwillow legal strategy, 95; and Title VIII, 97
Abbonizio Recycling Corporation, 35, 36, 39
Abernathy, Ralph, 20
Abrams, Kathryn, 154
academics: early meetings of on environmental justice, 21; role in Environmental Justice Movement, 24
advisory committee. *See* local advisory committees
African Americans: analogy to Latinos, 7; and Civil Rights Movement, 20; and consequences of segregation, 69; disproportionate exposure to toxic waste sites, 57; employment vs. whites, 67; and expulsive zoning, 69, 73; having less residential mobility than whites, 62; impact of stereotypes of, 68; as majority near Genesee Power Station, 124; migration to Chester, 37; protests in North Carolina and Texas by, 19; racism experienced by, 32, 63; realizing their power, 53; relegated to least desirable neighborhoods, 61; segregation and exposure to pollution, 59; systematic disregard of, 115; as target of uranium enrichment facility, 74; and toxic waste sites, 55; and whites living together, 66
agency, 153–154, 162; incomplete, 154; internal, 154
aha! moment, 152, 165
air pollution, 54
Alaska Native nations, 144
Alatorre, Maricela, 4, 5, 7
Alston, Dana, 31, 194
American Apartheid, 66

American Indian Movement, 26
American Ref-Fuel, 53
anencephaly, 82
Angel, Bradley: arrest of, 91; invited to Dilkon, 136; and Kettleman City struggle 2; as outside agitator, 92
anti-nuclear activists, 144
anti-toxics movement, 164; as origin of Environmental Justice Movement, 12, 22; and siting of waste facilities, 17; structural understanding of power, 23; using scientific and technical information, 23
anti-Vietnam War movement, 29
Appalachia, 154, 156, 157
Arctic National Wildlife Refuge, 144
Asian Pacific Environmental Network, 132
Atomic Safety and Licensing Board, 74
At-Sea Incineration, 158–159
Austin, Ben, 91
Austin, Regina, 62, 190

Bakersfield Californian, 94
Balanoff, Clem, 5
Balter, Jerome: on community reliance on the law, 47; and Thermal Pure appeal, 44; and Thermal Pure lawsuit hearing, 46
baseline, 58
Bear Butte (S.Dak.), 140
Bechtel, 164
Been, Vicki, 56
Beltran, Francisco. *See* Beltran, Paco
Beltran, Gabriel, 98
Beltran, Lydia, 98
Beltran, Paco, 85; application to LAC, 88; demoralization of, 102; son going to college, 98

Index

Crest Street Community Council, 127
Critical Race Theorists, 120
CRJ. *See* United Church of Christ Commission for Racial Justice
cyanide heap leach gold mine, 144, 147

DDT, 27
decision-making. *See* environmental decision-making
De Chiro, Giovanna, 14
Deep South Center for Environmental Justice, 26
Delaware County (Pa.): demographics of, 34; permitting Westinghouse incinerator, 38; Regional Water Control, 36, 39, 51–52; waste facilities in, 35; waste of, 36, 51
Delaware River, 34, 37
Delaware Solid Waste Authority, 53
DELCORA. *See* Delaware County (Pa.), Regional Water Control
Delgado, Richard, 120–121
Denton, Nancy, 66, 68
DEP. *See* Pennsylvania Department of Environmental Protection
Dilkon (Ariz.), 134–136; as host of Protecting Mother Earth Conference, 139; and incinerator, 138; and recycling plant, 134
dioxin, 158, 164
disproportionate impact. *See* environmental hazards
distributive outcomes: patterns of, 79; underlying social processes, 54
District of Columbia, 108
Durham (N.C.), 127

Earth Day, 29
Eastern Cherokee Defense League, 144
East Liverpool (Ohio), 86
East St. Louis (Ill.), 4
El Pueblo para el Aire y Agua Limpio, 185; appeal of incinerator permit by, 7–8; formation of, 3; lawsuit by, 122; postcard campaign by, 9; research by, 4; techniques used by, 19
Emelle (Ala.), 4

environment: Environmental Justice Movement definition, 16; redefinition of, 19
Environmental Appeals Board, 124–125
environmental decision-making: as "announce and defend," 111; causing distrust of government, 155; environmental justice inquiry into, 79; as forum, 107; and the law, 122; pluralistic processes, 110, 121; replicating constraints of social structure, 104; structure of, 13, 103–104; theory vs. reality, 109
Environmental Defense Fund, 29
environmental equity, 15
environmental extortion, 77
environmental hazards: disproportionate distribution of, 21, 54, 65, 76; disproportionate impact of, 24, 25, 59; disproportionate impact by income, 55; disproportionate impact by race, 55, 62; distributional inequalities exacerbated by law, 71, 75; distribution of, 10; empirical studies of distribution of, 17, 54, 70, 79; inequitable distribution of, 54, 58; multiple exposures to, 59; naturalizing disportionate exposure to, 59–60; political economy of, 155; segregation causing disproportionate exposure to, 66
Environmental Health Coalition, 23
environmental injustice. *See* environmental racism
environmental justice: authors' choice of term, 15; concept of, 14, 16; and decision-making processes, 79; feminist scholars and, 154; as goal, 10; groups and movement-building, 131; ignored by traditional environmental movement, 30; and industrial development, 77; lawsuits, 127; and models of power, 153; networks as transformative, 151; as political and economic struggle, 65; research, 62; struggle in East Liverpool, 86; struggles and litigation, 122; struggles influenced by laws, 103; Summit attendees' understanding of, 32; and

| 234 |

ABOUT THE AUTHORS

Luke W. Cole is Director of the California Rural Legal Assistance Foundation's Center on Race, Poverty, and the Environment. Sheila R. Foster is a professor at Rutgers University School of Law, Camden.